# Roses

Questions and Answers

# Roses

## Questions and Answers

*Bill Swain*

CASSELL

Cassell Publishers Limited
Artillery House, Artillery Row
London SW1P 1RT

Copyright © Bill Swain 1990

All rights reserved. This book is protected by copyright.
No part of it may be reproduced, stored in a retrieval system,
or transmitted in any form or by any means,
electronic, mechanical, photocopying or otherwise,
without written permission from the publishers.

First published 1990

**British Library Cataloguing in Publication Data**

Swain, Bill
  Roses: questions and answers.
  1. Gardens. Roses. Cultivation
  I. Title
  635.9′33372

ISBN 0-304-31681-4

Designed by Simon Bell

Photographs by Michael Warren, Michael Gibson and John Glover

Filmset by
Litho Link Limited, Welshpool, Powys

Printed and bound in Great Britain
by
Richard Clay

# Contents

|    | Introduction                                   | 9   |
|----|------------------------------------------------|-----|
| 1  | The Rose: As Interesting as it is Beautiful    | 11  |
| 2  | The Different Types of Rose                    | 15  |
| 3  | Choosing Where to Buy and What to Plant        | 32  |
| 4  | Preparation Before Planting                    | 42  |
| 5  | Planting and Staking                           | 47  |
| 6  | Pruning                                        | 54  |
| 7  | Feeding                                        | 73  |
| 8  | Pests and Diseases                             | 81  |
| 9  | Propagation                                    | 98  |
| 10 | Exhibiting                                     | 113 |
| 11 | A Work Calendar                                | 118 |
| 12 | Questions and Answers                          | 121 |
|    | Bibliography                                   | 263 |
|    | Rose Nurseries                                 | 264 |
|    | Useful Addresses                               | 266 |
|    | Index                                          | 268 |

# Questions and Answers

|   |   | Page |
|---|---|---|
| 1 | Controlling greenfly. | 123 |
| 2 | Not so super 'Super Star'. | 126 |
| 3 | Where to find old favourites. | 145 |
| 4 | A fresh rose bloom for Christmas morning. | 146 |
| 5 | Can blooms be kept in the deep freeze? | 147 |
| 6 | Are roses afraid of ghosts? | 148 |
| 7 | Improving clay soils for roses. | 150 |
| 8 | Why remove old flower heads? | 153 |
| 9 | Cutting blooms does no harm – unless . . . | 153 |
| 10 | Rejuvenating an old veteran. | 154 |
| 11 | Moving old established plants. | 155 |
| 12 | A rose without thorns is still a rose. | 157 |
| 13 | Coping with an enforced second move. | 158 |
| 14 | Don't bother to move it. | 160 |
| 15 | Underplanting roses. | 160 |
| 16 | Drought and roses. | 162 |
| 17 | Moving an established standard. | 163 |
| 18 | Can rhododendrons kill roses? | 164 |
| 19 | Buds will not open. | 165 |
| 20 | Suckers. | 165 |
| 21 | Use of horse manure. | 168 |
| 22 | Use of seaweed. | 169 |
| 23 | Use of peat and pulverized bark. | 170 |
| 24 | Limited usefulness of bone meal. | 171 |
| 25 | Tell-tale signs of potash deficiency. | 173 |
| 26 | Purple spot. | 174 |

|    |                                                          | *Page* |
|----|----------------------------------------------------------|--------|
| 27 | Roses and acidity.                                       | 175    |
| 28 | Roses in tubs.                                           | 176    |
| 29 | Climbers in containers.                                  | 178    |
| 30 | Schumacher was right – small is beautiful.               | 179    |
| 31 | 'Queen Elizabeth' as a hedge.                            | 180    |
| 32 | Roses as a subject for hedges.                           | 181    |
| 33 | More on rose hedges: do they sucker?                     | 183    |
| 34 | No flowers on a climber.                                 | 183    |
| 35 | Pruning 'Canary Bird'.                                   | 184    |
| 36 | Pruning a standard 'Ballerina'.                          | 185    |
| 37 | Pruning China roses.                                     | 186    |
| 38 | Rose die-back.                                           | 187    |
| 39 | Help for crash victims.                                  | 191    |
| 40 | Propagating shrub types by cuttings.                     | 191    |
| 41 | Propagation by seed.                                     | 193    |
| 42 | Dealing with mare's tail weed.                           | 195    |
| 43 | Buttercups and other persistent weeds.                   | 196    |
| 44 | Safe weedkillers for rose beds.                          | 197    |
| 45 | Moss and what it indicates.                              | 198    |
| 46 | The causes of mildew.                                    | 200    |
| 47 | Black spot.                                              | 202    |
| 48 | Can black spot spread to other plants?                   | 203    |
| 49 | Fungicide deposit.                                       | 204    |
| 50 | Rose canker.                                             | 204    |
| 51 | Rose rust.                                               | 206    |
| 52 | Leaf-roll sawfly.                                        | 208    |
| 53 | Capsid bug.                                              | 209    |
| 54 | Egg-spangled rose.                                       | 211    |
| 55 | Scented roses for the blind and partially sighted.       | 211    |
| 56 | Mixing roses.                                            | 212    |
| 57 | Going too far with technical standards.                  | 213    |
| 58 | The astonishing story of the Banksian rose.              | 214    |
| 59 | Dangers of mixing fertilizer chemicals.                  | 216    |
| 60 | Recipe for a safe rosehip syrup.                         | 217    |
| 61 | Modern varieties do not live so long?                    | 218    |
| 62 | Roses in a waterlogged situation.                        | 219    |
| 63 | Coping with a rose 'that round the thatch eaves runs'.   | 220    |
| 64 | Soap in the rose garden?                                 | 222    |
| 65 | What is whalehide?                                       | 223    |
| 66 | Is a thornless rose a chimera?                           | 224    |

|     |                                                                          | Page |
| --- | ------------------------------------------------------------------------ | ---- |
| 67  | Can rose colour be changed by colourants?                                | 225  |
| 68  | A blue rose?                                                             | 226  |
| 69  | How do they get roses in bloom for Chelsea?                              | 227  |
| 70  | Scented leaves.                                                          | 228  |
| 71  | Roses in shaded positions.                                               | 228  |
| 72  | When they become 'old and past it'.                                      | 229  |
| 73  | Rose petal pot-pourri.                                                   | 231  |
| 74  | Rose petal wine.                                                         | 233  |
| 75  | Is there such a thing as a green rose?                                   | 235  |
| 76  | One for Gracie Fields: 'the biggest bloomin' rose in all the world'.     | 235  |
| 77  | Smelling of bananas?                                                     | 236  |
| 78  | A 'Wedding Day' argument.                                                | 237  |
| 79  | Stars and stripes – and blotches.                                        | 237  |
| 80  | Hanging gardens.                                                         | 239  |
| 81  | A lemon-scented rose?                                                    | 240  |
| 82  | The rose with only four petals.                                          | 241  |
| 83  | A real rose hedge.                                                       | 241  |
| 84  | Double or fully double – is there any difference?                        | 243  |
| 85  | The dutch hoe – a dangerous tool for roses.                              | 243  |
| 86  | Robin's pin-cushion.                                                     | 245  |
| 87  | Plant Breeders' Rights – what does it mean?                              | 246  |
| 88  | Mineral deficiences – the tell-tale signs.                               | 247  |
| 89  | The legendary black rose.                                                | 249  |
| 90  | Miniature, patio, ground cover: what's the difference?                   | 250  |
| 91  | 'Bi-colour' and 'multi-colour'.                                          | 252  |
| 92  | Will the thorns ever be bred out?                                        | 253  |
| 93  | Why not put rose leaves on the compost heap?                             | 254  |
| 94  | The strange markings of the rose leaf miner.                             | 255  |
| 95  | Chopped straw mulch – a load of trouble.                                 | 256  |
| 96  | Grey lichen-like tents of the lackey moth.                               | 258  |
| 97  | Do coins in the vase water do any good?                                  | 259  |
| 98  | Magnolia – not a good climbing frame.                                    | 259  |
| 99  | Clematis not happy on a rose pergola.                                    | 260  |
| 100 | Moles in the rose beds: how to send them packing.                        | 261  |
| 101 | The biggest pest of all – deer!                                          | 262  |

# Introduction

We live in a world of rapid change. Every new year brings its own progress, something else new, something else to get used to. One of the most obvious changes, an inevitable consequence of an exploding population confined within the shores of an island, is the galloping spread of bricks and mortar across the landscape. Many more houses means many more gardens – and places to grow roses. Of course, there are still people lucky enough to have older, larger gardens, and still some with gardens so large that they have to employ others to do the work, but these days, the newer the garden, the smaller it is. The beauty of growing roses is that virtually every garden has room for at least a rose or two, and there isn't a single garden that doesn't look better for its roses. If the reputation of the British as a nation of gardeners is being squeezed by the physical constraints of twentieth-century progress, our love of the rose is still as bright as ever.

My intention in this book is to help you enjoy your roses to the full, whatever size of garden you have, and whatever your previous success, or otherwise, in growing roses. It will help you to plan and get the best from your roses, to plant wisely and over later years admire and enjoy what you have planted. It will help you to recognize some common sense about roses, and avoid costly mistakes. Enjoyment can be marred by problems and failures, and from a long experience of having answered thousands of gardeners' questions, I know that many of the difficulties that beset gardeners can be avoided, once the principles involved are understood.

Solutions depend not so much on knowing what to do, or when, or how, but *why*. If you understand the reasons why problems occur, then you can solve them, and your gardening becomes that much more interesting, successful and enjoyable. The roses you plant in your garden will be with you a long time; the wise gardener chooses and tends his roses well, gets to know them closely, and will be rewarded with season upon season of beautiful bloom.

So sit down, relax, and do some armchair gardening with me. From a lot of experience, I can tell you that it is the most important you will ever do.

BILL SWAIN<br>
St Leonards

# 1

# The Rose:
# As Interesting as it is Beautiful

Perhaps if we can parody the eight gramophone records, and ask the question, 'If you were cast away on a desert island, which eight plants would you wish to have with you?' there is no doubt that the rose would be the first choice for most people. That should not be surprising, because when asked to name one favourite flower, beautiful above all others, again there can be little doubt that most people – in Britain at any rate, and whether gardeners or not – would choose the rose.

So it has been for centuries, yet the multi-petalled bloom of modern times, epitomized by the modern Hybrid Tea rose (or, as it is abbreviated, H.T.) and probably most people's mental image of all that a rose is and should be, is a product of modern hybridizing and cross-breeding that did not exist even as recently as medieval times. Long before then, however, the rose had already found a place in the heart of man. To the human eye and senses, even the simply constructed single bloom of the hedgerow wild rose is so sublimely beautiful in the bud that it is represented in the earliest forms of art and pictorial decoration. The common use of the rose in heraldry illustrates how deeply and firmly it became associated with and identified as a symbol of family arms and crest, class and dynasty. In the twentieth century the rose is still regarded as something basically British, regal and exalted; it symbolizes quality and superiority.

It is one of the more perverse facets of human nature that the more we have, the more we want – and so it is with the rose. Never a season passes without something new being set before us; the resources of the rose seem limitless. As it does with anything that is widely liked and appreciated, this modern money-mad world has made the rose big business, and the plant obeys all the ups and downs of fashion, high pressure competition and selling – even racketeering – as do pop records, clothes and motor cars. It is so easy to be caught up in the whirl.

Why is the rose so universally admired and so highly cherished? A famous psychologist (he was a customer of mine before he took his talents to America) once suggested in conversation that it was largely due to the contradiction between the beauty of the flower and the beastly danger and hurt of the thorn. More important than all that, however, what is it that you, the reader, like about the rose? Is it the wide range of colours, the beauty of the bud opening into full bloom, or the scent? These are all factors that are essentially personal, and we are all different in our likes and dislikes. It is this width of opinion and preference, and the infinite variety and ability of the rose to supply and please all tastes, that makes possible the incessant striving to breed, introduce and sell something new.

You don't have to be a historian to know a pretty flower when you see one, and although this is not intended to be a text book – there is more than enough literature available to fulfil that function – I do suggest that your enjoyment of roses can be enhanced by knowing just a little about the many different kinds, and such matters as why they are cultivated in certain ways, why they are pruned, and so on – and to see a strange word, and know what it means!

The genus has extraordinarily wide origins, with different species coming from the whole length and breadth of Europe, the Middle East, Persia, Afghanistan, India, China, Japan and across to the North American continent. The Orient had well-developed civilizations long before anything in Europe, and they too appreciated the qualities of the rose and its potential when cross-bred and hybridized – a process that was well in advance of the horticultural achievements of European civilizations by the time the latter's explorations brought East and West together.

As with so many other plants, and indeed with many other arts, the developments that followed the introduction of oriental blood to the West were enormous and revolutionary. The extent of cross-breeding and hybridizing has been an explosion that continues to this day. Indeed, far from all the possibilities and permutations becoming exhausted, modern understanding of hereditary principles plus enormous advances in scientific techniques has, if anything, quickened the pace and extended the possibilities of the rose, more than with any other single genus on Earth.

Of course, some people take hobbies, pastimes and other activities to incredible lengths, but you don't have to be able to converse knowledgeably about all the different types to enjoy an exquisite bloom. If you are to enjoy the satisfaction of growing one, clearly it helps to know how to combat all the pests and diseases that conspire to stop you. Succeeding against challenge is part of the satisfaction – if a rose were to grow perfect blooms every time without problems, that would be too easy and give no sense of achievement.

There is one word to cover our liking of roses, our desire to discover the different kinds, and ability to overcome the difficulties of growing them, and that is interest. Unfortunately it can be very dull when you are faced with a dry reference book that retails facts and information and talks at you, not with you. Good rose-growing should be about enjoyment as well as understanding. Understand why something happens as it does and you are your own master, able to use your common sense and logic to make judgements and decisions. Add a touch of background, humour, a whiff of romance, an anecdote or two, and you have the stuff of interest and enjoyment. Is that not what all gardening is about?

I cannot tell you everything about roses, because I don't know it all – nobody does, or ever will. However, there is plenty here that you will find interesting because, despite all the books, journals, newspaper articles, radio programmes and so on, gardeners still have problems and ask a lot of questions. A lot of them are concerned and confused with the many different types of rose, so we will begin by describing them and explaining the meaning of many of the names you will come across – that will help you choose wisely, and without regretful afterthoughts.

Unusually, you may think, I shall not be listing and suggesting varieties for you to grow because I think that can be a misleading business and is not really helpful. In the final analysis, beauty is in the eye of the beholder, and essentially a personal matter. What pleases me may not please you, and my recommendation may disappoint you – and then what would you think?

Furthermore, new varieties come into the lists in such numbers that the same numbers have to be deleted, otherwise the lists would become far too long, and the nurseries quite unmanageable. All too often, a 'best of all time show-stopper' is difficult to find only a few years after its introduction, superseded by yet another new name. Not only would a list of varieties make a book like this out of date in a short time, it would not help you either. A comment here and there on a classic will not be out of place, but a list of recommended varieties is out!

Planting, staking and feeding have been talked and written about so frequently that it really is astounding how many questions and problems still occur about these subjects. Instead of repeating all that has been said and written before, we will therefore discuss these matters in a way that enables you to use your common-sense judgement and understand why you decide to do something. It is your garden; you do the work and make the decision according to your judgement. You can never experience the real satisfaction of growing roses well by following a list of step-by-step instructions.

As with planting, so with pruning: hundreds of books, millions of words, lots of diagrams and illustrations, and still the questions come! So, we will tackle pruning in a different way, one that takes the mystery out of it. Propagation – by seed, budding, or grafting – will concern only the minority of rose gardeners, but has to be included, even if rather briefly. So too with exhibiting: somewhere a reader may be able to grow significantly better roses than his or her neighbours, and he or she would like to put it to the test of the show-bench.

Pests and diseases have had innumerable volumes devoted to them, and still remain a never-ending source of trouble and worry. Almost like new roses themselves, chemical insecticides and fungicides come and go with remarkable rapidity. Some arrive in a blaze of publicity and promise, only — like DDT and many others – to be banished in disgrace for creating insufficiently researched 'side effects'. How, then, can one be definite about recommending chemical preparations? How can I be sure that this year's cures will not be in disgrace and condemned by the time you read about them? Such is one of the consequences of 'progress'.

Following pests and diseases is a section that will interest those who would like to try their hands at raising their own new plants, and perhaps even achieving fame in the process! The biggest section follows; this is a selection of the many questions received from readers – the more important, the most often asked, and therefore the sort of **thing most likely to be worrying you – with 'reason why' explanations.**

# 2
# The Different Types of Rose

Many thousands of years of natural evolution and hybridization, helped in recent centuries by the bringing together of species from widely separate parts of the world, and in modern decades by the attentions of the human mind and hand, have produced a multitide of rose forms, shapes, colours, habits and abilities. With such diverse origins it is not surprising that occasionally some unsuspected gene from a complicated ancestral past asserts itself and a deviation pops up.

Such skeletons from ancestral cupboards can be most welcome – for example, a docile bush form may suddenly want to climb about, change colour, or show some other perverse side of its nature that we find attractive and wish to keep. Sometimes the variation is slight, and a new variety is born, but occasionally variations are so great and distinctive as to found a new race, a new type, something quite different to anything seen before. Catalogues, lists, the literature of the rose: all use a lot of words to classify the different kinds, but seldom tell us much about how they differ. It will be helpful, therefore, to know something about what these words and classifications mean before setting about choosing what to grow.

For this purpose, I propose first to discuss the several bloom shapes and forms, then the growth and habit forms and variations, and then progressively to pass on to the many breed and race classifications. That way we shall have a good idea of all the different kinds of rose, where to look to find the right variety to suit a particular purpose, and more importantly, where not to look, and what to leave alone. Before looking at the bloom shapes and forms, we need to clarify a few terms which are not as simple or straightforward as might be supposed.

# Clarification of terms

A **single** bloom is one with a single circlet of five petals, as you will invariably find in the wild rose of the hedgerow and, of course, in a number of the modern bred varieties as well. In many cases, the anthers at the centre of each blossom are highly coloured or contrast with the petal colour to add to the attractiveness of the flower.

Single
(a)

Double
(b)

Semi-double
(c)

Quartered
(d)

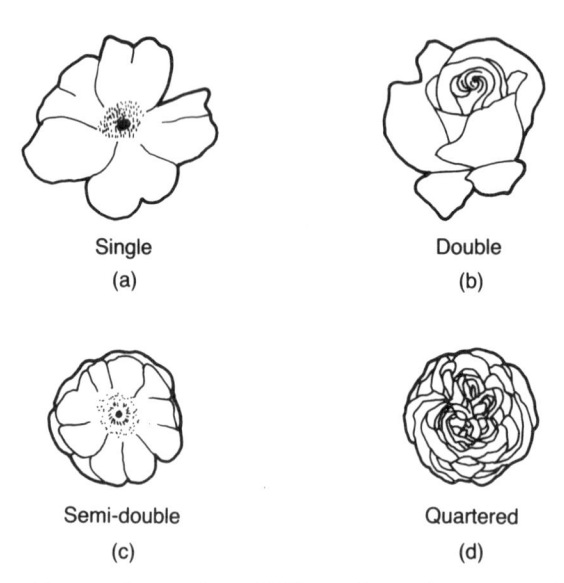

**Figure 1.** Rose blooms take a variety of different forms, best summarized as (a) single, with a single circlet of five petals, (b) double, with anything from 10 to 30 petals, (c) semi-double, with up to 15 petals but opening more like a single than a double, and (d) the old favourite quartered rose, with its many petals curled into four 'quarters'.

As 'single' means five petals, you may deduce that the word **double** would mean ten – but not so. 'Double' *can* mean ten petals, but it can also mean 15, 20, 25, 30, 35 – nominally any multiple of five. Some petals do not fully develop and may be only partial petals, so in practice the actual number can mean pretty well anything. There is no precise meaning to 'double' with regard to petal number, and the word is taken to mean a number of petals so closely packed that until the bloom fully opens and then 'blows', it is virtually impossible to see the anthers and other sexual parts of the flower – they are quite hidden.

A **semi-double** bloom, of which there are a great many, is somewhere between, but tending more towards 'single' than 'double' so that, although there may be as many as 15 petals, the flower opens more loosely than a double and reveals the anthers more readily. (See also question number 84 on page 243.)

Especially in the description of the blooms of older breed types, you will often see the word **quartered**. This is a rather apt description of a bloom that is flat, (compared to the high central point of the Hybrid Tea, for example) and in which the many petals seem to curl and divide into four sections or quarters. This was a favourite feature in olden times, and a similar petal formation can be seen in some modern bred fuchsias.

Weather, temperature, position, fertility and such factors all have an effect upon the flowering period, but by and large, most roses will begin to bloom, or be almost ready to do so, from late May into June. There is not so much variation at the front end of the flowering season as there is in autumn and winter, when some varieties and types show a marked reluctance to end their activities. Indeed, a few are notable for their apparent determination always to herald the New Year with a fresh bud! That apart, we should bear in mind that roses vary greatly in their ability to bloom more or less continuously after the first flush. Those that do are described as **perpetual flowering**, and those that bloom in short repetitive bursts are called **repeat, recurrent,** or the French **remontant**. Many roses, especially the ramblers, have one single flush and no more.

# Growth form and habit types

The **bush** – or, as it used to be called, dwarf (misleading these days in view of the growing popularity of the miniature and patio types) – is the form that is most popular and commonly planted in gardens everywhere. Its branches fork from an implanted bud just above ground level and normally make 2–4ft (0.6–1.2m) high, although – and this has to be said – too often encouraged by incorrect and only partial pruning that permits new growth to break not from near ground level but from 1ft (0.3m), 2ft (0.6m), or even higher, they are frequently to be seen consisting of younger bloom bearing growth on top of old barky stems, the whole reaching 5ft (1.5m), even 6ft (1.8m), or more in height.

This kind of mistreatment highlights how descriptive words and terms can be confusing if they are taken to mean anything more than a means of distinguishing form – and not size, for instance. If mistreatment and eventual size confuse matters, those catalogues and articles that lump bush and shrub roses together only add to the confusion. Some shrub types can be quite small compared to a mistreated overgrown bush type.

Most often identified with the widely known and popular Hybrid Tea, the bush form includes many different kinds of so-called 'Old' roses as well as 'Moderns'.

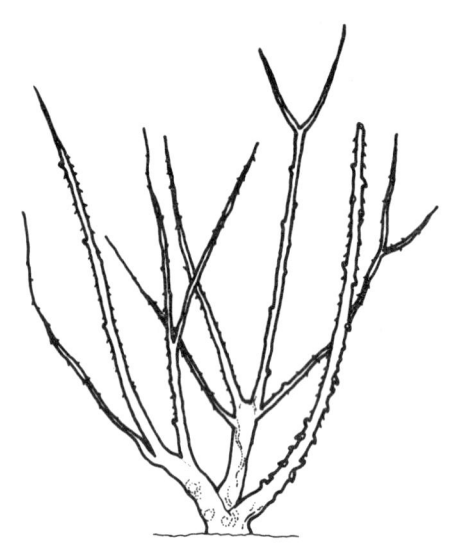

**Figure 2.** The bush rose, usually 2–4ft (0.6–1.2m) high, is the most popular type.

**Standards** are basically bush forms that have been budded, or less often grafted, on to single stems anything from 2–2½ft (0.6–0.8m) high (**half-standard**) to 3½ft (1m), 4ft (1.2m), 5ft (1.5m) and sometimes even a little higher than that. The objective with half standards is mainly to lift a particular plant above its neighbours, and add height and variation in an otherwise uniform bed. They are also used in pots and containers on patios and courtyards, where they look attractive and are not so liable to be blown over as the taller full standard. With the standard rose, apart from the aesthetic beauty of its form, the main purpose of the extra height is to lift blooms to eye and nose level where they can be more easily appreciated. The standard is really an aberration of the natural form – a manufactured monstrosity albeit a beautiful one – and, as so often happens when man confines, restricts and changes the shape of plants, there is an inherent structural problem, which we will discuss when we come to aftercare, pruning and feeding.

**Figure 3.** The standard rose is really a bush rose growing on a single stem. Heights of 5ft (1.5m) or more call for strong staking; this standard has three ties to a stake carried well into the head, for extra protection.

A **weeping standard** achieves a different form by having not a bush type but a rambler budded into the top of the stem, from where the long flexible rambler stems hang and drape down like a floral curtain. Regarded by many as the most beautiful form of all, it is usual to enhance the curtain effect by budding 1–2ft (0.3–0.6m) higher than the normal bush type standard – 6ft (1.8m) or even 7ft (2.1m) from ground level – and to spread and support the draping stems from a wire umbrella like a large floral crinoline.

**Ramblers** are for the most part hybrids of the Japanese species *Rosa wichuraiana*, or have it somewhere in their not-too-far-distant

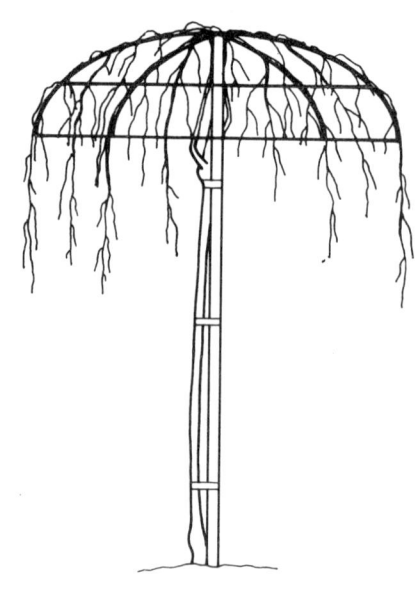

**Figure 4.** A weeping standard rose – a rambler growing from the top of a single stem – is especially beautiful when draped over a shaped top support, as here.

ancestry. In their natural environment, ramblers spread and sprawl over the ground or up into and over other plants or objects that offer support – a more literal name would be 'scrambler' – and their frequent use is to be tied to and draped over arches, pergolas, fences and similar supports. They have one short season of bloom, with large trusses of relatively small flowers, then all is over, and they have to be cut back to produce new growth for next year's display. Perhaps for the sake of brevity, although not for precision and clarity, it is not unusual in some catalogues and lists to find some species roses included under the rambler heading, which like *R. wichuraiana,* have the same sprawling habit and are sufficiently vigorous to get up into trees.

**Climbers** are often confused with ramblers, which is perhaps not altogether surprising in view of their similarities, and is not helped by the practice in many nursery catalogues and garden centres of grouping the two together. However, without being too pedantic about it, there are clear differences which it is as well to realize and bear in mind. The typical climber develops a thick strong stem which, although pliable enough when young to be bent and trained to a support, becomes woody and rigid by its second year. They are more suitable, therefore, for straighter runs and flatter surfaces, like fences, house walls and trees, than to being turned, twisted and trained to an arch or pergola. Another effect of the development of the hard woody stem is that, as soon as they are established, climbers drop the tendency to put up new growth from ground level (as ramblers do) and so pruning has to follow a different principle (see pages 54–72). Normally, climbers produce larger flowers than ramblers, and quite often several times again during a season – hence the description 'repeat' flowering.

**Climbing sports** originate for the most part from bush types 'sporting' extra long canes which still bear the same flowers as the parent. As we have already discussed, the ancestry of the rose is extremely wide and complicated, and although extraordinary genealogical detective work has been carried out into many family trees, one wonders how it is possible to be sure of the right direction when travelling through the mists and fogs of time, especially during the period before copyright was extended to plants, when secrecy was a safeguard against competition. Occasionally, a hiccup in the genetics occurs. If the aberration can be propagated and maintained, we have a climbing version of a conventional and matching bush type. However, climbing sports differ from true climbers in that invariably they do not bloom until the second year wood, and then only on side shoots, and seldom repeat much after the first burst of bloom during June.

**Pillar** roses are in the main simply less vigorous ramblers – climbers and climbing sports are sometimes included – that normally do not reach more than about 9–10ft (2.7–3m) in height or cane length. The term 'pillar' indicates the purpose for which they are well suited – tying and training to a pillar, pole, tree stump or whatever – although of course they will also do quite well on a fence or wall.

The term **shrub** rose is often used confusingly with bush rose. There is no clear definition of precisely what is, and what is not, a shrub rose – indeed, some catalogues, from quite reputable houses too, describe the shrub type merely as one that differs from the bush, the climber, the rambler, the miniature and others, and cannot be conveniently classified with them. Smaller forms can be interplanted with bush roses, but normally shrub roses grow much larger than the bush forms – 8ft (2.4m) and 10ft (3m) high and wide being quite common – with considerable variation in habit and the way they carry their branches and blooms. A shrub rose may be a true species, pure and simple, it may be ancient, or it can just as well be a highly cross-bred product of more recent times. By and large, however, shrub roses are not so far from their natural origins and include many that are perpetual or recurrent flowering.

**Miniature** roses, sometimes not more than 6 inches (15cm) high when full grown, are often denigrated and derided as toys – which is most unfair because a great many people with the most limited facilities who would otherwise miss out are thus enabled to experience the satisfaction of rose growing. It is not surprising that the demand for and popularity of miniature roses have increased as garden sizes have diminished. For a long time the type remained quite insignificant, but in recent years the increasing attention has added many new varieties, and a few miniature standards are also now available.

The same circumstances that have brought more attention to the miniatures are no doubt a big factor in the development of a grouping as yet not officially recognized, but being listed and offered by more and more growers. **Patio** roses occupy a small niche between the true miniatures and the ubiquitous bush size, and are therefore eminently suitable for planting in and around patio paving, pots and containers.

## 'Breed types'

As stated earlier, the vast numbers of rose species and natural hybrids have been multiplied out of all knowledge by the intuition and skill of the human mind and hand. It is not possible here, neither is it necessary for our purpose, to attempt a historical analysis of the evolution of the rose genus into the many classifications, types and kinds. However, what I feel will be of interest to many rose gardeners, bearing in mind the many questions asked, is an explanation of terms like Hybrid Tea, Floribunda, Polyantha, and the rest.

The **Hybrid Tea** (abbreviated to H.T.) is the type most gardeners regard as the epitome of all that a rose can and should be. Whether the bloom shape is the ultimate, only time will tell, for there have been other occasions in the development of the rose when a new type has been regarded as the last word. In recent years the H.T. has been grown more than any other, both as bush and standard, and such is the sublime beauty of the opening bud that H.T.s invariably take all the prizes at the shows. They are in such demand that we have the phenomenon of an industry geared to satisfying a craving for new varieties every year. So many thousands of differences have been hybridized and bred for that it has become well nigh impossible to find a variation that has not been tried before, but which is new, and can reap a rich reward for the nursery that is first on to the market with it. Today, the rose, especially the H.T. and its offspring, the Floribunda, is very big business indeed, and played for huge winnings, with large multi-national companies paying fortunes to have a new rose variety given the company name.

The basic characteristic of the H.T. is that the flowers are invariably double with so many petals – sometimes to their detriment in wet weather – that the centre becomes pushed up to a high point – in the classic shape that everybody likes to see. We have run the whole gamut of colour with the post-war American varieties, then the swing back to Europe for scent with the colour, then the bi-colour with the petals showing contrasting colours on each side, revealed so attractively as the petals curl back on themselves. We have nearly every colour of the spectrum from purest white and cream through yellow, orange, pink and scarlet to deepest velvet black crimson. Barring the almost frantic effort in the search for the elusive clear and genuine blue, it must be a colossal headache to the raisers to think up something new.

And yet, the astonishing fact is that the H.T. that we know and take for granted today is not much more than a hundred years old, generally accepted as having originated in 1867 with the variety called 'La France'. It is quite certain that the poets Shakespeare, Keats, Byron and Wordsworth never saw a Hybrid Tea rose. Even the early varieties developed in the time of Browning and Tennyson were nothing like the splendours of today, and one wonders what the genius of their poetic expressions would have made of the ethereal glow in the half light of 'Super Star' (see page 129), the exquisite shape and deepest of all crimson-black red of 'Charles Mallerin' or a hundred and one other modern marvels.

As we have said, the ancestry of the modern H.T. is a genealogical maze – not to say minefield – and although tracing parentage is an absorbing passion for some, going to that extent is not the purpose here. The point to bear in mind is that all that glisters is not gold, and there has been a price to pay for all the splendour. The more the hybridizing and crossing back and forth has concentrated on the spectacular, the further it has taken the plants from the vigour of their **natural origins, and the less resistant many have become to pest and** disease. Evolved in the cut and thrust of nature, 'wild' plants have to fight and resist – or perish. The high society platinum beauty brought up in a secluded hot-house may look a million dollars on the show stand, but is all too liable to fall flat on her face at the first pinprick of adversity and does not stand a chance unless she is cocooned in protective sprays.

**Hybrid Perpetual** (abbreviated to H.P.) is a term not much used now. This grouping derived primarily from the Tea, Pernetiana and Bourbon roses, all with their origins in China, were the parents of the Hybrid Teas and naturally bear a close resemblance to them, having passed on much of their form, fragrance and perpetual or recurrent flowering. Because of the popularity of the Hybrid Tea, H.P.s have been largely superseded by their offspring. Not many growers offer them any longer as a separate classification, and there is a general tendency to lump a few – if any – with others in a rather cursory grouping as Old roses. Any collection worthy of the name, and the space of course, should contain a representative or two, but you will probably have to go to a specialist grower like David Austin to find a decent descriptive list from which to choose.

**Floribundas**   If there was one criticism of the H.T. it was that, although the blooms were undoubtedly beautiful, there were not many of them – not enough at any rate to satisfy many gardeners who simply wanted more on each plant. So, the H.T. was cross-bred with Polyantha varieties derived from *Rosa multiflora*. This has produced a type with the upright carriage and bearing of the H.T., but which flowers in clusters like the Polyantha. The individual blooms can be single, semi-double, or fully double like the typical H.T. – although normally just a little smaller – and the clusters succeed each other almost continuously, or at least are recurrent, from early summer to November.

The Floribunda has become very popular, and as this has increased so has the H.T. influence increased over the Polyantha to the extent that we now have H.T. type roses being borne in abundance. Nowadays vying with the H.T. for the most varieties offered and space occupied in many catalogues, the Floribunda is available in bush and standard form and, more recently, in patio and miniature forms.

The **Polyantha** was developed from *R. multiflora*, a white multi-flowered climbing species from China and Japan. It is now available in a wide range of colours, small flowered clusters, and in bush form.

As you might expect from such headlong cross-breeding and

hybridizing in the incessant search for something different and new, the various types are so widely stretched that the edges tend to run into each other and merge, and the dividing line becomes ever more difficult to discern. The genealogist has a job to sort it all out, so it is no wonder that many rose lists get into a mess and tend to lump types together more for brevity and convenience than for strict botanical clarity. Bear this in mind when you peruse the catalogues and the plants on offer in the nursery garden centre plunge beds.

Alas, in most gardens, especially suburban, most of the Old and shrub roses will hardly be thought suitable (size alone rules them out) but that is not to say all will be unsuitable, any more than all H.T.s and Floribundas are really suitable. Whatever we may think of their evocative names, 'Queen Elizabeth' and 'Peace' are much too boisterous to be given room in genteel society. But if you are prepared to spare the time, settle down in an armchair and explore among the oldies in a good descriptive catalogue like David Austin's *Handbook of Roses* (see Bibliography), who knows what nuggets of gold you might find to fit into your garden? In gardening, he who does not seek, does not deserve to find.

# Breed and species names

In many catalogues you will find exotic-sounding breed names and references to them, but seldom much explanation of just what they amount to. Here we look at the more important names.

**Alba** is a very old breed, originating from a European species dating back at least to medieval times. The flowers can be semi-double, double and quartered, but have a limited colour range from the white of the base species through blush to pink – which is attractive when seen against the grey-green foliage. They require little or no pruning or other attention, being remarkably resistant to disease, and are among the hardiest of all roses, thriving in conditions that would frighten the life out of most others. They will make from 4–6ft (1.2–1.8m) high and wide, with a tendency to branch and spread at the top, so are not really suitable where space is limited. The fragrant large blush-tinted but rather ragged double *R.a. maxima* is the emblematic 'Jacobite Rose' often seen in Scottish gardens.

The **Bourbon** group derive from a cross between two Chinese species, but took the name from the Ile de Bourbon, later renamed Reunion Island, in the Indian Ocean, from where they came to Europe in 1817. They can make large shrubs – some will get up to 7ft (2.1m) high and as wide – with large flattish blooms and a colour range from white through pink and red to deep crimson. Heavily scented, they share the parentage with another scented Chinese species of the Hybrid Tea. The Bourbon variety 'Mme Isaac Pereire', with huge crimson blooms, has for long been widely regarded as the most powerfully scented rose of all. Be careful however; it is vigorous and can make 7ft (2.1m) high and wide without trouble (see page 132).

The **China** roses derived from *R. indica* – one of the parents of the Bourbons, and thus the H.T.s – have small blooms that are borne regularly and repeatedly throughout the entire flowering season. They are often listed with others of similar appearance but not the same derivation, consequently causing some confusion to the purists. The old and still very popular variety 'Old Blush China' is reputedly 'The Last Rose of Summer' of the nineteenth-century poet Thomas Moore, no doubt due to its remarkable reluctance to stop blooming each autumn.

Mostly twiggy bushes about 3–4ft (1–1.2m) high and wide, although some are larger, China roses must have full sun. In fact, that is allied to their one main fault: they are rather tender, don't like exposed positions and can be badly cut about by cold winds. They require very little attention – the only pruning needed is the removal of old barky wood, and of course that cut back by wind.

The **Damask** rose grouping is characterized by an elegant, upright, stately growth, taller than wide, and holding its double, semi-double and quartered flowers, all with a pleasant fragrance, more in open bunches than tight clusters. The 'Versicolor' form of the species type *R. damascena* has flowers sometimes white, sometimes rose-pink, sometimes a mixture of both, and is reputedly the origin of the emblems of the feuding York and Lancaster families. A smaller-growing, more compact form, the **Portland** roses, are closely related and are often listed with the Damasks. They are distinguished by bearing their blooms very close to and within the foliage, but are repeat flowering.

The **French** or **Gallica** roses are probably the oldest cultivated roses of European origin, and can arguably be traced back for 3,000 years. They were much favoured by the French (hence the name), who developed and raised them to prominence in the seventeenth and eighteenth centuries, until the introduction of the Chinese wonders. Mostly short bushes, seldom over 3–4ft (1–1.2m), they are notable for crimson and purple single and semi-double blooms, all having the typically 'French' perfume.

Included in this grouping is the celebrated 'Rosa mundi', with single crimson cerise flowers vividly striped with white – a showy flower beloved of the Elizabethans and Tudors. Incidentally, although sometimes called the Tuesday rose, it has nothing to do with the French words for either Monday (*lundi*) or Tuesday (*mardi*). It is much more likely that the name commemorates 'fair Rosamond', the mistress of Henry II. However that may be, there is no doubt at all that it is still the most popular of the Old roses.

The **Noisette** roses are an old cottage garden favourite of yesteryear, consisting of repeat and perpetual flowering climbers, invariably of considerable beauty. However, there is wide variation in the group, and care is needed in the selection. All have fragrance, some very strong. Some are vigorous and will make 15–20ft (4.5–6m) with ease; others will have difficulty making 10ft (3m). Some are remarkably hardy, whereas others need the protection of a warm wall or even a greenhouse.

The **Japanese** or **Rugosa** rose grouping contains some very attractive dense rounded shrubs with longish stems, furry with innumerable small thorns. In addition to single blooms, there are several semi-double and double kinds that open wide and full with a 'mop' of smaller curled petals at the centre, sometimes shading to a deeper colour at the base that suggests bi-colour, a different and almost foreign appearance. All are vigorous, forming tough prickly 5–6ft (1.5–1.8m) shrubs – and one or two up to 8ft (2.4m) or more – so read the individual descriptions very carefully when choosing. The species type is very resistant to disease and is used extensively as a stock root for budding bush types.

The basic species type of the **Musk** rose, *Rosa moschata* originates from southern Europe, has white-yellow blooms, and can easily reach 30ft (9m) high. The type was developed considerably by German growers, with more amenable size, choice blooms and scent, becoming known as **Hybrid Musks**. Not a little confusion followed the development in the early 1900s of a distinct group by a clergyman gardener, Joseph Pemberton. Sometimes the **Pemberton Musks** are listed separately, sometimes they may be listed in with Modern Shrub

Roses as well as Hybrid Musks, or they may be listed in with it, which is all very confusing. However, we don't have to be exact and precise to enjoy this very fine group of roses with their large bunches of fragrant bloom.

The Pembertons clearly have the edge over others in the group, bearing much more bloom on long arching canes, and heavily scented. They require little attention beyond cutting back long canes by about a third in early spring, just as growth begins to stir, and then trimming back any remaining side shoots to no more than three buds, taking out old wood that becomes dark and barky to promote new growth from the base – and, of course, removing the flower trusses as they fade.

The basic species of **Provence** and **Moss** roses, *Rosa centifolia*, forms a wide, loose, open bloom (an influence to be seen in some modern hybrids), which has given them a rather derogatory name 'cabbage rose'. Being heavy, the blooms have a very pronounced tendency to hang their heads, which has passed on to its derivative the Provence rose. *R. centifolia* is also called the 'Painters' Rose' as it became a favourite still life subject with French and English painters.

A mutation that became popular in Victorian times was called the 'Moss Rose' because of a minute thorny, moss-like growth that forms on and around the bud scales, in some cases very heavily, and which is coloured. It is curiously attractive.

Although not large shrubs, there is considerable variation in size: some are no more than 2ft (0.6m) high and wide, and others three times that. Take careful note of the potential size – it is very easy to go wrong with these.

**English** and **New English** roses  One of the more diverting, interesting, and some will say downright difficult to explain, trends in the midst of all the modern development, breeding and hybridizing of H.T.s, Floribundas and the other Modern types has been the steady unrelenting interest of a sizeable body of enthusiasts in older rose types. Perhaps this is due to a reluctance to let go of the past, and perhaps too there is a parallel in other parts of the garden with the modern revival of interest in 'wild' and 'natural' gardens and plants.

In the past 30 to 40 years or so, one of the ways that interest in Old rose types has been manifested has been the crossing of modern hybrid varieties directly with old varieties and species. There is little doubt that this particular development was motivated largely by the wish to restore something of the vigour and resistance to disease of the older types to modern colours and shapes. In the event, the crossing of the very new with the very old has produced an entirely new race of roses that combine the softer colour and fragrance charms of the old with the advantages of the modern forms.

A common criticism of the early varieties was that they were only 'once flowering', and that the colour range was rather limited – but no more. The Wolverhampton rose-grower David Austin (who has led the way, and to whom the world of roses owes a vast debt of gratitude) has continued and persisted, with the result that what have become known as English and New English roses now contain recurrent flowering varieties, a very wide colour range, fragrance, vigour, and an undefinable but strangely characteristic old-fashioned charm and flower formation. English roses now include bush growth forms – both large and small – climbers, singles and the fullest possible doubles. They are a race of roses that are well worth exploring and are yet another example of the inexhaustible resources of the rose to come up with something new and different.

**Species** roses   As remarked with regard to the English roses above, and in addition to the crossing back of the new with the old, there has been a return to and seeking after the more simple and unsophisticated beauties of the species roses, their forms and near hybrids. Most of the true species are single-flowers, and seldom bloom beyond the one initial burst – this showed out in the early English crosses. However, we shouldn't grumble, because that is all that we get with many other plants, and at least the reason of interest and attraction is extended by colourful fruits (hips) in autumn.

Many nurseries are adding species and Old varieties to their lists and you may well find shrub forms, ramblers and climbers all grouped under the one heading. Be very careful if ordering from a catalogue and not actually seeing the plants in full growth; read the descriptions most carefully. There are some very distinctive and interesting roses to be found among the species which are well worth exploring and looking for, as you will see from the following examples.

*Rosa ecae* from Afghanistan, a 5ft (1.5m) shrub with fern-like foliage. Although the flowers are only 1 inch (2.5cm) across, there are lots of them, and they are the deepest, purest yellow.

*R. hemisphaerica* is the very old 'Sulphur rose' associated with the Redouté pictures of the art world. The large, full, double, pale yellow blooms are heavy and turn over to hang down. It makes a beautiful 6ft (1.8m) shrub, but it does need dry sunny weather to get the blooms to open.

*R. moyesii* is a well known species name, with large 3 inch (7.5cm) deep red flowers and contrasting centres followed by large conspicuously coloured and shaped fruits. The type has long arching canes and easily makes a 10ft (3m) shrub. It has several forms – of which 'Geranium' is perhaps the best known – that are of smaller stature and more amenable to the average garden (see pages 138 and 142).

*R. primula* from Turkestan (6ft – 1.8m – tall with small yellow flowers and fern-like foliage), and *R. rubiginosa* from central and eastern Europe (an 8ft – 2.4m – thicket smothered with single pink flowers and, later, with red hips), are both noted for the scent not of their flowers but of the foliage. This will pervade a surprisingly large area with fragrance, particularly on a warm moist evening.

*R. rubrifolia* is the rose much beloved by flower arrangers for the copper-mauve foliage. In themselves, the cerise-pink flowers are insignificant, but seen contrasting against the foliage colour they are very, very attractive. It makes a 6ft (1.8m) shrub that produces a second fine display in autumn with masses of dark red hips.

Finally, *R. xanthina* 'Canary Bird' is one of the most popular of the species roses, having 2 inch (5cm) bright yellow flowers on 7ft (2m) shrubs clothed with delicate fern-like foliage. It is an apt and evocative name – but do try to see potential purchases in bloom before you buy, as it is not always reliable and can disappoint (see pages 139 and 140).

There are very many more species, but I believe enough have been indicated to let you see that the rose is by no means restricted to the Hybrid Tea – there are many other kinds to provide variation and interest. Just how much you can have depends on what you have space for and the kind of garden you have. I cannot emphasize enough, however, the importance of learning all that you possibly can about the varieties you are interested in before you buy and plant. Modern H.T.s vary considerably in their vigour and size, the Old and species types even more so, and it is a simple matter to run into problems.

A few years ago I saw a catalogue offering Scotch, sometimes called 'Burnett', roses. There are several forms and variations of size, bloom colour and form; the variety 'Double White' has the added attraction of a sweet lily-of-the-valley scent. It is very easy to respond to brief descriptions in catalogues that are not fully descriptive. The basic species type, *Rosa pimpinellifolia* (or, as it used to be called, *R. spinosissima*) grows very well in most soils, but flourishes particularly in light sandy soils in which it can indulge its natural habit of spreading to form large prickly thickets by means of underground runners and suckers. Hybridizing with other species and forms dampens this ardour to some extent, but some varieties on offer are merely forms of the base species, and therefore can present problems in a small garden where space is limited. This is an example of why you should judge catalogues – and nurseries – by the candour, honesty and fullness of the information they provide.

Selection is not a matter of having everything that takes your fancy. If you are to get the maximum enjoyment from growing roses, just as much care is needed in choosing one as a hundred, and it is to selecting what to grow – and where to buy – that we now turn.

# 3
# Choosing Where to Buy and What to Plant

The previous chapter shows that there is an extremely wide range of roses, and although buying one may not seem a major event, costly mistakes can be made. Even this simple job can be a pitfall for those who do not pay due attention, so let's discuss a few salient points. We have some armchair gardening to do, a thoroughly enjoyable pastime and most important if you are to get the best from your roses.

There will be gardeners with established rose gardens who can only introduce a new plant at the expense of something else – a replacement of a loss perhaps, a substitution for something better, an extension or changed layout. Some readers will have been growing roses for years, others may be starting for the first time from scratch, with no preconceived ideas, pattern or convention to adhere to, and a great many more will be at every stage in between. No two readers are the same, any more than their gardens. All will want something different, and the only way to help everyone, whatever they might already know about roses, is to start at the beginning.

The first thing to do is to rephrase the question that everyone asks themselves, not 'what would I like to grow, what do I want to grow?' but 'what do I have space for, and how much time am I prepared to devote to looking after what I plant?' This means that, before you begin to think about colours and the names of varieties, you have to be clear about what you would like to do and what it is possible to do, perhaps planting kinds and types about which you may have heard but are not familiar with and which would add variation and interest to your garden. H.T.s and Floribundas are glorious, but there is such a thing as too much sameness, as the saying goes: 'having too much of a good thing'. Planting one rose or a hundred makes no difference – you have to think about it if you value your garden.

Replacing a loss is straightforward enough, but a new planting, a new feature or breaking new ground in a collection all need even more careful planning. This is why we have discussed the many different types first, and thus have some idea of all the possibilities available to us.

Relatively few amateur gardeners will be in a position to plan an entirely new garden of any serious size, so it would be rather academic to the majority of readers to go too much into siting and orientation of north, south or other aspects. Ninty-nine gardeners in every hundred have to put up with the garden they have, facing the way it is, and cannot pick and choose or move it around. In any case, even for those with the extent and shape of garden to be able to consider size, shape of beds, borders and orientation, aspect is not of crucial major importance, because with very few exceptions, roses are hardy and do not need mollycoddling. Indeed, several are at the other extreme and are so hardy as to be used for screening and protection in exposed positions.

Except for the climbers and ramblers, which are amenable to being trained and grown on walls and fences, roses can be said to positively dislike being shut in. They like open situations where fresh air can move through and circulate freely. Any obstruction and tendency to stagnant air conditions is an encouragement to the arch enemies of pests, like aphids, which get the chance to settle, and fungus diseases like mildew and black spot which also are able to settle, spread and press their attack. By and large, roses are for open situations and full sun, not dappled sunlight or shade.

For those gardeners able to cut out and plant up new beds, the nature of the rose does impose certain conditions if it is to be appreciated fully. Compared to many other flowers which achieve greatest effect when planted *en masse*, the rose is essentially an individual beauty which has to be seen and smelled close to. Admittedly, one has to stoop down to smell a low shrub, but that is not such a problem for most of us as it is to struggle through to the middle of a bed. Imagine a collection of a dozen roses, planted in four rows of three in a nearly square block – two plants are beyond reach in the middle, and the inner sides of the others are not easy to reach. The nature of H.T. and Floribunda bushes suggests that they should be planted in isolation, or in long and narrow strips where they can be approached both sides. At the least they should be planted no wider than two abreast where each plant can be approached from one side.

Of course, some kinds, particularly the Floribundas with their abundance of bloom, are suitable for mass colour effect, especially when colour is vivid but individual bloom quality and scent are not pronounced. The problems that then have to be borne in mind, as with large pads of H.T.s, are access for dead-heading, protective spraying and, if not weeding as such (they should be suppressed anyway), regular hoeing to keep the soil surface open. It is one thing in a park, where gardeners are working full-time, but for the average amateur with a job to go to five days a week, these are the sort of things one should think about even before placing an order, let alone planting. Roses need looking after, and it is no good at all planting a collection, or any number of them, if you are not going to be able to give them the time and attention they need.

Borders at the edge of the garden are usually fairly narrow; fences and walls at the back of a border may need thinking about. Pergolas and arches are not so bad for accessibility, but dead-heading means work above your head and that entails the use of steps, which require a firm path or surface before you place yourself at risk on them. The time demanded in maintaining roses is not great, it does not mean a number of hours or days a week, but it does mean a regular tour around, if only of a few minutes' duration, perhaps in the evenings, with secateurs in hand to snip or prune away faded flowers, and a puff or spray here and there as and when you find aphids or other pests.

Over the years, I have seen so many private gardens and advised so many gardeners on labour-saving tools and equipment, and what comes through loud and clear is that the biggest problem facing gardeners is that they are caught in the trap between growing all they would like to grow, doing all they want to do and having the time to do it. Too many take on too much, for the time they can or will devote. This leads directly to a situation that you should avoid. All too often, shrubs, including roses, conifers and the like, are planted not for their intrinsic beauty, not for an attractive combination of colour, but because 'they do not need so much looking after as plants that have to be lifted before the frost, and replanted fresh each year'.

We might almost call it 'convenience gardening'; whatever takes the least time and trouble. The times I have heard: 'We want it to look nice, mind you, but not take a lot of time. What about a few roses?' This is hardly the best of reasons for planting, and not the right attitude. If you just plonk roses in the ground and leave them to get on with it, they will probably get by somehow and you will get some blooms for a season or two, but if you are to get the very best out of them, roses most definitely should not be chosen, planted and forgotten about.

One point that is appropriate to bear in mind at this juncture, and that is often overlooked, is the difficulty, because of their nature, of mixing H.T.s and Floribundas with other plants. Somehow they just do not look right and blend. Old roses do mix much better, the Albas, Centifolias, Bourbons and Gallicas are happy in a mixed throng, but the H.T.s and H.T.-type Floribundas are more formal in carriage, and need a more formal setting.

Underplanting is another association with other plants that has its problems. I do not think that there can be any combination that we did not try during my time in the parks, and the only thing that did not look positively awful were the short growing, pale, less intense blues of violas and lobelia under pink and red roses – other colours and growing heights were invariably a tasteless rag-bag. Even these plants are difficult, because there is the practical problem of keeping the soil surface hoed loose and open with underplanting in position, and mulching becomes quite impossible. By all means try underplanting if you prefer, but without question bulbs of any kind should not be grown under roses. For one thing, they do not look right; for another, the decaying foliage makes an awful untidy mess. Furthermore, lifting the bulbs for dividing is bound to disturb the roots of the roses, which is just about the worst thing you can do to them.

This is an appropriate place, perhaps, for a few words about the use of roses for hedging and screening. No doubt the thorns are a very useful asset in providing a child and dog barrier, but there are a few points to bear in mind. First, make sure that a barrier – or any other rose for that matter – is entirely within the confines of your own boundary. Growth that overhangs a pavement, footpath or anywhere to which the public have access renders you liable for damage or hurt to passers by.

Secondly, the impression created by some advertisers, invariably at one end of the quality table, of a clipped formal hedge covered in double blooms, is an improbable exaggeration, if not a downright falsehood. Do not be taken in! There was a practice at one time – no doubt it still continues in certain quarters – of collecting the rootstocks in which implanted buds had failed, bundling them up and selling them off as hedging. These are no good for trying to implant a second time because the wood is a year older and much less likely to 'take'. As at any other self-respecting nursery, we always gathered ours up and burned them – but not these lads. If there is a bob or two to be made, old rootstocks may be sold as 'hedging roses' with a bit of brash advertising – it does not matter if the illustration is nothing like the truth, the media do not know any better – and somebody will buy them, they always do.

True enough, the stock species *Rosa rugosa* is often used for hedging, but if that is the hedge you want, you will do much better to buy plants raised for the purpose. There are much better ways of creating a rose hedge anyway; ramblers on a low supporting frame provide a more impassable barrier, with better blooms than *R. rugosa*'s singles.

So much for some of the more salient principles in deciding what you would like to grow, what you have the space for, and what you are letting yourself in for in terms of looking after them. Let's bear them in mind while we turn to the next step in choosing. Quite often, this begins with looking at the enticing pictures in the catalogues.

Most catalogues begin, usually with some proud and flamboyant phraseology, by describing the new varieties being introduced for the first time, and invariably, because they are the kinds that get most of the breeders' attentions, these will be H.T.s and Floribundas. However, I must warn you to be on your guard and to approach the picture gallery with caution.

An enormous amount of skill, equipment, patience, money and sheer luck goes into the breeding of new varieties, and if it has become customary to have to be seen to be introducing six, eight, ten, a dozen or whatever new varieties every year in order to be regarded as one of the top flight nurseries, then that is what they have to do – and who can blame them for wanting to recoup their investment by selling all they can? There is no doubt also that there is a peculiar element of 'one-upmanship' among many gardeners in being able to boast of having the very latest rose in their gardens. You may be affluent enough, in space as well as money, to be able to indulge in such fancies – and run the great risk of finding, in a year or two, that your early triumph turns to sad disappointment.

One of the most frequent questions I have been asked about roses goes something like this: 'I bought some of the variety *x* when it was first exhibited at Chelsea and the other shows. It was hailed as a new sensation and we thought so too. Now we have lost one and want to replace it but the nursery do not grow it any more, and we cannot find one that does.' (See question 3 on page 145 for the solution to this.) The most important duty that I owe you, the reader, is that I be absolutely honest and candid, and therefore, although I have no doubt that the growers will not like me for saying so, I suggest that unless you aspire to the show bench, or base your gardening on taking chances, you should not heed the blandishments but look instead for the shortcomings.

There are so many things that can go wrong. The new show-stopper may look a million dollars on the show bench and the exhibition stand, but be of little value in your garden. The prima donna admired by the crowds in the marquee may give up outside in the rain – like the glamorous film star whose bikini must never be allowed to get wet! The advice is often given to see roses at the shows, and make your selection there. There's no doubt, of course, the big shows like Chelsea, Harrogate and Shrewsbury are evidence of the remarkable skill and ingenuity of our rose breeders and growers in producing something new, and assorted tribes of writers, scribes and newspaper correspondents vie with each other to find extravagant superlatives to describe them – but it is all delusion. Fed, pampered, cosseted, all 'psyched up' for show day, what is the show-stopper like a day or two later? Does the exquisite bud become a floppy washed-out rag? Does the colour fade? Does dew or rain reduce it to a sodden pulpy mass? How many plants were needed to furnish the buds for the exhibition vase? Is it mean and sparing with its flowers? Is it soft and prey to pest and disease?

Be warned: time is a great leveller and it takes a few seasons in the hard world outside the show marquee for a new rose to find its true level. Five years can change opinions; ten years can erase memories. In all honesty, the history of commercial rose-growing is a trail of trumpet-blowing and publicity, so often followed by silence as the subjects ran out of steam and fell by the wayside. It is difficult to find out about such things; catalogues need to be read between the lines and the shows are full of razzmatazz. Of course – and especially when you only want a single rose to fill a gap – it is all very easy to succumb to the highly coloured and neatly packaged entreaties to impulse buying, conspicuously displayed in supermarkets, DIY garden centres, and even the local street market. You will find precious little information there – they stock quick-selling commodities, not the kind of roses we are looking for.

The basic principles in deciding what to grow remain unchanged whether one is growing one, a hundred, or a thousand. The only difference is that, the fewer roses you have space for, the more certain you have to be that the varieties you grow give the greatest possible pleasure, for the longest possible period and with the most resistance against pest and disease. Small gardens should not carry passengers or invalids with a limp. Naturally, we look for deportment and how the flowers are carried, for colour and splendour, for abundance, for the sweet scents and the period over which the bloom is carried, and for resistance to rain, pest and disease.

The rose fulfils these desirables more than any other flower, but we should not deceive ourselves. Of the vast multitude of varieties that are available, old and new, and despite the astonishing achievements of the modern breeders and growers, not many varieties match up to all or even most of the desirable specifications, and it is difficult, nay, impossible to name one that does not have some fault somewhere. For this reason, instead of joining in the stampede for the latest and newest, I suggest it would be more prudent to wait for a year or two to see if the strawberry blonde holds her place as a glamour queen, or in reality is a blowzy old dame hobbling into the has-beens in the back row of the chorus, where she will find plenty to keep her company.

Let's turn to practicalities. It is clear that we should not be led astray by glamorous starlets. By all means we may admire, but it is prudent not to judge by what we see at the shows. We should read the catalogue descriptions with circumspection – what they do not say is invariably more important than what they do – and we need to be more guarded when reading articles by newspaper reporters whose effusions are often more flamboyant than they should be.

The best and most reliable way to get good information – there is no comparison – is to go and see roses actually growing. It is rather like something that I used to do as a young groundsman coming up through the ranks, when I applied for vacant jobs all over the place, the bigger and more prestigious the place the better, and more often than not without the slightest intention of taking the job if it had been offered! Apart from the invaluable experience thus acquired of conducting oneself at interviews, I was able to walk over grounds and sporting venues and to compare the standards with my own at home.

Without being in the least conceited about it, I soon was able to judge whether my cricket square was as good as some county grounds, whether my soccer and rugby pitches compared to professional clubs, and whether my tennis courts were as good as the big venues seen on TV. That was the best way to find out how good you were at your job, whether you could regard yourself as being on a par with the best – or still had a lot to learn. I learned a vast amount!

I wasn't the only one to do this. Other young fellows were doing the same thing; we used to meet and recognize each other and compare notes – and pretty scathing we were at times with what we found. If that was revealing in its way, then it is just as revealing to see roses actually growing, and not just read what others say about them.

Without a doubt, if you can make the journey from where you live, the very best thing to do is to visit the Trial Grounds of the National Rose Society at St Albans, Herts, – the Mecca of the rose – where you will be able to get as much information as you want, and straight answers from knowledgeable staff. If St Albans is beyond your reach, perhaps you are better positioned for the gardens of the Royal Horticultural Society at Wisley in Surrey, or those of the Northern Horticultural Society at Harlow Car, Harrogate, in Yorkshire.

The respective national capitals each have rose gardens that are well worth visiting: Regent's Park in London, Saughton Park in Edinburgh, and Roath Park in Cardiff. You would be wise to phone ahead, especially if you are coming a long way, to check opening times because they vary from time to time. Another avenue of enjoyable information-seeking – sadly, not as well-known and patronized as it deserves to be – is the programme of private gardens opened in aid of various charities like the Gardeners' Benevolent Fund, from whom you can obtain a county-by-county week-by-week guide giving details of location, times of opening and points of interest. Many of these have roses in mature growth, and this is where you not only see potential sizes but can also get ideas of settings of other roses or other plants that you can copy in your garden. This is throughly enjoyable and could not be more informative. Always carry a notebook with you!

Finally, there are the several nurseries which specialize in roses – indeed, some grow nothing else – and which welcome visitors to walk around the pads and fields to look at what they are buying. In the reference section on pages 264–5 is a list from which you may be able to find one or more near you. They are given in alphabetical order, and **from my own experience I know them to be absolutely reliable.** In fact,

I knew the principals of all these nurseries personally, and enjoyed a mutual respect with them. Of course, there are many more very good rose growers around the country, some relatively new on the scene, just as many old and respected names have moved aside for one reason and another. I cannot get around now as I was once able to for my newspapers – but I stick to my policy now, as then, of wanting to see and size up would-be advertisers beforehand, so beg the pardon of the newcomers not included in my list.

Even if you cannot reach any gardens or nurseries to see roses in action and have to rely on catalogues and lists, there is a great deal of enjoyment to be derived from weighing up the pros and cons and in the anticipation of the pleasures to come, just like choosing a holiday from the glossy brochures. The parameters one will use to decide where to place an order are somewhat similar to choosing which holiday and which brochure. Essentially, you will be looking for the fullest possible information, not only about how fantastic the colour is, but about all the other factors we have been discussing, and how candid are the comments on the shortcomings. A good rose-grower is proud of what he grows and what he sells. He earns the right kind of reputation not by extravagant claims and dressing-up, but by reliability, interest in and service to his customers. Any fool can go out, ring a bell, shout his head off, and get some new customers, but will he keep them in the future? Will they come again? And will the repeat business keep the nursery going for many, many years? That is the acid test.

And then comes the hard work as, like packing your holiday case, you have to whittle down all that you would like to take – or in our case, grow – to the short list. All the things you 'ought' to take on holiday – just in case it turns chilly, rains, is too hot, or whatever else – have to be reduced by sheer practicality, when forced to it, of deciding what you can possibly do without and leave behind. For most gardeners, a garden is like a pint pot – you cannot get a quart into it.

Which catalogue helps you most in this respect? There is no better way to compare them.

One way or another, you place your order, but the wise gardener does not just sit and wait for it to come. He gets ready to receive it, and we will discuss this most important aspect in the next chapter. However, before that, we have to deal with an aspect of buying roses that we have scarcely mentioned yet: 'container grown' plants at garden centres. There are garden centres – and for the most part, they will be attached to nurseries where the plants are propagated and grown, not just bought in wholesale – where 'container grown' really does mean grown in a container, and not potted up a few days beforehand. This is not to disparage growing in containers. It has several benefits, such as being able to slot a ready-growing plant into a gap to replace a loss or, on a bigger scale, plant up an entire bed, in bloom, overnight! The entire 1951 Festival of Britain on the South Bank was organized and dependent upon container-grown plants, shrubs, even trees 30ft (9m) and more high – I was on the preparation end of all that!

But 'container grown' means planted, established, growing away and capable of being planted in the open ground without root disturbance and without check. It does not mean – what it all too often has become – an aid to impluse buying, 'immediate' gardening, and the idea that 'if we lift them and pot them up instead of leaving them in the ground, we can sell them in a couple of weeks time as "container grown"'. Because of the very obvious advantages of growing in containers the practice, in far too many hands, has become a circus. I am anxious that no reader of this book becomes a clown.

If, for whatever justifiable reason, you consider buying a container-grown rose, or any other plant for that matter, turn it on its side, and look for fresh root action around the drainage holes. If it is in a whalehide pot, you will be able to plant the root ball and the pot because this will rot, without disturbing the root. If it is in a smooth plastic pot, and there is insufficient root coming through to prevent movement (i.e. the plant is pot bound), it should be possible to slide the pot away just enough to see if the root ball is held intact by root action. If it is not, and the root ball crumbles, you are not going to be able to plant it in the ground without disturbing the roots. It was potted up too recently, so reject it. If the nursery or garden centre do not like the idea of you looking, walk out and go somewhere else.

The best way to buy roses is still 'bare root'. They will be sent to you during the dormant season, and assuming that you have bought some in this way, we will now turn our attention to our preparations to welcome them.

# 4

# Preparation Before Planting

As soon as your order is placed, you will have to give some thought to the welcome your plants will receive. Catalogues come out early – you may have ordered as early as the Chelsea Flower Show in May – and although you know that the plants will not arrive before the back end of October at the earliest, more likely into November, you will have to plan where the temporary reception centre will be placed. You are going to need an area about a yard (metre) wide, for as long as you need to accommodate the plants – and that you will be able to judge as you read on. Whether you will be able to do the job in a vacant spot in the vegetable plot, at the back of a border or wherever, a suitable area has to be earmarked and reserved so that it can be empty and vacant from the second half of September on.

You can have no idea at all what the weather will be like when the plants arrive: it could be wet and the soil like a quagmire, it could be too dry, or frozen hard, and planting quite out of the question. Good nurserymen watch the weather forecasts, and do not despatch when cold weather is imminent. However, like a bad-tempered dog, the weather can turn very quickly, and whatever the weather charts show, by the end of October you could have frost and a covering of snow.

The better nurserymen pride themselves on their packing, so much so that they often advise you to leave the plants in the packing when planting is delayed, and to lay them up in a cool garage or shed. That probably is the best procedure if you don't prepare properly, in the time-honoured way, by 'heeling in'.

At the end of September, dig out a trench two spits wide (the width of two spades) and pile the soil in a ridge on one side. Trench and ridge will occupy about a yard or a little more at this stage; you will judge the length. Dump alongside a barrowload of compost, peat or fallen leaves or, failing that, old newspapers or straw. If you can lay your hands on some old sacking or cardboard cartons, so much the better.

When the order arrives, unpack it carefully and check the contents against your order and the condition of the plants. If the order is wrong, or if the plants appear badly dried, shrivelled, broken or in similar bad condition, now is the time to say so, and not weeks later, when they are not growing well or are dead, as so many complainants do! It is unlikely at this time of year, and so soon after lifting, but if the plants do show signs of dryness and shrivelling, immerse them in water as completely as possible before heeling in.

Quite often, you will find that bush and shrub roses have been cut back to maybe half their height in order to reduce the overall size so that they fit into the sack or bag – perhaps to get this through the postal system. This is usually done by a guillotine that cuts back a bundle of a dozen or so plants at a time, and it is not unusual to find the cut ends chopped and bruised rather roughly. Use your sharp secateurs to trim such stems to the first next bud, as if you were pruning, where the wound will heal quickly. Don't shorten the stems, just tidy them to a clean cut, and do the same with any broken roots. Make sure that the identity labels are securely attached, and take them out to the heeling-in trench.

Bush and shrub roses you can lay with roots in the trench and the top growth laid against the soil ridge, standards will probably need a third spit out so that they can lie supported and not blown around and damaged. Once the plants are laid in the trench, turn the next spit of earth loosely over the roots. Keep it loose, you are not planting yet; the purpose is simply to hold the bushes steady, to protect the roots from drying out and keep them in an environment that will encourage them to begin making new growth. If they have to stay in the trench long enough for new roots to develop, they are not so likely to be damaged if you lift them from loose, friable soil. Throw over a covering of compost, peat, leaves or newspaper, wrap with sacking or cartons, and hardy plants will then be happy enough, for a few weeks if need be.

Planting, the make-or-break job, follows as soon as conditions allow, but there is still a lot of preparation that should have been completed beforehand. By and large, planting roses will be in one of two ways: either planting into fresh ground, a new collection perhaps, where they have not grown before, or you may be making a replacement of an old worn-out plant, or where one has failed. The very first and most important principle to bear in mind when planting a rose or any other shrub or tree is that this is the last opportunity you will have to do anything basic about the soil underneath, where the roots will have to work.

We can do a lot after planting, but in no way so fundamental as doing the job properly beforehand. If the ground is vacant, and can be dug over, this is by far the best policy; the time and effort is worth it. The usual advice is to prepare the ground by digging two spits deep, but we are rarely given an explanation why, and for that very reason, therefore, we do not see the correct way to do it. It is hard work for most amateurs, using unaccustomed muscles, to double dig a whole plot, and although it undoubtedly improves fertility, the effort and perspiration always feels more justified when you understand why you are expending it – so here is the explanation.

The ability of soil to support plant life is an extraordinarily involved and technically complicated science, and although you do not have to become a scientist in order to grow roses well, you do need to use a lot of judgement in all sorts of situations. In order to do that, you need to know what you are doing.

Soil is comprised of several component parts that combine and behave together in a most remarkable way. The first component, the basic rock particle, can be large like sand and grit or microscopically small like the individual grains of clay, thereby imparting respectively much of the basic behavioural characteristics of different soil types: light and quickly draining, heavy, sticky and liable to waterlogging, or a happy medium in between.

Plants live with their roots in soil, which enables them to anchor themselves and stand upright. Through their roots they absorb nutrients that have to be in water solution – so water is the second component. Plant nutrients are derived in the most part from the decomposition of plant and animal remains, during which process they reach a peat-like structure that has remarkable powers of moisture absorption and retention, and at the same time has considerable influence on the physical texture and structure of the soil. In the final stages of decomposition this once-living (organic) matter, the third component, becomes jelly-like and is then, and correctly not until then, called 'humus'.

The decomposition process is the function of a whole myriad of microscopically small living creatures, bacteria, which must have access to the fifth component, air. All five component parts react with and are interdependent upon each other, so much so that all five behave as a single living entity. Remove any one and the interdependence breaks down, and is no longer able to support plant life. Generally, infertility does not come as a sudden cut-off point; rather it declines gradually, and when it is observed we have to look for the cause in the interdependence breakdown, and not just regard it as a shortage of one or other nutrients. Fertility is not restored merely by putting down chemical plant nutrients or fertilizers, neither is one component more vital than any other. Interdependence is interdependence of *all* components in a living working relationship.

Students are generally taught that soil consists of these five components, but actually, there are two more, the larger macroscopic animal life like earthworms, grubs, larvae and such creatures, and the living plants – but we need not get any more deeply involved. Just a point however, about 'soil-less composts' – this is really a misnomer. The term is used mainly for made up composts in which the rock particle is the missing component, usually to avoid the risk, despite sterilization, of introducing disease. However, the basic structural principle remains, and the primary constituents are present: air, humus, bacteria and moisture.

To the extent that a soil fulfils this interdependent function, it is fertile, not so fertile, or not fertile at all. To the thoughtful reader, it will be interesting – and sobering – at this point to interject an observation for your contemplation. In some places, this living layer of fertility exists less than an inch (2.5cm) deep, in other places at a depth of several feet, but in relation to the overall dimensions of Earth, it is very, very thin. Within this incredibly thin and fragile veneer lies the entire capacity of this planet to support land-based life forms as we know them, and that includes you and me.

Extraordinary as it may seem, it nevertheless is a fact that plants breathe through their roots, not in the same way as you and I with lungs, but the same chemical process of respiration goes on and, unless like seaweed and water lilies they are adapted to do so, plants can no more live in an airless waterlogged soil than you can live with your head under water. Apart from other mechanical purposes like weed removal and the admixing of organic matter, the main purpose of digging is to greatly increase the air content and revitalize the bacteria. Of course, if we do this two spits deep, so much deeper do we increase the potential for fertility.

However, all too often when two-spit digging is recommended, the point that is not made clear is that we should be thinking primarily about the needs of the plants that are to grow in the dug soil. Compared with a lettuce, for example, our rose roots are going to work at a lower level, and at planting time are going to have to work and make fresh growth (become established) in that second spit region. As a rule, and with regard to its proximity to the free atmosphere, air content and organic content derived from leaf and debris fall – and perhaps your cultivations, such as mulching – the top spit level is always more fertile than the spit under it. It makes sense, therefore, if you are going to be a hero and dig a plot two spits deep, to know whether to 'double dig' (reverse the spits) or to 'bastard trench' (leaving them in the same position).

To 'double dig', dig a trench two spits deep and barrow the soil to the other end of the plot, keeping the spits apart. Throw the next top spit into the trench bottom, and then the second bottom spit on top. Work your way to the end of the plot – top spit into the bottom, bottom to the top – filling in the last trench with the barrowed soil.

To 'bastard trench', take out the top spit of the first trench and barrow it to the end of the digging area. Instead of digging out and removing the bottom spit, simply fork it up, break it open and leave it where it is. If you can fork in some compost, so much the better, but the bottom spit stays down, and the second row top spit goes over on top. Work your way to the other end – the last trench is simply filled in with the barrowed top spit from the first row.

If you decide to dispense with a thorough dig through the whole plot and merely take out planting holes, at least try to follow the above principle: dig two spits deep, and reverse them with the more fertile top spit going down to root level. Under the new planting, work in a good lump of compost, moist peat, or contents from a spent growbag; this will serve as a moisture-absorbent reservoir to guard against the arch enemy of new plantings: drying out.

# 5
# Planting and Staking

Planting roses or other shrubs and trees, whether bare root or container grown, is a two-stage job if done in the best possible way, and an art in itself. Dig a hole wide and deep enough to accommodate the root system without undue bending and fill it with water. If you have time and can take a couple of days over the job, wait until the water has drained away, and fill the hole again. Do this a day or two before planting, so that after one or two waterings, the soil under the planting position is thoroughly wet, with the moisture where it should be – deep under.

Lift the plants from the heeling-in trench very carefully. Roses do not like root disturbance at the best of times, and any damage at this stage is another shock that they can well do without. Trim any broken or damaged roots cleanly and, if you are planting a bush, hold it up and look at it carefully. Visualize how it is going to fit in with its neighbours: the stems may be rough-trimmed, but you will prune them later in early spring, not now, and then the new growth will follow much the same line of the present branches. Some budded bushes like roses can be a little lop-sided at the start, and tight packing in the nursery rows does not help. Decide which side to 'face to London' for the best viewing position.

It may help to build a shallow cone of soil around which to spread the root system evenly. Then spread a little soil covering, shake it through the roots, put on more soil, firm, and when there is sufficient covering for you to firm without damaging the roots, tread with the heel, not the sole, of your foot.

If the filling-in soil is a little moist, so that a moisture contact is made with the wet soil underneath, there should be no need for further watering. If the filling-in soil is dry, watering is needed only to make this contact, and no more. The bulk of moisture should be underneath, which is why you filled the planting hold beforehand, so that root action is encouraged to work down to seek it and in so doing become established.

There has been much advice given in recent years to plant with the graft bud just at or below the soil surface. The explanation is usually that the top variety – the scion – is encouraged to put out its own roots, and then you have two lots of root and a better plant. To put it mildly, this is misguided and misleading nonsense. Good roses obtained from a good grower are on reliable vigorous stocks which need no help from the 'weak top half'. Indeed, a good strong stock needs to be able to get rid of all it has to push into the scion, without any hindrance. Any resistance or reluctance by the scion to take everything, perhaps because it is getting some of what it needs from its own roots, and the stock has to start looking for ways to get rid of the unused energy, and that means making its own top growth, which takes the form of suckers or 'briars'.

The old practical experience is still the best advice: leave a good clear inch (2.5cm) or more between bud and soil when planting, and make quite sure it stays that way, especially when mulching later. It is a good idea to lay a thin cane across the planting hole, as an indicator where the soil level is, and as you plant and firm, adjust the plant height accordingly.

Climbers, ramblers and larger growing shrub roses can be expected to grow away and quickly make more top growth early on than the bush types. The demand for moisture at root level is therefore greater, and the pre-planting organic input and soaking needs to be more carefully attended to. Planting of standards and standard weepers is basically the same as far as soil preparation is concerned – the essential difference being that the plants have to be staked, and staking is something that has to be done properly.

You will need to have your stake ready well before planting begins because it will have to be prepared properly if it is not to be a waste of time. A stake is there to hold up the tree and not, as is so often seen, the other way round. Furthermore, a stake has to be substantial enough and in good enough condition to prevent the tree from breaking its neck. This can happen, and all too often does, in two ways.

Nine hundred and ninety-nine standards in every thousand are staked in a dangerous, albeit orthodox, manner – it is a wonder that losses are not much greater. The normal procedure is to link a standard to a stake with the top tie just below the head of fanned out branches, and very close to the implanted bud or buds. The sail effect of wind on the top foliage therefore concentrates stress at the top tie and in the vulnerable buds, which will be weak anyway for at least the first year or two. There is no recovery; the loss is total. The solution is to take the stake a foot (0.3m) or more higher and to loop branches to it so that the head cannot be turned over. The extended stake can look rather unusual, especially for a while after pruning, but that is a small price to pay to ensure safety. When you pay good money for a standard rose, you don't expose it to this kind of danger for the sake of short-lived appearances. The long stake is ridiculed by the theory merchants, and no doubt will be so again, but when they have had the practical experience, as I have, of losing hundreds of trees through their necks breaking under the weight of an Easter snowstorm, they will learn the commonsense of long staking.

The second type of breakage occurs not at the top tie but near ground level, when the extra leverage imparted by wind on the long stem reveals the weak spot in a stake that has been allowed to rot and deteriorate. The danger area is at ground level where wet soil and air meet, where rot sets in and where a wind-blown standard leans heavily on its 'support'. If the stake cannot take the strain and goes at the ground level weak spot, the plant stem has to bend sharply where it is trapped between its firmly-held root and the bottom tie. The result is then a nasty looking and virtually impossible to repair greenstick fracture.

Where stakes are needed, preparation for planting therefore includes preparing stakes of sufficient length and strength, and protecting them against rotting. A rose stem is not very thick, and it does not look very nice to use a stake so thick as to be out of proportion to the stem it is supporting. Ash stakes 1¼ inches (3cm) square are best – they will be expensive, but cheaper softwood stakes are treacherous and a waste of money. You will need each stake to be at least 2½ ft (0.75m) longer than the height of the standard from ground level to bud to give 18 inches (45cm) in the ground and another 12 inches (30cm) up into the head; a 5ft (1.5m) standard would therefore require a 7½ ft (2.3m) stake. If you can find a stake that long at the garden centre, it will probably be painted green, with perhaps a black painted end for the ground – don't be deceived. Invariably, this is ordinary paint and not protection against rotting.

If you cannot find ash stakes, use square planed hardwood – usually beech – from a DIY centre. Point one end and paint with Cuprinol green – make sure it is the green kind for garden use; the brown wood preservatives are very like creosote and can be harmful to plant life. Paint the entire stake liberally, especially the ends where end grain is exposed. Three days later, give the pointed end another coat along 2 ft (0.6m) of its length, to protect it to 6 inches (15cm) above ground level, and repeat again three days later so that there are three coats all told.

Standard weepers will be very much more 'top-heavy' and require a much more substantial stake. Bearing in mind that it will be mostly hidden by the curtain that will fall around it, and that it may also have to support a wire umbrella frame, a 3 inch (7.5cm) diameter or square stake is not too big. Protect it with Cuprinol green in the same way, similarly the timber of rustic arches and pergolas. The section that will be in the ground definitely needs three coats of Cuprinol treatment, but if you don't particularly want the part of the stake among the foliage to look green, use clear Cuprinol or varnish. Never, under any circumstances, use creosote.

Pillar rose plantings do pose a special problem, because they will grow so much taller and wider, and thus need very much bigger and stronger staking. Bearing in mind the awful job involved in renewing or replacing the pillar stake, you can see the sense in putting up a concrete post, or at least a concrete spur to which a timber can be bolted.

Stakes protected in this way should have a reasonable life. You will have to prepare them beforehand, of course, and have them ready for use before planting – plus the material to make the ties. The one thing you do *not* do is to plant your tree and then start looking for something to use for ties, any more than you bash a stake in afterwards and damage the roots.

Preparation for planting means having everything ready to hand before you start the job. I dislike plastic ties – and you will see why as we proceed. Making tree ties properly is an art, and it needs practice to do it well. You will need hessian sacking, soft string (called 'fillis') and thick 'tarred string', both of which you can obtain from the garden sundries store. You will also need scissors, which are more convenient for this job than a knife.

A standard stem should be between the stake and the point from where you will normally view the tree, so that the stake is out of sight behind the stem. Begin by offering up the tree to the hole, some root systems will be rather one-sided and you may need to adjust the hole accordingly. If the standard is single budded, the bud should be on the side away from the stake, and therefore 'facing to London'. When a standard is double budded, these are usually on opposite sides, one an inch (2.5cm) or so above the other. In this case, position the tree with the buds to the left and right, and the stake behind facing bare stem. You can thus arrange the tree in two positions, so try to have most bloom-bearing wood towards the viewing point, and away from where the stake will pass into the top growth.

When you are happy with the exact planting attitude, mark the stake position in the planting hole and, using a crowbar or pointed pole, make a hole some 12 inches (30cm) deep into the hole bottom to receive the stake. If you use the stake itself to make the hole, you could easily split it. Drive the stake in and tread it firm. With the stake firmed in the hole, hold the tree up with a simple string loop, and plant it just as you would for a bush – except that, without the bud to go by, you will have to look carefully for the soil 'tide mark' where it was growing in the nursery and finish off to that height, with the standard stem about 1½–2 inches (4–5cm) from the stake. Again, you may find it helpful to lay a cane across the planting hole.

At this point, whatever you are planting, take a firm hold of your plant with a gloved hand and give a gentle but firm pull, as though pulling it up again! If the plant lifts, you have not firmed enough and will have to do the job again.

Now for the ties, an aspect of planting and staking that is widely underrated. Ties can be literally of make or break importance, and many a fine tree is scarred for life and ruined by carelessness and neglect, purely as a result of not doing this part of the job properly. When I took my practical working examinations, making tree ties was worth a lot of marks and considered so vital that candidates who failed their tying failed tree planting, however well they did otherwise. Harsh, you may think, but that was as it should be. This is how to do it – and earn high marks! If you value your trees, you will take pains to master this art. It is worth it, believe me.

For a standard rose, cut a strip of hessian sacking about 3–4 inches (8–10cm) wide, and long enough to go round the plant stem twice. (Other standards like fruit and ornamental trees will be thicker and the sacking strip will need to be wider and the actual tie bigger, but the principle remains exactly the same.) Fold the edges over ¾ inch (2cm) top and bottom, so that you now have a double thickness 1½–2 inches (4–5cm) wide with a clean folded edge top and bottom. Starting with an end between stem and stake, wrap the rose stem twice, snipping off the excess at the same point opposite the stake. Tie the wrapping in position top and bottom with the soft fillis string. This first collar is made as high as you can work, just below the buds or branches, and tied firmly so that the hessian is not loose, which can lead to twisting and rubbing. Under the string will be four layers of sacking and this provides cushion enough for the stem to grow and swell without restriction until you remake the tie – in a year's time, at the most.

Now for the tie itself. The purpose of a tie is not, as you might think, merely to hold a stem upright, but also to hold it firmly away from the stake and so avoid any possibility of chaffing or rubbing. As we proceed with making a tie, the purpose of it will become apparent – as well as the reason why plastic straps, loops of string and, worst of all, wire loops, do not do the job and can be so dangerous.

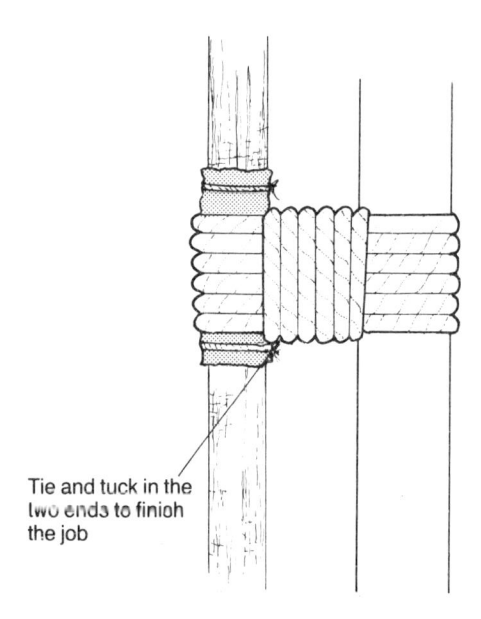

Tie and tuck in the two ends to finish the job

**Figure 5.** A properly made tie keeps your standard rose safely secured to, but not rubbing against, the stake. Ties should be inspected regularly and renewed annually, so as not to constrict the stem.

Make a hitch with the tarred string around the stake adjacent to the top of the sacking collar, lock knot it between stake and stem, and leave 3–4 inches (8–10cm) hanging (you will need this for tying off at the end). Use a piece of wood – or, better, a block of polystyrene – 1½–2 inches (4–5cm) thick, held between stake and stem as a distance piece. Wrap the string around four or five times, with the loose end dangling down in between. As you pass round the plant stem for the last time, turn the cord through between stem and stake and wrap the turns, pulling the cord tight to form a firm collar as shown in Figure 5. Finish off by tying with the hanging loose end, cut away the surplus, and tuck it up into the collar out of sight to leave a neat and tidy tie. Remove the distance piece – the softer polystyrene block is easier to remove without damaging the stem than a harder wooden block.

It will take a little practice to get right, but a tie made properly and firmly in this way will 'feel' right, and it will at once be clear how and why this method does a job that other methods and materials do not do. Make another tie about 6–9 inches (15–23cm) from ground level. Two ties may be enough for a 3ft (0.9m) stem, a 4 or 5ft (1.2 or 1.5m) stem will require three, and maybe even a fourth if you also need to pull in a bent stem so that it can be held straight to grow out of its misshapen state gradually. Loop in top growth using the fillis soft string, to prevent the head swaying about, check over for any broken or split damage and, finally, make quite sure that the identity label is legible and attached securely.

No pruning is done at this stage. Never mind what you read and hear to the contrary; your plants have had quite enough shock as it is without adding to it. Give them time to settle, make new roots and get established. Spring, when the swelling buds indicate movement and rising sap, is quite soon enough to direct their energies by pruning – and that is the area to which we will now direct our energies!

# 6
# Pruning

If there is one aspect of growing roses that creates a degree of bewilderment – if not actual fear – in the minds of gardeners, it is pruning. The reason, quite simply, is that pruning is little understood – again that word *why*. Understand what it is we are trying to achieve by cutting off a lot of top growth, and the where, when and how of it lose much of the mystery. As always, we have to be prepared beforehand, and as we cannot start the job without tools, this is the place for a few dos and don'ts.

For a long time the professionals had a preference for a pruning knife over secateurs. To what extent this was a natural conservatism and reluctance to use a different method of cutting, or a preference for the clean cut of a knife in skilled hands over the often not so clean cut of earlier designs of secateurs, or a bit of both, I'm not so sure. However, 'skilled hands' were the operative words, and because most amateurs found secateurs easier to handle and use, whether they were good, clean, bad, or indifferent in the cut, secateurs – often of the most inexpensive and dubious quality – have always been the amateurs' cutting tool. Modern secateurs are now so good, however, that professional opposition to them has virtually disappeared, and it is a rare sight indeed to see a knifesman carefully honing the curved blade with his special fine-grained carborundum stone, invariably kept in an oilskin tobacco pouch in his apron pocket. That is another old skill that has gone!

Without a doubt, the Rolls Royce of secateurs (incidentally, not 'a pair of secateurs') are those manufactured by Felco in Switzerland, and readily available in Britain. The *crème de la crème* of their range also solves the problem of blistered hands by removing the cause of blisters – sliding friction between skin layers under frequent and repeated pressure – through the design of a revolving handle, and is used, I think it is fair to say, by professional rose-growers and other nurserymen more than any other. They are rather expensive, but the best never comes cheap, no matter what it is.

Less expensive, but very good and popular among amateur ranks, is the range of secateurs produced by Wilkinson Sword. Both they and Felco achieve their cut by curved blades that slice with a scimitar-like action. Less expensive still, is the 'rolling cut' action of a blade against a broad anvil – the Rolcut is the best-known example. This cutting blade has to be kept sharp to perform its job properly without undue pressure in the hand, and is therefore made from a very hard steel – so hard in fact, that it can be brittle when subjected to a common form of misuse: the correct action with all secateurs is a firm steady squeeze, with no wrenching and definitely no twisting, which can cause the blades to break.

Unless you are snipping soft growth where there is little space between stems you wish to prune and those that you do not wish to harm, always cut with the object wood well back in the blades to reduce stressing the blades and their pivot. If this does not cut cleanly, never use excessive force – you are using the wrong tool. Put down the secateurs, and use long-handled pruning loppers – the type made by Wilkinson Sword are as essential to rose-growers as secateurs.

While on the subject of secateurs, if you cannot rise to the cost of the revolving handle type, at least make sure that the handles are polished smooth. Keep a little box of french chalk or talc handy to keep your hands 'lubricated' so that the skin slides as easily as possible over the handles, and so reduces the likelihood of friction. To meet this problem, most makes have polished smooth plastic handles – unlike one well-known manufacturer who, for many years and until only relatively recently, proudly proclaimed the brand name by imprinting it deeply all over the handles – which gave the user a good 'grip', but therefore virtually ensured sore, blistered hands whenever there was much work to be done

Sometimes, we have to deal with very old hard and thick wood that taxes the strength of even the loppers. Usually, such wood will already be redundant and dead, and a saw is needed. The 'pruning saw' normally sold for such work has teeth on two edges and, used in tight positions where it is invariably needed, great care and patience is essential to avoid the back edge causing damage to stems and growth that should not be harmed. You will find it very much safer to use instead the thin blade known as a 'key-hole saw' or, as it is called in the form in which the blade passes into the handle and is gripped by a screw, a 'pad saw'. These blades are very thin, and although the metal is often a little softer to allow for bending without a dangerous snap, they therefore bend that much more easily and should be used carefully.

Unless you are forced to do so, never use a saw on live green wood – the roughly cut surface it leaves is not conducive to healing – and you definitely will need a pruning knife to pare the surface clean and smooth. If you have to use a knife anywhere in the garden, and for whatever purpose, keep it sharp, very sharp. A blunt knife is a dangerous knife, because you then have to use excessive pressure, which makes a slip more likely, and then you will be lucky to avoid hurt and damage. On the whole, good secateurs are safer and cleaner for your roses, as well as yourself. They are one of your most important tools, so always keep them clean, sharp and oiled, and use them with care.

Finally, the rose-grower's tools will include a pair of leather gloves – not those flimsy rubber gloves used for washing up. They will have to stop thorns getting through to your skin – otherwise you had better also equip yourself with a fine needle, tweezers, and a strong light!

Right! You are ready to prune: how and when do you do it? There is an old adage which runs: 'If you don't know why you are pruning, don't prune'. It is certainly true that more roses are ruined by incorrect or purposeless cutting than any other cause. The basic purposes of pruning are two-fold: first, to divert and concentrate sap flow and energy into the buds and shoots that will grow in the direction we want, to promote or provoke new growth from dormant buds, and to better utilize energy by removing growth that has borne bloom, will not bear more, and cannot make worthwhile contribution to the plant's processes; and secondly, surgically to remove dead, diseased and infected wood.

Left to their own devices, most roses tend to develop new growth into which they direct their sap and energy, bear bloom, and which then – as it becomes old and tired – gradually either becomes starved, by-passed, neglected and finally aborted as the plant constantly turns its attention to new growth, or it develops a barky exterior layer as it settles down to becoming no more than a main road communicating between the raw material goods received from the warehouse in the soil and the production factory upstairs – quite often, a very long way upstairs.

In the natural course, a lot of the energy of the rose is directed into new growth – after all, the plant's continued and future existence depends upon it – but not all. The older growth of roses becomes bypassed, deprived and finally starved to the point of die-back only slowly; the transition is gradual, which means that some not inconsiderable part of the plant's energy is wasted in trying to sustain growth that can no longer produce the best bloom.

The primary purpose of pruning, therefore, is to prevent this situation and anticipate the plant's own eventual rejection or abortion of its aged growth by hastening its removal, and utilizing the energy to better advantage, diverting it into the production of new growth, shoots, stems and blooms. In the case of bush and shrub types, this will ideally be from the base of the plant to avoid the main road from becoming any longer than it need be, and to preserve and constrain the overall size of the bush.

Some species and types bear the best bloom on the current year's growth, others on the previous year's wood, yet others on short side shoots of current growth from last year's main stems. Some have a marked reluctance to break out new growth from the base, and are more ready to sprout shoots from growth high up. Some varieties, even compared with close relatives in the same group or type, are much more vigorous than others. Clearly, you have to know about the strengths, tendencies and habits of a plant before we even open the secateurs, or you could be cutting away the best bloom-bearing wood! It is absolutely essential, therefore, that each plant carries a durable and legible identity label, perhaps also a code or indication as to the pruning degree and method. Failing that, you must at least keep a detailed plan or map of your rose garden with such information.

If we may define the purpose of pruning as stimulating, promoting, maintaining, directing and prolonging the vitality of the rose, it becomes evident that we can segregate a great many principles, dos and don'ts into those that are general and applicable to all roses, and those that are specific to particular species, types and varieties. We have already been using a few special words, and as we shall be using several more, let's define the meaning of some words and phrases connected with pruning. The following are not in alphabetical or order of importance, but of convenience so that we may keep our discussion in an interesting and logical sequence.

# Definition of terms

**New wood** means stems and branches of the current year's growth. Most types, including H.Ts and Floribundas, develop their flowers on this new wood – in other words, new shoots and stems form and bear bloom during the one season. **Old wood** means a stem or branch of the previous year's growth, or earlier. Thus, by this definition, and for pruning purposes, late produced growth in autumn will have become 'old' as distinct from 'new' by the following spring, when it is scarcely six months old! Ramblers and many of the climbers flower on year-old wood: new stems grow out to their full length one year – and in the more vigorous kinds, this may be very long indeed – and then bear bloom the following year.

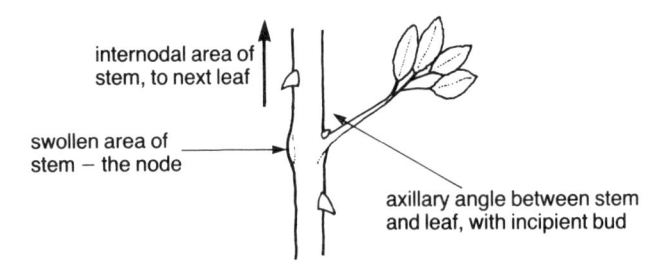

**Figure 6.** The eye forms in the angle between leaf and stem.

The **eye** is the infantile, incipient and sometimes scarcely discernible growth bud that forms in the **axil** or angle of a leaf where it is attached to a stem. Usually, the word is applied at the immature stage before the eye swells with rising sap, often changing colour a little – which helps to identify it on a leafless stem. **Bud** is also applied to a more developed eye as above, especially when one is implanted in a stem in the process of 'budding'. Of course, we also use 'bud' to describe an unopened bloom.

**Figure 7.** The eye grows out from the stem to become a bud.

**Budding** is the process by which an eye or bud is inserted in a slit made in the bark surface layer of another, usually more vigorous, type (see also Chapter 9 on propagation). **Grafting** is a similar process to budding, but not often used with roses. Instead of inserting an eye as in budding, the shoot tip of a host plant is removed and replaced with that of another. A **scion** is the growth that arises from an implanted bud or graft, whereas the **stock** – sometimes referred to as the **rootstock** – is the host plant that receives the bud or graft, with its own top growth removed so that its sap and energies are made to support the new guest.

A **leader** is a main or central stem that extends and grows along its own line of growth. This may be vertical as in a typical tree, or horizontal as in a trailing or rambling plant. **Lateral** is the word given to a shoot, also called a **side-shoot,** that arises sideways from a leader. Invariably, this is an axillary shoot.

A **sucker** is a stem growth arising either from a previously dormant eye in the stem or the root-stock, or from the healing tissue (**callus**) that follows a wound and damage to stem or root, and they occur in many plants, not only roses. Sucker top growth is often called **briar** in the case of roses, after the name by which the wild rose was known, and following the old practice of using rooted briar stems dug out of hedgerows for budding and grafting – at one time this was one of the chief occupations of gypsies, who would 'hawk' them by the bundle around less reputable nurseries. Briar growth is easily recognized by the different foliage, usually lighter in colour, and with seven or more leaflets to each compound leaf. Scion varieties are normally darker with leaves of only three or five leaflets, but this is not absolutely the case.

In some parts of the country **spur** and **snag** can mean the same thing, and in others have quite different meanings – but they are still caused by the same thing: bad pruning. A spur, sometimes inappropriately called a snag, is the result of either a breakage not being cleaned back properly to an eye or growth bud, or of pruning too far above a bud – a common case is cutting a bloom, and not paying attention to what is left behind on the plant. When a stem is cut midway between nodes, there is nothing the plant can do with the stem part above the last growth or eye, and so it dies back. In most cases, the stem simply withers back to the first node, and remains as an unsightly brown spur. It is then dead tissue, and open to attack by coral spot fungus. However, the withering or die-back can run back beyond the node before the plant is able to form a self protective barrier of special cells, and keep on running, even into the main stem, and obviously cause serious trouble. This is most likely to occur in weak sappy growth that has grown fairly recently, like a flower stem, and where leaves on that stem have not yet had time to make the carbohydrates and store the energy in the storage cells of the node. With insufficient resources stored ready to hand, healing tissue, callus, cannot be formed quickly enough at the exposed cut, which remains wide open to infection.

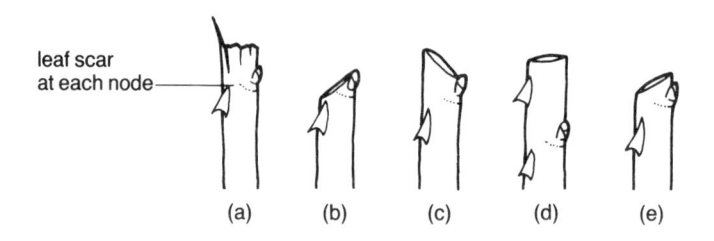

**Figure 8.** Pruning faults can be easily identified.
(a) This ragged cut, more of a tear, is too far above the node, and is certain to cause unsightly die-back.
(b) This stem has been cut at too sharp an angle, and too close to the bud.
(c) Here the cut slopes towards instead of away from the bud.
(d) A flat and internodal cut won't encourage bud growth but will cause die-back.
(e) A correct cut, properly angled, just above the bud.

Like a wound in your own flesh, a clean cut heals quickly, but a jagged, ragged, bruised gash can take a long time to heel and is open to infection all that time. Whether it is a spur of useless stem which does not, cannot, heal quickly, or a bad cut from blunt secateurs, disease spores are ever ready to accept the invitation of a door carelessly left open.

**Node** is the name given to the swollen area of the stem at the base of each leaf created by the special cells which store carbohydrate energy elaborated during daylight by the green leaf. For the most part, a node is a staging post area, collecting energy during daylight, and passing it on to other parts of the plant during darkness, when the elaboration stops, and there is not so much traffic on the stem main road. It does not all go, however; there is always some energy left in store for emergencies like leaf fall or breakage that needs sealing with callus –

no fools, these plants! –and it is this stored energy in the node that is utilized to form firstly healing callus tissue, and then 'adventitious' tissue, such as roots when we make cuttings with stem growth above a node, or growth buds when the cut is above the node and its attendant eye. **Internode** and **internodal** simply relate to the stem area between nodes and where the energy storage is minimal or absent.

# General principles

- Always, and without fail, remove dead, diseased and ailing wood, and spindly, feeble growth. Whatever other pruning is done or not done, this first principle is obligatory – even when the catalogues and reference books state 'no pruning needed'.
- Always make cuts clean and smooth with no ragged, broken edges to the cut, or slivers of stem left exposed.
- Always cut back to clean, healthy wood, with no discolouration or other sign of disease. Healthy, clean wood can heal – sometimes you may be trying to get ahead of spreading disease as it works its way into a plant, and pruning to discoloured, infected wood or leaving bruised, sawn and anything other than clean cuts only causes more trouble.
- Always make cuts at a slightly sloping angle – as shown in the sketch, and never at an angle that would allow rain, dew, and heavy moisture to lie on the open cut.
- Always make a cut just above a bud or eye where the exposed surface is near the nodal storage cells and will quickly form healing callus, and where the growth bud will receive the diverted energy. Never leave a snag or spur.
- Always remove suckers and briars thoroughly and completely. They have two sources of origin, above and below ground level. Briar shoots on standard stems and from the base of bushes should be rubbed off while still juvenile and 'finger and thumb' fragile. Don't leave them until they are so developed and tough that they will not easily pull away and have to be cut; this is merely pruning and you will thereby ensure that several adventitious shoots will grow to replace the one being removed. Stem growth originating from the root-stock below ground can be a problem because, by the

time these shoots push their way up through the soil and show out, they are well advanced and reluctant to 'let go' – gloves are essential. Clear the soil down to the point of origin, take a firm hold and wrench the growth away – never cut, no matter how resistant it is. Occasionally, you will meet a brute that refuses to pull away, or can even break or lift the root. Don't struggle: take a grip with pincers or pliers and remove the sucker as though pulling out a nail.

- Unless you are growing a rose specifically for the hips, always remove spent blooms – or the entire truss in the case of cluster-flowering types – a job called **dead-heading.** This is to avoid the plant needlessly spending energy on making seed. Even if you want the hips, never let a rose take on this effort until it is well established – three years old at least. Furthermore, especially when blooms are double or have many petals, it is quite likely that spent blooms will collapse into a rain-soaked soggy mess that quickly becomes a haven a breeding ground for mildew. This fungus is problem enough without encouraging it.

- Always, when dead-heading or taking flowers as cut bloom, observe the above principle of cutting or cleaning back to just above a node. Casually snipping off 'a nice bloom here, and a nice bloom there' may be very enjoyable, but unthinkingly can leave an internodal spur.

- Always clear up fallen material. Dead-heading climbers and ramblers can often be a massive job involving step ladders to reach up to pergolas, arches and walls, and the larger shrub types can present the same problem. If you have much of this kind of work to contend with, you may well find it worthwhile to invest in a 'pole pruner'. This is literally secateurs on the end of a pole 6ft (2m) long or more which enables you to reach up, with your feet safely and firmly on the ground. The main problem then, inevitably when cutting at this distance from your eyes, is to make pruning cuts as clean and precise as when the secateurs are actually in your hand. It is generally much easier simply to let cut material fall with this kind of work, but remember that clearing up every scrap afterwards is just as important as cutting it off in the first place. Old leaves, twigs and bits and pieces left lying about are the ideal propagating material and position for mildew, black spot, coral spot and all manner of troubles.

- Always remove rose prunings, leaves, blooms and other bits to the **fire and *not*** to the compost heap. Even if you are confident of your ability to manage a compost heap so that it becomes hot enough to cleanse itself of disease spores, there remains the risk of the subsequent compost matter containing thorns which are extremely resistant to decomposition. Handling such compost is then dangerous, because any wound in your fingers and hands, a splinter perhaps, has to be a dirty wound.

So much then for what may be regarded as general principles, applicable to all. It is when we come to the particular that you have to use your own personal judgement, opinion, interpretation of what you observe and experience. You will be concerned with what may be called the degree of pruning: do you prune hard, ruthlessly to ground level, or not so drastically? When do you prune? Just as many experts advocate autumn pruning as waiting till spring – who is right?

Gardening, and rose growing, is all about opinions. No two gardeners are the same, so how can their opinions be identical? What is certain is that, although a lot of 'experts' are ready to tell you what to do – and you may be the kind of gardener who merely wants a set of step-by-step instructions – the point entirely missing is that it is you, and only you, who has to use your judgement and make the decisions. So before moving to the particular let's see if we can draw some general conclusions regarding degree and timing.

It is true that much of the subsequent shape and form that a rose assumes is determined more during the first year or two of pruning than any subsequent factor. Most amateur gardeners are 'afraid of the knife' and do not prune hard enough, leaving too much old wood, with the result that the growth buds that grow on are at the top end of 3 or 4 or more inches (8 or 10 or more cm) of the previous season's growth. The base wood of the plant therefore grows higher each year and we get the familiar 'bush rose' consisting of 1 ft (0.3m), 2 ft (0.6m) or even more of old, bare and barky wood, with the current year's bloom-bearing growth starting from way up in the air! All this is the result of being afraid to prune hard enough early enough.

The inevitable result is that a plant young in years becomes old and senile in form and shape. When, in desperation, this kind of badly pruned bush is cut back hard to retrieve the situation, the base is so old and hard, that any dormant bud buried within is quite incapable of awakening and breaking out. The root-stock then has no option: with no or insufficient shoots to take the upthrust, it has to get rid of its energy with top growth of its own. This explains why so many drastically cut back plants respond by sending up suckers.

Bushes, standards and most shrub and Old roses should be pruned to outward-facing buds that will emerge to form an open 'shuttlecock' or cup-shaped structure, which is open in the centre. This not only produces a balanced form to the plant, carrying and showing the blooms to advantage, but reduces hindrance to air movement to a minimum. A stagnant, slow moving and bad circulation of air is a direct encouragement to disease spores to settle and take hold.

The 'open cup' principle holds good for most types – there are just two or three growth habits like Bourbons and Musks that do not lend themselves to it too well, and we will deal with them later. A rule that does hold good, however, concerns crossing branches and stems; these inevitably result in rubbed, chafed and damaged stems. Crossing is difficult to avoid in some of the larger shrub types, and in these cases, the stems should be pulled and held apart by a judiciously placed loop of twine.

The object is to promote stem growth in the desired direction line, but this will not be achieved if, as sometimes happens, a dormant eye emerges as two or three buds, or as not infrequently occurs on too weakly pruned stems, growth emerges in a completely wrong direction from lower buds. If this should happen, carefully rub out the unwanted shoots while still very young, leaving the strongest among multiple buds.

The first pruning after planting is the important formative prune – the plant cannot be expected to grow right if it does not start right. All first year pruning should be harder and closer to the base than in subsequent years. Bushes are on short, almost non-existent, stems, whereas standard top growth is exposed high up, and is more vulnerable to the consequences of weak and incorrect pruning. When in doubt, and given a choice of bud direction, always choose to prune standards a little harder rather than softer than bushes.

Some varieties have a weaker, less vigorous growth disposition than others and, even on the same plant, some stems and branches will be somewhat weaker than others. Contrary to what might be expected, these do not want mollycoddling or softer treatment – in fact the reverse. We have to make them concentrate what they have on the job in hand. Clearly, then, you have to know your individual roses to get the best from them, know their strengths, and their weaknesses.

The response to pruning is a concentrated and redirected burst of growth which will be more readily sustained by good, fertile conditions than can be expected on sandy, barren and infertile soils. Fertility conditions play a part then, and as hard pruning provokes the greater growth response, we should judge to ease back a little on poor, dry soils compared with more fertile conditions. It is all judgement and decision, weighing up many factors that all have varying influence, and you do what your commonsense tells you is the logical and rational thing to do.

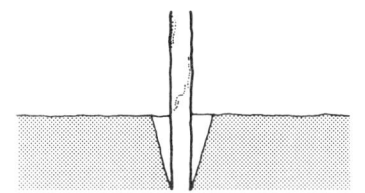

**Figure 9.** An unpruned bush may suffer from wind rock over winter, opening up a funnel around the base of the stem which could fill with water and freeze. Prune the bush and firm the soil.

Especially in exposed positions, it is sensible, for example, to trim back long stems and tallish growth in order to reduce the sail effect in wind and the resulting problem called 'wind rock'. This is a particular risk also with stakes – when wind blow rocks the plant or stake, there is a likelihood of the stem or stake opening a funnel-shaped hole around itself as it rocks and compresses the soil. In clay and heavy soils the risk is increased that the hole will then hold water for considerable periods, with the plant and stake actually standing in water. If it freezes, a collar of ice is then so much the worse, so it is a wise precaution to go round your roses after windy conditions and tread firm and close out any 'funnels' – but of course the danger to taller bushes can be much reduced by shortening sail.

When should you prune? Timing has always been, and no doubt will always be, a subject of debate. Extreme opinions are taken up – which is not easy to understand when you consider the principles involved. Fundamentally, roses are as much shrubs as any others in the garden and, like them, divide broadly into two categories as far as pruning is concerned; those that flower in spring and summer on wood developed during the previous growth period (i.e. last year), and those that flower, necessarily a little later, from mid summer on, upon wood that has developed during the current season. In the former case, the plants are pruned as soon as flowering has finished in order to divert energy into producing new wood to bear next year's flowers. Roses in the second category – including those that have been repeated flowering well into autumn — are pruned towards the end of the winter dormancy period when the sap begins to move, and the axillary growth buds begin to swell.

Ramblers, weeping standards – which are for the most part rambler types budded into tall standard stems – climbers, climbing sports and several species types all fall largely within the first category, but so often have peculiarities of their own that we should not generalize. It is wisest to treat each variety according to the details and information that will be contained in the better kind of catalogue – the sort of information which will also influence your decision where to order.

The overwhelming majority of bush and shrub roses come within the second category, that is, they are pruned towards the end of the dormancy period. When is that? I don't know – nobody does, and I cannot resist a smile of despair every time I see one of those gardening page headlines that advise us to 'prune those roses now' and such like. It is evident that the experience of those responsible for such advice has not extended to the fact that the north and south of Britain are as much as 500 miles (800 km) apart, and the climates can be very different. It is quite impossible, and very misleading to suggest, that pruning can be done according to the calendar. Winter dormancy may be ending in February in the balmy south-west, not till a month later in the northern counties, and weeks after that around Aberdeen. How can any writer know where lives the reader for whom the advice is intended, and what the weather will be? You have to use your eyes, watch points and, again, use your judgement.

Some varieties are early birds, and anxious to lead the way. Make a note of these in your garden diary, and watch carefully for the first sign of bud swelling, for they will need pruning first. Many gardeners will argue that there is a risk in pruning very early, that frost can burn and shrivel young foliage that unfolds as the buds expand. True, it is a risk – many a spring in Britain has thrown a frost at us in April, even May is not unknown – but you are not going to be so daft as to muffle up and go out to do the pruning just because the date or some idiot article says the time is right. If you are unlucky and suffer a bad frost-burn, be prepared to prune the stems further back to the next dormant eye, whatever its direction, and whatever the date.

# Pruning specifics

One of the rules of gardening is that all rules have an exception! Bear in mind that, while we may group and classify according to this or that pruning rule, you must expect to meet exceptions. When they occur, your catalogue and reference list will point this out – you really cannot know too much about each and every rose in your garden.

**Hybrid Tea bush types** After attending to the basics or primary aspects – removing completely all dead, diseased and feeble wood (you won't find much of this in the first year) – seek to prune to outward-pointing buds that will grow out along the line of growth, not sideways, so that this growth leads to an open cup or shuttlecock shape. At the first pruning, take each stem down to a suitable bud, so that ideally it is reduced to no more than 3–4 inches (8–10 cm) in length. At the second and subsequent prunings, a widely advocated rule of thumb guide is to reduce the stem length by about a half. As I mentioned earlier, you must always bear in mind the effect of poor fertility, and less vigorous habit. If you cultivate and feed your plants well – we shall discuss both later – you should be able to make heavier demands. My personal preference and practice – but it has to be supported by very fertile conditions – is to prune much harder than many think that a rose can stand (remember, don't be afraid of the

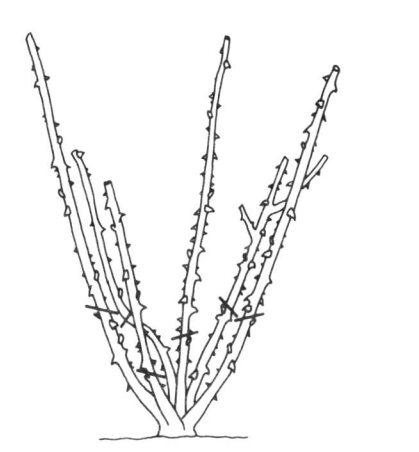

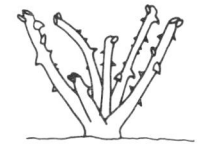

**Figure 10.** First year pruning will take each stem of a bush rose down to no more than 3–4 inches (8–10cm), cutting where possible to suitable outward-pointing buds.

knife, to three or four buds as necessary to find the outward pointing direction from the previous year's prune.

Pruning does not end with the use of your secateurs; you will need to watch that the growth bud develops properly, reducing any multiples to one single and strongest. Watch also that the cut surface dries and heals. Any sign of browning or other discolouration could be the onset of die-back, and if this is confirmed, you may be able to trim it away, but if it goes back below the node, you will have to prune back to the next growth bud irrespective of its direction. Remember also that cutting blooms for the house and dead-heading are forms of pruning, and the general principles should be observed, particularly with regard to leaving spurs.

**Floribundas** Pruning for Floribundas follows the same general principles as for H.T.s, except that it should be not so hard – the first year cut-back should be 1–2 inches (2.5–5cm) longer, leaving some 4–6 inches (10–15cm) of stem from the base and still aiming for outward-pointing buds to develop the open cup shape. Particularly in secluded, well sheltered, and not so well ventilated gardens, the open centre – and perhaps also the planting distance between plants so that they do not merge and clash – is more important with Floribundas. They bear more blooms than H.T.s: some are very floriferous indeed, and bear large clusters which in stagnant air conditions, can increase the risk of diseases like mildew and those pests that don't like being blown about.

Before leaving the pruning of H.T.s and Floribundas, here are just a few words about some popular varieties that are examples of exceptions proving rules. Not all catalogues draw attention to the fact that extra vigorous varieties will be overpowering when planted alongside less precocious members of their own family. Pruning to the same hard degree invariably results in an explosion of growth, and such varieties are really much better given enough space elsewhere to do their own thing, and be treated as shrub roses. The variety 'Queen Elizabeth' is a case in point and is the cause of not a little correspondence. Nearly in the same class are 'Peace' and, the purest white of all, 'Iceberg' (see page 130).

**Climbers** Some climbers are so strong-growing – almost rampant – as to be unsuited to being kept on a lead, restricted and cramped to the confines of arches and pergolas. They need the wide open expanses of a high wall, fence, side of a house, or even trees, where they can fling out and stretch their long stems – 30ft (9m) high is by no means unusual. So it behoves you to be wary when planting. It is no good thinking that secateurs will keep a 30ft (9m) monster down to 10 or ft (3 or 4m) – the plant will take on the challenge, break forth with even greater vigour, and fight you all the way.

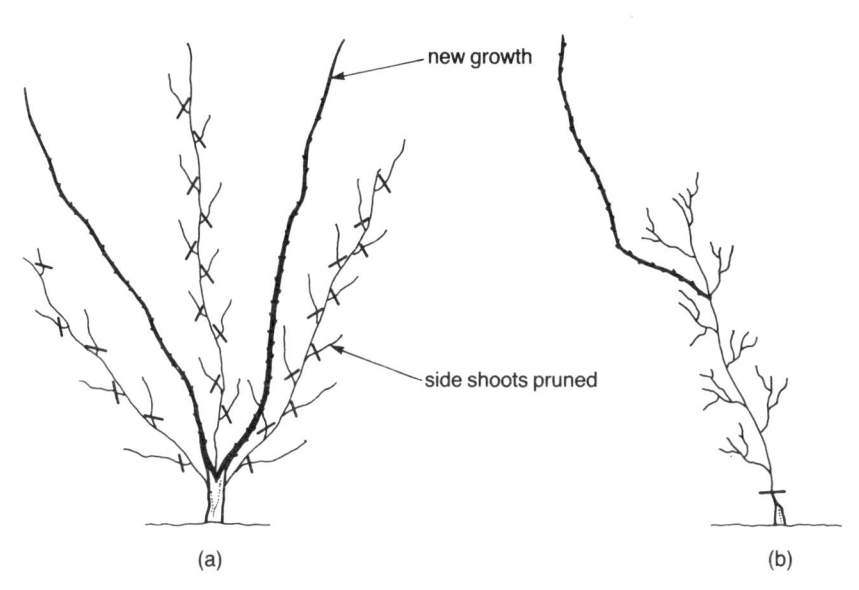

**Figure 11.** Climbers usually need only a light pruning, (a), to build up strong main stems and develop lateral side shoots. But if new growth breaks out too high on older wood, (b), the stem can be cut out to encourage new growth from the base.

As they age, many climbers – especially the 'climbing sport' variations of H.T.s and other bush forms that develop a liking for wanderlust and travel – get into the habit of flowering mostly, if not only, at the growing extremities of their stems. Depending upon each plant, where it is planted and how it is supported, this tendency can often be countered by cutting back hard, encouraging the break-out of new growth from the base – and then using a little plant 'psychology'. Given full rein to run as far as they want, the plants are living very well and don't feel in any particular danger, so there is no need for them to waste energy by perpetuating the species and going to the trouble of producing flower and setting seed. So, we give them cause to fear, and reason to give attention to reproducing themselves. This is done not by more pruning, but by making life distinctly awkward. The long stems soon become woody and resistant to bending, so while they are still new, young and supple, the growing tips are bent repeatedly – at right angles, or thereabouts if you can – every foot (30cm) or two, left and right, up and down. You may be able to accommodate this bending by tying in to a longish pergola or trellis on a wall or fence.

The bending and difficulty for the plant of getting sap through the restriction constitutes a threat, and the reaction to this is to try to make sure of the perpetuation of its own species by making seed – which, of course, has to be preceded by flower, and lots of it! Unlike the true rambler types with only one flush of bloom, the climbers group contains varieties that flower more or less continuously, and others that make two or more bursts or displays with periods between, during which little or no bloom is carried. The continuous types are usually described and listed as perpetual flowering, whereas the intermittent types are called recurrent, repeat flowering or, as the French call them, *remontant* (see also page 17).

Apart from the name of each variety, it is clearly important to know exactly the type and habit of each climber you grow. You may have only two climbers, but their habit, and pruning therefore, can be quite different. Generally, then, the basic objective is to build up a strong framework or system of main stems, and to develop lateral side shoots which are pruned back each spring to 3 or 4 inches (7.5 or 10cm), with a terminal bud pointing in the right direction to fill spaces and gaps. Only occasionally does it become necessary to cut out main stems, such as when they become old, gnarled and barky.

When grouped together with others, the climbing sports are correctly prefixed by the word 'climbing' to distinguish the subject from the bush type, for example 'Shot Silk' and 'Climbing Shot Silk', or sometimes less noticeably by the word abbreviated to 'Clg' after the name, for example 'Shot Silk Clg'.

**Pillar or 'short climbing roses'** By and large, training and tying into a single pillar or post is only suitable for shorter growing climbers that do not grow long enough to clothe larger areas like walls and pergolas. They are virtually a border line grouping between the strong climbers and the ramblers inasmuch as they need more use of the knife to keep young stems coming from the base.

**Ramblers** With very few exceptions, the ramblers are distinguished from the climbers by flowering in one display of bloom and then no more, on long flexible stems that have developed the year before. The basic pruning principle, therefore, should be to remove wood as soon as it has flowered in order to divert energy into the production of good strong stems to carry the next year's bloom. However this should only be in proportion to the individual plant's

PRUNING

new growth

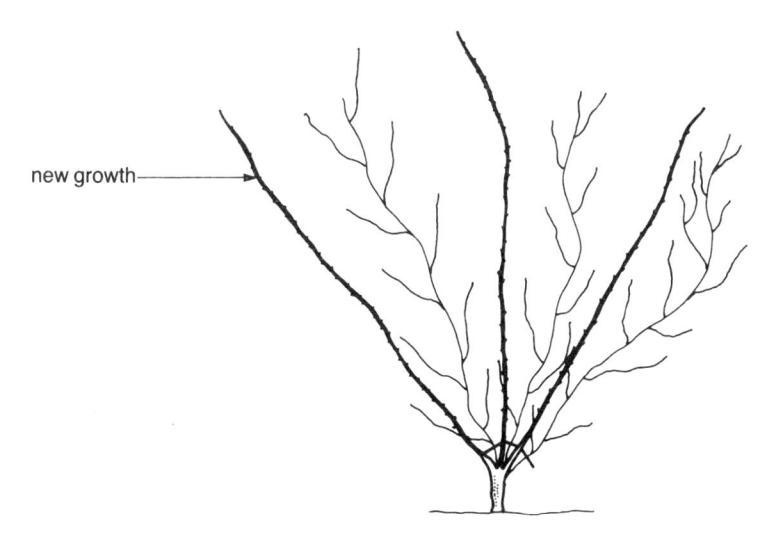

**Figure 12.** Wood is pruned from a rambler as soon as it has flowered, to divert growth into strong new stems for the next year's bloom.

capacity to produce new wood, and you may have to compromise and resort to some lateral side-shoots like a climber.

A good performance in later years means the sacrifice of bloom in the first year from planting. As soon as the growth buds begin to show signs of movement in spring, take the existing canes down to about 15 inches (38cm) from ground level. If you have prepared really well with a good wodge of organic matter underneath and a 'starter' of Humber or Growmore, you can ask rather more of a good strong plant by taking it down a little more – and, of course, to outward-facing top buds. This will remove any possibility of bloom in the first year, but it will concentrate the plant's mind on good long stems which will need tying in to a support like a pergola or arch to show next year's bloom to best advantage.

Pruning in the second and subsequent years should try to begin a routine or system – and only your cultivation and experience will determine this – of removing wood that has flowered in proportion to the amount and vigour of new wood that the individual plant puts up. Even in the same garden, plants of the same variety will vary. To get the very best results you will need to observe closely, compare, make notes, and use your judgement while bearing in mind that if you make heavy demands you will have to feed well. Producing this amount of new growth also means adequate moisture below: when weather is dry, remember the thirsty ramblers; lay the hose out and let it dribble for a few hours. Fast cars drink petrol, and if you don't fill up often, your roses will become stranded with empty tanks.

If you are hesitant about pruning flowered wood hard, some of the more vigorous varieties will reflect your hesitancy by sending out new growth from half way along old stems. If this happens, it is usually better to leave things for that year, and to take them right down after the next flowering. Always try to encourage growth from the base, and never let wood become old, brown and barky – that shows you are timid. Until a young planting gets into its stride and you feel confident, a fair enough procedure would be: if the plant made three new stems last year, it should be well established and capable of making three this year, so three oldies to come out. Next year, it could make four or five, and you can then decide whether to push it gently by taking out three stems, or harder by removing four or more.

**Shrub roses** Most, but by no means all, shrub roses rule themselves out of small and average size gardens by their dimensions, but some are small enough to be captivating and defy rejection. In fact, the range of size is exceeded only by the range of habit. Accordingly, it is impossible to generalize a policy or principle for pruning. The first step, of course, is to tidy the shrub by removing dead, diseased, weak and crossing stems. After that, the framework of garden size and the plant's neighbours constrains the subject from spilling over the edges. In general, a reasonably safe procedure would be to prune back main stems by a third during the dormant season plus, with shrubs that are well established, a somewhat vigorous removal of old, spent stems before they become senile.

**Species roses** These and varieties of species, being much nearer to their natural original, are capable and best left to do their own thing. They will need little or no pruning beyond dead-heading and keeping them within bounds.

**Miniature and patio roses** Pruning of the miniature and patio forms should follow the same general principles as for bushes, standards, climbers and the rest. The size is different, of course, but the scale remains.

# 7
# Feeding

In Chapter 4 I stressed the importance of preparation before planting – what you do afterwards cannot put right what you fail to do before a plant is in the ground and growing away. A rose is like a dog: you do not and cannot get back more than you put in and, in the same way that a dog is more rewarding than most other animals, you get more back from a rose than other flowers. Roses are heavy feeders at the best of times, and pruning for more and better bloom drives a plant even harder.

A good balanced meal for yourself is traditional 'meat and two veg.' and not tonics and pep pills. Plants, particularly roses, are no different, they need good and balanced feeding just as much as you do; nitrogen for leaf production, phosphate for root growth and potash to keep the system toned and resistant to sickness and disease. Too much nitrogen encourages an abundance of leaf tissue that is not balanced by enhanced root activity to support it, or enough potash to keep the plant structure hard. Soft flabby growth in plants is as much at risk to disease attack and structural collapse as it is with ourselves and other animals.

Also vitally important is the way in which the chemical nutrients are presented. It is perfectly possible, for example, to analyse your meat and two veg. and to give yourself a tablet containing the chemical contents in a concentrated form. That would provide the nutrients your body needs, but whether the mechanics of your digestive system would be happy with a diet of tablets and pills instead of bulky food is of course more than doubtful, as our bodies are not constructed that way. But that is precisely what happens when we expect plants to live and thrive, not as nature intended, but on chemical fertilizers.

A fertile soil is dependent upon its physical structure just as much, if not more so, than upon its mere plant nutrient content. It has to contain organic matter, which is at once the moisture-retentive component and the source of plant nutrient as it decomposes to its simple chemical components. It is the haven, therefore, for the bacteria that perform the decomposition process – they need air, and we can say that, in order to be fertile and support our roses, the soil has to contain organic matter, moisture, air and bacteria.

The bacterial reduction of organic materials to simple compounds that dissolve in the water content of the soil is a long and slow process. Only in the final stages of breakdown does the nutrient become available for uptake by living plants, and this can take weeks or even months. The nutrient availability, as an end product, is therefore gradual and prolonged in contradistinction to the availability of artificial chemical fertilizers which are manufactured to be quickly soluble, and are as quickly washed out of the soil. By its very nature, the organic content in a fertile soil constitutes a reservoir, a bank balance that will stand withdrawals for some time with little or nothing going in, which explains why fertility can often be maintained for a while by replacing lost nutrients with straight chemicals. But that cannot continue forever.

It is more prudent, more rational and more natural to use organic materials – manures. They may be concentrated naturally as in animal tissues like bone, blood, hoof and horn, or processed to contain a high proportion of one or more nutrients, or they may be bulky and contain very little as in plant tissues like peat, compost and leaf mould. Any organic material must inevitably reflect its origin, and cannot contain what it wasn't in the first place. Horticultural peat, for example, is derived from mosses and sedges, both of which are lowly forms of plant life that live in areas of poor fertility. Consequently, their partly decomposed forms – peat – cannot contain much by way of those nutrients that are required by higher plant forms like roses. You will have to add that.

Compost, leaf mould and rotted manure all derive from varied sources and the residual content will therefore be greater and wider than peat. The greatest value of all such bulk matter, however, is not in the nutrient content, but in its effect on the soil structure, its retention of moisture and harbouring of the bacteria. Natural materials like 'blood, bone and fish' will between them supply nitrogen (N), phosphorus (P) and potassium or potash (K), hence (NPK), but how do you ensure the diet is balanced? You can buy a proprietary mix that will provide end residues that balance reasonably well – eventually. The problem is that, for example, the nitrogen in blood can become available to plants in days and continue for a week or two, whereas the phosphate in bone cannot possibly become available for several months.

You could use a largely inorganic balanced source like Growmore, and rely on the bulky peat or compost for the organic input, but better still is to use organic matter like sewage sludge, poultry, farmyard and animal manures, blend them to achieve balance both in content and time, and to dry and concentrate them so that they are pleasant to handle and easy to spread. This is a manufacturing process, and of course a proprietary product. By far the best I ever used was 'Humber Eclipse Fish Manure' which used the waste from the fishing industry as the raw material, but it is no longer obtainable as such because the fish content is redirected to cattle and poultry feeds. Other materials have to be utilized, and although not quite so good as the old fish manure, it is still way out in a class of its own.

Humber Manure is not easy to get because it has a strong smell and shopkeepers think it drives their customers away! Personally, I do not find it objectionable, and in any case the smell goes off very quickly when it comes into contact with the soil and bacteria get to work on it. If you cannot find it locally, contact Humber direct – the details are given on page 267.

Tests show that, after a slow beginning, availability of the nutrients rises to a peak in about 80 days and then tails off with the potash being held late, when it is needed. The steady release and peak indicates the best way to use this manure: if it is put down at the end of March, the peak comes towards the end of June. Similarly, if we want the food supply to tail off in September, the last application must be spread during June. No autumn dressings are needed – the late potash takes care of that. I find that 1 ounce (28g) to the square yard (square metre) as a starter, towards the end of March, then a little more – 1½ to 2 ounces (43–57g) – at the end of April, May and June is all that is required. If you can spare the time to sprinkle out ½ ounce (14g) every week, that is even more gradual. Lightly scratch it into the soil or mulch the surface so that the bacteria can get at it – they are the chaps that do the work and unlock it.

Alternating periods of flood and drought are not to the liking of any plant, certainly not to roses. They do best not only with a steady food supply but also with a steady moisture availability at root level. There are two ways to ensure this: one is to make sure that there is plenty of moisture-retentive organic bulk under each plant at planting time, and the second is a steady carrying down and mixing into the soil by worm action from a blanket cover on the soil surface, a cover that also drastically reduces evaporation. This cover, called mulch, can be peat, compost or even material that is not well rotted (see question number 21 on page 168). Pulverized bark or even wood shavings can be used as it is so exposed to the air that denitrification is avoided. A layer 2 inches (5 cm) thick suppresses weed growth, reduces moisture evaporation, is easily scratched open to help air penetration, and as it decomposes is pulled down into the soil by worms.

I have had many letters asking for advice and questioning the use of bark and shavings because of coral spot fungus appearing. This invariably only occurs when the mulch is allowed to pack and remain undisturbed – mulching is not intended as a boon to lazy gardening by putting an end to the need for hoeing. The cover has to be disturbed and scratched open by frequent hoeing; a claw hoe is ideal for this, as it is less likely to snag and damage the root stems. Any weeds that are able to get through the cover are knocked over, but the important purposes for keeping the mulch jostled about are air penetration and the prevention of rain run-off from a packed surface. Saprophytic fungi like coral spot on mulch are an indication of insufficient hoeing.

If there is one overriding golden rule with feeding any plant, but especially with roses, it is the meaning of the old saying 'you can lead a horse to water, but you can't make it drink'. Unfortunately, this is not quite true, we can – and it is possible to overfeed one or other of the three main elements and so cause what is called an 'induced deficiency' of the other two. You can create this situation quickly, by providing, say, a highly nitrogenous chemical like sulphate of ammonia, or much more slowly by lashings of the ubiquitous bone meal under the mistaken impression that it provides all the major elements and is a balanced feed (see also question number 24 on page 171).

Several proprietary fertilizers, mixed and formulated specifically for roses, show a marked bias in favour of one or other element. They are far from being the same or even similar, and you can check this by comparing the analysis on the packets. Whether you feel that these cocktails are what your roses will be happy with is very much like you considering whether you would be happy and healthy on a diet of fast and convenience food like hamburger and chips and little else. Balance is the key – and moderation at all times.

We shall be taken to task if we disregard foliar feeding. It has its proponents, but has become all out of proportion, I feel, and needs to be put into correct perspective. See what you think.

Unless they have evolved in such a way that they are specially adapted to do otherwise, most plants – and our roses certainly – naturally absorb nutrients through their root systems. Several deficiencies, particularly of trace elements, which frequently cause characteristic blemishes and structural damage to leaves and stems, can often be remedied quite quickly by spraying a solution of the appropriate element directly on to the foliage. The speed of absorption and remedial effect can be astonishing. Without doubt, when the need occurs, this method of by-passing the roots and 'injecting' deficient nutrients directly into foliage is extremely valuable and cannot be denied. It has been known for a long time, and has led to the more modern practice called 'foliar feeding', in which the purpose is not so much to correct deficiencies, but to encourage a boost in performance, yield and so on by spraying major element solutions on to the leaves in the same way.

There is no doubt that performance can be improved in many cases, but the fundamental question has to be asked whether such foliar feeding or boosting is merely making up and filling a gap left by normal cultivation that is not as good as it could be. Plants have evolved to live according to certain natural laws and procedures, and it is no logical solution to improving cultivation to ask plants to live differently to what nature intended. Foliar feeding may be good for emergencies, but not in my book for basic cultivation of roses.

Perhaps this is an appropriate place for a few brief notes on the more common chemical fertilizers and organic manures of plant and animal origin.

# Chemical fertilizers

**Sulphate of ammonia** is perhaps the most commonly used nitrogenous fertilizer. Nitrogen becomes available very quickly because the two fractions break apart readily in the soil. It is best used on calcareous soils – chalks and limes – and light soils that can stand being made a little more heavy and sticky. It is very easy to cause scorch (plasmolysis) if used too strongly – never exceed 1 ounce (28g) per square yard (square metre).

**Nitrate of soda** is another common nitrogenous fertilizer. Very quick acting, it is quickly soluble and liable to cause scorch. Never exceed the equivalent of ½ ounce (14g) per square yard (square metre) dissolved in a gallon (4.5 litres) of water, and never allow direct contact with stems or leaves. If used with care, it is to be preferred to sulphate of ammonia on heavy soils.

**Nitro-chalk** was at one time a by-product of the gas and other industries, but now that manufacturing methods have changed, it is not so plentiful or cheap. It breaks down to provide both lime and nitrogen, and is therefore most suitable for use on heavy acid soils. It is least effective, even counter-productive, on chalky soils. Not so quick acting as sulphur and soda compounds, it is a lot safer. As with all nitrogenous fertilizers that boost leaf growth, use this only in spring and summer when growth is fastest and can respond and absorb the spur. A dose of 1 ounce (28g) to the square yard (square metre) 3–4 weeks apart is the maximum rate, otherwise scorch can result.

As can be seen from Chapter 7 on feeding, high nitrogen can produce imbalance and soft, lush, disease- and pest-prone foliage with roses. If they need any bias at all, it is towards potash for hardening and ripening leaf and wood, and phosphate for stimulating root activity.

**Basic slag** is another by-product of industrial processes that has become scarce due to changed methods. It is mainly used as a phosphate source which, as it also contains some lime, has an alkaline reaction. Slower-acting than most artificials, it is best hoed or dug in during winter, some months ahead of renewed springtime growth and activity. The strength can be variable depending on the source, and it is therefore wise not to risk damage by exceeding a maximum rate of 4 ounces (113 g) per square yard (square metre).

**Nitrate of potash, saltpetre and bonfire ash** supply both potash and nitrogen, and a lot of it, which, when released very quickly by reaction with other chemicals and ignition, provides an explosion like gun powder. They are very soluble, hence the admonition to 'keep your powder dry' and why bonfire ash is very quickly spoiled if allowed to become damp with rain. They are liable to scorch (plasmolysis), so use sparingly and keep them away from leaf and stems. The straight chemical should be used dissolved in water no stronger than ½ ounce (14g) per gallon (4.5 litres) per square yard (square metre).

**Iron sulphate's** main use is as a quick-acting source of iron in cases of chlorosis on soils where iron is either in short supply or is locked away and unavailable to plants by a chemical combination with lime. It is one of the main constituents of the old lawn sand method of weed-killing in lawns. The inference is clear to keep the application rate very low – no more than ½ ounce (14g) in 2 gallons (9 litres) of water per 2 square yards (2 square metres), and applications at least 3 weeks apart.

Most samples of **muriate of potash**, a commonly-used potash source, also contain enough common salt (sodium chloride) and other salts to constitute a danger to shallow root activity. It is normally used in association with ripening and colouring, and for roses therefore apply in June onwards – hoe and water in ½ ounce (14g) per square yard (square metre) at no more than 3–4 week intervals.

**Superphosphate** is the most commonly used phosphatic fertilizer to promote root activity. Use it at 1½–2 ounces (43–57g) per square yard (square metre) in spring and summer, hoed or dug in to the soil.

# Organic manures

**Bone meal** is basically a phosphate source, but with sometimes a little nitrogen depending upon the source. Universally used, especially at planting time – which is something of a hoot, as it needs a long and involved bacterial breakdown process for the phosphate to become available for plant uptake. The coarse grist can take as long as six months, by which time many plants that are intended to benefit will have long since gone.

**Dried blood** is another animal product from the abbatoir, this time to supply nitrogen. It breaks down readily – indeed, if allowed to become damp it invariably smells of ammonia, which is the indication that the nitrogen is already being released and lost into the air. It is best used after being steeped in water for a few hours. Use it at 1 ounce (28g) to the gallon (4.5 litres) per square yard (square metre) or 5–6 yards (5–6 metres) row run.

**Hoof and horn** is yet another animal end product valuable as a long-lasting slow-release supplier of nitrogen, and in the same class as bone meal for the length of time it takes. It is rather expensive – there are so many competing demands for the raw material – so you will naturally be sparing with it. Useful in composts for potting up plants that will need nitrogen later on, I wouldn't use it for roses – it can lead to soft leaf growth just when you don't want it.

**Farmyard, horse, cow, pig, sheep, goat, poultry and similar 'raw' manures** are all very variable because they must depend upon the food intake of the animals concerned, and the age of the manure – the time it has been stacked for nitrogenous urine to have drained out or been decomposed. It is best stacked and composted beyond the denitrification stage (well rotted). The one exception, if you can get it, is goat droppings. Unlike the others, the goat is a ruminant, and will eat almost anything given half a chance. The result of browsing off hedges and other plants, not just grass, goat manure normally has the most balanced NPK content of any, and is worth its weight in gold.

**Mushroom compost** is the material from mushroom beds after cropping has finished, by which time the urine content has gone, but it still needs composting if it is to be dug in. It is ideal as a mulch, where the bacteria can get all the air they want to break it down, but often contains limestone chippings or a residue, and therefore needs watching for use on the acid-lovers. Best bought in by the load, it becomes expensive when stacked, composted, mixed with a little poultry, bagged up and given a fancy proprietary name.

By and large, the above are 'natural source' materials, with little or no attempt to balance the NPK content, and you will need to take this into account when you use them for whatever particular bias they give. Balance is better achieved by a mixture – often sold as 'blood, bone and fish' – although in recent years the fish content has been considerably reduced as it is used more and more in animal and pet foodstuffs. However, the problem is not so much the balance, but the varying times taken for the raw materials to complete their respective breakdowns and become available to the plants. True balance in this respect is only achieved by composting, processing and blending, and that means a proprietary product such as Humber 1–1–1 Garden compound.

# 8
# Pests and Diseases

If your efforts at feeding and cultivation are designed to make your roses happy, there are plenty of creatures and other life forms about whose objective is to give them hell. The rose is on one of the higher rungs of the evolutionary ladder, and its sap stream and physical structure contain many complicated chemical compounds that are particularly attractive and useful to insects. The high proportion of carbohydrates in the leaves makes them an ideal target for creatures that bite and suck out the energy rich sap. Others find in the rose elaborated chemical compounds readily available that they can utilize for colour pigments, their own body structures – and even scents to attract each other!

A list of only the more common villains and what they get up to reads like a catalogue of horrors enough to intimidate anyone and put them off rose-growing for all time. Greenfly, with their extraordinary reproductive method that enables millions-strong plagues to suck the sap from young shoots and buds, are described in the answer to question number 1 on page 123. Aphid attack is crude flat-out assault by hordes that can quickly replace their losses. Others are more subtle, if not downright clever, like the frog-hopper or spittle-bug that, instead of spitting back the sap it doesn't want – like greenfly – uses it to surround itself in a frothy mass that hides and protects it from predatory birds and also prevents the soft-skinned body from drying out. Another is the sawfly, which lays its eggs always along the midrib of the leaf, and with them a hormone that causes the leaves to roll up from the edges in to enclose and protect the emerging larvae in a neat tubular hideaway. There are many more, and to them have to be added the spores of fungal diseases, always produced in countless millions and ever-present, carried on the wind, ready to take advantage of easily-penetrated soft flabby tissue, a wound or a point of entry perhaps left open by insect damage, to invade, debilitate, deface and even destroy an entire plant. The rogue's gallery is formidable, but help is at hand, because we have friends, both natural and those of our own devising.

The very first rule, as with all sickness, is that prevention is better than cure. Pests and diseases are clever enough, persistent enough, and serious enough to need no help from us. It is one of the primary purposes of cultivation that we affect and change conditions in favour of the plants and to the detriment of their enemies. We readily accept the need for digging the soil to open it to the air, for good drainage and manuring, for the elimination of weed competition and for the provision of nutrients for our plants. Just as important, but generally not accorded due attention, are such factors as the clearing up of fallen and accumulated debris from under shrubs, hedges, fence bottoms and odd corners, all of which are hibernating havens and breeding grounds for all manner of enemies. It is not very clever to spray and fight off enemies from the front door, while letting them take up residence outside a wide open back door.

No matter how thorough our precautions, however, trouble will strike from time to time and, as with all forms of sickness, the very first thing we then have to do is diagnose or identify the cause. What are we faced with? The maladies of the rose separate into three basic groups: insect pests, fungus disease, and physiological (that is, internal structural) disorders. Some readers will hasten to add children and animals! My goats used to adore roses and hawthorn: how their tongues, throats and stomachs dealt with the thorns never ceased to amaze us.

Distinguishing the problem area and making a diagnosis should not present much difficulty. Insect damage is usually fairly evident – the physical damage can be seen, the creatures themselves can be seen, and even those that hide or run away cause tell tale signs that can be noticed and recognized. Similarly, fungal diseases show characteristic effects that reveal both presence and identity. Physiological disorders, like cancer in humans and animals (according to the present state and progress in scientific knowledge and understanding), are not diseases caused by other life forms like bacteria, baccilli, fungus or virus (although cancer opinion is beginning to waver with regard to virus).

Structural, cellular disorder and collapse in plants is usually a reflection of old age, bad growing conditions or inadequate feeding. True, pest and disease may follow, but we should always keep in mind the possibility that the initial breach in the defences is due to physical disorder. The signs are not always immediately apparent or indicative, and can easily lead us up the garden path; we have to learn to recognize the various spots and blemishes, however small. Let's look at the groups and the enemies in more detail.

# Insect pests

As control of pests and diseases consists basically of subjecting them to conditions or substances that are harmful to them, we have to recognize that, as they have all evolved defences of one kind or another – and very successfully too, which is why they are still on this Earth and contending with us for our roses – somewhere in their life cycles are periods and stages when they are more exposed and vulnerable. It is no good throwing things at them when they are safely in their dugouts and shelters, but at some time they have to come out into the open, if only to change their clothes and appearance, and that is when we can get at them. It may be with a contact poison that quickly enters a soft-bodied creature like a greenfly and kills on contact, a stomach poison that works through the digestive system, a neurotoxin that paralyses the nervous system, or an asphyxiant that enters through the creature's respiratory system, or we could encourage a natural predator. Less practical is physical destruction like squashing or bashing them on the head.

Insect pests sub-divide into three groups: those that bite, those that suck sap, and those that do both or either, but from within the soil. The biters are usually the easiest to detect because they eat away the foliage. They are normally found on the plant, exposed as with caterpillars, or concealed, like sawfly and tortrix larvae. They bite, so the obvious step is to make sure that they bite poison.

Instead of chewing into or biting off the leaves and shoots, the suckers are interested only in the liquid sap, which they obtain by probing a very fine tubular proboscis into the surface tissue cells. The typical examples are greenfly, the frog-hopper, and capsid bug. As they do not actually devour the tissue but merely pierce through the skin to get at the sap inside, the problem of making contact can become a little more difficult. For a long time, control was confined to contact killers – effective enough with greenfly, less so with frog-hoppers, and hardly at all with capsid. However, the relatively recent development of toxins that enter the plant sap stream without harming the plant enables us to kill all who dare to suck.

The third group are the creatures that still bite and suck, but from the safety of beneath the soil surface. Physical contact by means of drenching the soil to a requisite depth is expensive in terms of quantity needed to thoroughly soak deep enough, and the consequences from those it does not reach. Contact killers are therefore problematical, and we have to adopt a different technique. All these soil-inhabiting creatures have to breathe, not with lungs like us, but by a process called diffusion through their porous skins or through special breathing pores. This is a much slower atmospheric change than lungs, of course, and is suited to the confined and restricted conditions of a 'soil atmosphere', which is just what we need for them to breathe in poison. Let's deal with them all in a little more detail that will enable us to recognize them and understand how to deal with them, beginning with the biters. There are many more pests than those we shall discuss here – but these are the most serious, and those you are most likely to meet.

## *The biters:*

**Leaf-cutter bee**  There are many kinds of bee, and they do not all swarm and live in hive communities. Some are solitary, and this one constructs a nest for its eggs and offspring by cutting away half-moon shaped pieces of leaf, carrying them away and sticking them together like bricks! One or two bits chopped out is not too serious, but a really big attack is another matter and has to be taken seriously. The old DDT sprays got into them through their feet and through the biting jaws but, like so many poisons, just as many friends are knocked over as foes, and the indiscriminate use of DDT is now banned in this country. Systemic poisons will not stop the bees from taking a building brick, but they will be feeling pretty queer by the time they want to come back for more.

**Leaf-roll sawfly**  This clever little beast is given a fair description and discussion in the answer to question number 52 on page 208,

PESTS AND DISEASES

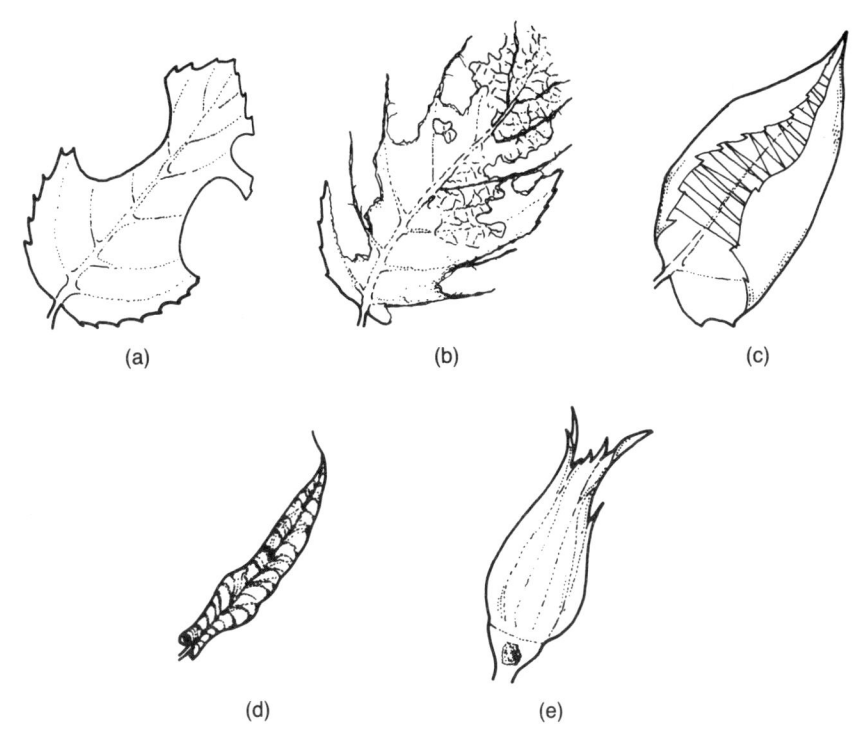

**Figure 13.** Pests make their unmistakeable marks on the host roses. These leaves are the work of (a) the leaf cutter bee, (b) the rose slugworm, (c) the tortrix moth, (d) the leaf roll sawfly. The bud (e) has been burrowed into by the tortrix moth, and if it opens at all will be badly damaged.

which, with Figure 13 above, will enable you to spot that it has been on your plants. Another sawfly, the **rose slugworm**, chops out the soft parts of the leaf tissue between the veins to leave a skeleton. Yet another, fortunately quite rare, follows you around when it sees secateurs in your hands and drops a few eggs into the soft pith of the stem when you make a cut, before the cut wound has had time to callus and heal itself – another reason why you should always try to confine cutting to a fine dry day. The little larvae soon emerge – they know which way to go! – and bore down into the stem where they pupate and eventually emerge as adults.

**Tortrix moths** There are more than one kind, but the differences do not matter to us, they are all crafty and clever at hiding where you cannot see them. The damaging period of their life cycle for our roses comes when, as minute caterpillars and chewing for all they are worth, they can be detected by knocking a plant so that it judders. Alarmed, they drop quickly and remain suspended at the end of fine silk-like threads. Later, they will attach the threads to leaf edges, which will pull together as the silk dries and shrinks, and thus roll the leaf around themselves. You can distinguish this leaf-roller from the sawfly by the extent and nature of the curling. The serious damage occurs under cover of darkness, when the little blighters make tracks for the flower buds and burrow into them which, if it doesn't ruin them completely, means a damaged and distorted flower when it opens. When you observe leaf-roll, it doesn't take a moment to pinch the leaf firmly between finger and thumb or, better still, to pick it off and burn it.

All the biting pests above can be controlled by planned, routine, repeat spraying with systemic insecticides. These pests were a headache at one time, but the modern rose-grower has a much easier life – and there is no excuse!

## *The suckers:*

**Aphids**, or as they are commonly called, **greenfly** (and not uncommonly **blackfly**), are given a fair description and discussion in question number 1 (see page 123). They are soft-bodied and physically utterly defenceless. Being little more than thin skinned bags of sugary carbohydrate sap from the plants they are sucking, they are an easily taken source of energy for many predators, including other insects and birds – a slaughter that is countered by the extraordinarily rapid rate of reproduction.

The **spittle-bug** or **frog-hopper** is equally as soft as an aphid, but three or four times the size. Its defence mechanism is not rapid reproduction like the greenfly, instead it surrounds itself with the familiar frothy blob of air bubbles that it forms as it spits out the sap it has taken from the plant – instead of spitting it back into the plant. This not only hides it from predators but ensures that its soft body does not dry out.

Another sucker, the **capsid bug**, is very seldom seen. It must have telescopic eyesight and be extremely sensitive to vibration because it is off as soon as it knows you are coming.

There is a bewildering array of contact and stomach poisons based on chemicals such as lindane, malathion, nicotine, pyrethrum, BHC, Derris, and many more – indeed, rather like the introduction of new rose varieties, new chemicals become available and push others off the market with almost equal rapidity. Some are better at controlling one pest than another, and at one time a well-stocked garden shed contained enough chemicals to stock a chemist's shop – but no longer.

The control of both biters and suckers has been revolutionized by the advent of the systemic insecticide. The problems associated with achieving physical contact have been superseded and replaced by the certainty of killing as soon as the pests bite or suck. The plants' metabolism is not affected and absorption into the sap stream and tissues is effected from a simple spraying and wetting. The effectiveness usually lasts for some weeks, but is variable, depending largely on the amount of new growth being produced, and therefore the rate at which the toxic content is being diluted, and the speed of living – called the metabolic rate – which affects the rate at which the plant is able to break down and divest itself of what after all is a 'foreign body'. After an initial recommended strength spray, all that is needed is a 'topping up' spray every three or four weeks.

There are several systemics to choose from, but advisedly you should go for one that is compatible with systemic fungicides which you will no doubt need to apply and which we shall be discussing shortly.

## *The soil dwellers*

By and large, the soil-dwelling enemies of the rose are confined to the several kinds of **chafer**. These are flying beetles that begin their lives in the soil as the familiar white or cream-coloured grubs, fat from feeding on plant roots, horny headed, usually brown in colour, very slow and sluggish moving and curled rather like a large letter C. There are several kinds, from the large cock chafer to the much smaller greenish rose chafer. The adults emerge from the soil in May and June – hence the common name 'May Bug' when they at once attack open blossoms of many kinds.

It is better to control them during this 'in-ground' period, the best control being achieved by watering down a solution of a chemical, one of a group with the long name 'chlorinated hydrocarbons', and used primarily in this case on lawns as a wormkiller. Obtainable under the proprietary name Chlordane, the toxin gradually works down into the soil diffusing into the soil atmosphere. Taken in by the slow-breathing soil creatures, the toxin accumulates in their bodies until it reaches lethal proportions. The trouble with this, as with many another insecticide, is that there is no selectivity or distinction made between soil creatures that are harmful and those that are beneficial, like earthworms.

Finally, before leaving the harmful insects, mention must be made of horrid little blighters that for long were regarded as exceptions to the normal methods of control. **Thrips** or thunder flies as they are sometimes called because of their tendency to fly in clouds when thunder threatens – are minute midge-like flies that like to get into buds just as the bud scales (sepals) are opening and lay their eggs there. Minute they may be, but the effect is traumatic. For long it was thought that wet spraying turned the buds to a wet mash, and therefore dusting each individual bud was necessary. Imagine dusting each bud with a soft brush and malathion dust!

In fact, the collapse of the bud to a mash is a consequence of the egg laying. Dusting with malathion is probably still as effective a deterrent as any, but clearly it has to be applied early before the little blighters are on the wing. If you can spot the minute pinprick and area of discolouration around it – a magnifying glass is useful – the fly has already left a visiting card. The wisest course is to take off the bud and burn it – you will not get a bloom anyway.

# Beneficial insects

Not all small creatures are pests, some are predatory on the pests themselves, and we should regard them as friends. However, encouraging them to the extent that they can be relied upon to keep roses clean is hardly practical. Taking out some and reducing the number of pests is one thing, but reliable eradication can hardly be expected or hoped for, and much as it may displease those purists who do not like the idea of using poisonous chemicals in the garden, they have to be our main line of defence and protection of our roses.

Perhaps the one big glaring example where natural predation can have a significant effect, quite astonishing on occasions, is with greenfly, and no doubt the most familiar example – it seems to get the most publicity – is the **ladybird**. There are several forms of ladybird, with wide variation in colour and number of spots, but all remarkably similar in the voracious manner in which the dark, blackish larvae, which look like tiny crocodiles, gobble up the defenceless prey. Very soon, they eat enough to pass on to the next stage of their life cycle. It is worth getting to know and recognize the small black blob-like chrysalis that adheres to stems and leaf stalks because it can very easily be mistaken for caterpillar or similar droppings and knocked away. At the risk of being regarded as a gardening Miss Marple or Sherlock Holmes, it is a good idea to have a magnifying glass in your pocket when you take a turn around the roses.

In the opinion of many, even more effective than the ladybird beetles are the several forms of **hover** or **serphid flies**, and this opinion is growing following the work of the Henry Doubleday Research Association (HDRA) into other plants that attract and encourage creatures that prey upon pests. These remarkable flies with wasp-like markings hang motionless in the air – hence the name of hover fly – and suddenly shoot off to a different position; their flight is a series of sudden darting movements. Their larvae are small almost leech-like creatures, variously green, brown and grey, and all with an enormous appetite for greenfly. The research done by the HDRA has shown that the hover flies are much attracted by a bright little annual plant, much beloved in old-style cottage gardens, which rejoices in the delightful common name 'poached egg plant', as each whitish flower has a golden yellow centre just like a poached or fried egg. Correctly named *Limnanthes douglasii*, the seed is readily available and, when conditions suit, it seeds itself so readily that it becomes self-perpetuating and can even become invasive. Hardly a colour combination to enhance or blend with the pinks and reds of roses by underplanting (see question number 15 on page 160), but a nearby border or patch of it is widely being reported as being responsible for clearing out all the greenfly!

A creature of docile and fragile beauty when closely examined is the **lacewing**, with its thin pale green body, borne between two pairs of transparent lace-like wings. Gentle the adult may be, but the tiny yellow and brown larvae are definitely not, and is fiercely active as it attacks greenfly with relish. The eggs of the lacewing can often be seen as a tiny little cluster at the end of a thin hair-like little stalk usually attached to the undersides of leaves. When seen, they are all worth trying to preserve, perhaps by postponing cutting back until the eggs have hatched, or by hitching up the egg-bearing leaves among the remaining foliage.

Another predator – perhaps not quite in the same class as the others described here, but still worth a mention – is the **Ichneumon fly**. It looks like a slightly small-sized cross between a bee and a wasp, but with a longer drooping tail. It too regards greenfly as a good meal, so don't go bashing at everything that looks remotely like a wasp. There are other friends of the rose, but, for the most part, with less actual and potential effect. However, the hover fly and poached egg association shows clearly that this is a direction in which a great deal of research needs to be done. There is so much that we don't know, and the HDRA organization does nothing but good for our knowledge and understanding.

# Fungal pests

Pests and diseases are different forms of life, but they often go hand in hand. In addition to, and apart from, susceptibilities built into some varieties of rose (as a result of breeding for colour, habit, scent or whatever at the expense of vigour and resistance), growing conditions, cultivation and weather all have an important influence on the ability of the plants to withstand and ward off fungal attack. One of the basic factors we have to bear in mind about fungi is that, unlike insects, which make their attack at certain predictable times depending on their life cycles, fungal attack in one form or another is about and ready to take advantage of any weakness for much longer periods – in fact, at almost any time of the year.

It is not often that secateurs or the knife is proven to be the carrier of infection; of course, if you know you are working on infected wood, it is only common sense to disinfect your tools with Lysol or a similar substance before moving on to plants that are clean. By far the two most common and important fungal diseases are mildew and black spot, and both arise from microscopically small spores in the air being able to settle on leaf and stem tissue that is unable to offer sufficient resistance to their invasive germination. The first line of plant resistance is the surface skin layer, the epidermis, like your own skin. The tough leathery top surface of a mature leaf is not so easy to penetrate as the softer epidermis of the underside, which is why mildew in particular can often be found by turning over leaves that are glossy and apparently quite healthy, even protected by fungicidal deposit, on the top. Similarly, young emerging leaves and shoots that have not yet developed a tough skin are easier for fungus spores to penetrate as they are for sucking and biting insects, and this is why the first signs of mildew especially are always to be found on such tissue. Whether young leaves remain soft, flabby and vulnerable for longer than they should depends largely upon growing conditions, and essentially upon the toughening effect of potash.

Even so, tough or not, fungus attack is persistent, and the principle of prevention being better than cure means that we have to try to prevent the development and growth of spores into our roses by spreading a film of fungus-toxic material on leaf, shoot and other vulnerable parts – a contact killer – or, as we are now able to do for insects, we can render the sap stream and internal tissue poisonous to invading fungus by introducing a systemic fungicide. Contact fungicides can be general and fairly generally effective, or specifically designed for one particular fungus, and therefore very effective.

There are several fungi known collectively as mildews, the most common to attack roses being **powdery rose mildew** – which is not a bad description, because it has the appearance of a dusty, powdery covering on the affected foliage. It can develop strongly in almost any weather, but contrary to popular and widespread belief and advice, the conditions that most favour and encourage it are not damp and mugginess, but hot dry days interspersed with clear, cold, dew-laden nights. The reason is not hard to understand: hot dry weather puts great strain on the continuity of moisture supply at root level, and as a result the plants slow, the foliage flags, and in the wet dew the fungus runs like mad. Enclosed gardens in which the air cannot move freely are just what the fungus likes and increase the likelihood of attack. For the same reason of poor ventilation, the less resistant ramblers can suffer badly when grown against walls.

The one thing that can be said with certainty about mildew is that it is unpredictable. Glossy dark bronze-green foliage is widely held to be very resistant; in some places it is, but in others it can look as though a flour sack has burst. I had a customer friend high on Epsom Downs whose garden was the admiration of everyone – the passengers on the buses at the stop outside had a grandstand view. He planted a hundred 'Zambra' roses when that variety was first introduced by Wheatcrofts – the brilliant orange flowers against the bronze-green foliage were a show-stopper at Chelsea. In his windswept position he had never known a serious attack of mildew – but he did then! I have known gardens where the roses never had a moment's fungicidal attention and didn't know what mildew was, and there have been others where the roses received every care and attention, and each year the place looked like a flour mill. How do you find a reasonable and consistent thread of explanation through this? There is one: Epsom Downs may be high up with plenty of air movement, but there is only a thin soil cover on solid chalk. The natural organic content is thus very low, the moisture reservoir non-existent and, as is invariably the case in such conditions, there is a chronic shortage of potash.

Mildew is too prevalent and persistent to be wiped out completely, but those three factors are the key to helping our roses to resist it. The first visible signs of the disease are a slight increase in the red tinges and colour of shoots and young leaves, and of course that is very easily missed because it is the normal colouring of many varieties. Generally, there is also a slight twisting and distortion reaction in the way that the leaves are held, but again, this is difficult to detect unless you know exactly what you are looking for. Faint white spots next appear on the top surfaces of leaves, but turn the leaves over, and more prevalent patches will be found. If these first signs are missed, they are soon followed by spots on new shoots, buds and leaf stalks, by which time it is much too late for prevention and contact fungicide because the fungus is already well embedded within the plant tissue. The only hope then is rather like injecting antibodies into our own blood – a systemic fungicide.

Mildew is not so very difficult to stop in the early stages, and there are several fungicides that will give it a severe check – all the chemical manufacturers have their own products and trade names which, like everything else, are constantly being improved and changed – but by far and away the most important point to bear in mind is that it has to be hit early and repeatedly. Mildew is more debilitating and weakening than is generally realized. (See also question number 46 on pages 200–1.)

Another all too prevalent fungus that attacks roses, **black spot**, is a different kettle of fish. First appearing as tiny black spots on the upper surfaces of leaves, this is the outward sign that the fungus has already been inside the tissue and working for some time. Even so, it is worth getting to know and keeping a sharp look out for the signs from as early as May on, because if you act quickly enough it is possible to stop the attack before it spreads through the rest of the foliage by picking off, and, this is important, burning the infected parts. Left undetected, the spots will expand to discs, then to coalesce, by which time, as a rule, the fungus will already be on its way down the leaf stalks and into the main stems. Black spot has to be taken very seriously because, given the right conditions, it can ravage and virtually destroy a rose garden in just a few days – I have seen this happen, and it is not a pretty sight. It can occur much earlier, but the peak danger period for the disease generally begins from the early part of July, and may persist right through the growing season until the big temperature drops of late autumn upset it.

Three important factors encourage the disease: warm humid muggy weather, clean air, and lack of hygiene. The weather we can do nothing about, except to recognize what it can be letting us in for, and to take precautions accordingly by spraying contacts or systemics. The clean air is a little more involved – surprisingly, the disease was markedly less prevalent before the advent of modern clean air policies. The sulphur-laden dirty atmospheres of industrial localities virtually guarantee a grimy but effective fungicidal deposit – the indication could not be more clear that, whether accidental or intentional, a fungicidal film on the foliage does have an effect.

The third factor, hygiene, is perhaps the most insidious and difficult to control. While it is true that the spores can easily hop over the garden fence, and there is not a lot to be done about sources of infection further along the road, much can be done by being entirely ruthless in cleaning up your fallen leaves and rose debris. No matter if it does not appear to be infected, clear up all leaf matter and burn it. Don't put the debris on the fire heap to be burned later, which merely prolongs the possibility of infection, but burn it immediately. The spores of black spot are persistent, and accumulated debris and rubbish are perfectly capable of spreading the disease far and wide.

The two courses of defence are by contact and systemic fungicides, such as Maneb, Zineb, Dithane, Orthocide and others. This entails starting early and topping up with repeat spraying on the young growth every few days.

An old method that is still worth trying is to soak-spray the plants and soil all round early in the new year with Bordeaux mixture (this can be bought as a proprietary mixture ready for mixing) that combines the fungicidal properties of copper and sulphur. It is the same spray material that has been used for ages on potatoes and other crops, and can be a great help here also. A word of warning: don't use metal containers or sprayers because they can corrode. Wash out any containers thoroughly with hot water and make the spray fresh for every spray.

Systemic fungicides, especially those manufactured by Murphy Chemical, can sometimes be combined with systemic insecticides – a cocktail that simplifies preventive spraying and saves time – but do check very carefully for compatibility. Don't throw any two products into a bucket and mix them; they may well destroy each other.

Fortunately **rose rust** doesn't occur very often, but when it does it can be a killer. Treat it in the same way as black spot, with particular attention to clearing up fallen leaves on to the fire. Systemic application and Bordeaux mixture in the dormant period should keep it at bay. (See also question number 51 on page 206.)

## Other disorders

Now a couple of problems which are frequently taken for fungus trouble, but which in fact are not, so perhaps we should talk about them here, between the fungus diseases and the physiological disorders. An ailment, descriptively called **purple spot**, is caused not by fungus but by poor soil conditions and serious nutrient inbalance (see question number 26, page 174).

Another problem is **canker**. There are different kinds and, although the rose is ailing and liable, invariably the trigger is injury like hoe damage, rubbing and chaffing, bad stake ties and bad careless pruning (see question number 50, page 204). Amputation of all affected wood has to be ruthless and drastic – there are no sprays, dusts or systemic cures, because they do not affect the cause. Having regard to the causes, it has to be recognized that the conditions that lead one plant to canker are also putting others to the same pressure, so look to your overall cultivation methods.

## Physiological problems

Finally, a few words about some physiological problems which result from nutrient deficiencies and weather conditions. Sometimes these are confused with pest and disease.

First, the weather. The most common problem arises from that annoying characteristic of British weather, the **late spring frost.** Leaves scorch, mainly from the edges in, becoming crinkled and brown. It can look more serious than it actually is. Not very serious, the plant grows on unharmed, new growth soon takes over, and the damaged foliage, while a little unsightly, is eventually cleared away by dead-heading and cutting back.

You ought never to see **nutrient deficiencies** because they are a sign of incorrect feeding. However, it is prudent to become aware of the signs. Make a note of the symptoms, and pin it up in the garden shed – the remedies are self-evident. Main element problems are most often caused by the artificial feeding of fertilizers that are either unbalanced in themselves or become unbalanced because of the local soil conditions.

Phosphate is the least problem and, perhaps because of the almost profligate use of bone meal and the very long time it takes for the phosphate to be released by bacterial decomposition, is very seldom indeed the cause for worry. Nitrogen shortage normally shows out as small, sickly, pale green foliage. When it is serious, spots and patches of yellow and red appear as the green chlorophyll is not made, or breaks down. Potash shortage is often an induced condition caused by too much nitrogen reducing the potash content to an unbalanced proportion. In addition to the flabby growth and increased susceptibility to pests and disease that follows, the visible indications show out as brown patches which spread and coalesce round the leaf edges. These collapse, shrivel and dry as though scorched – but this is not to be confused with frost scorch. A further characteristic to aid a correct diagnosis is a marked shortening of the bloom stalks. Sandy, chalk and other quick-draining soils with low organic content are particularly prone to potash shortage and imbalance.

When they are experienced, the three trace element deficiencies you are most likely to meet concern iron, manganese and magnesium. Iron shortage shows out as an overall pale colouring in the leaves. Iron is a component part of the green colouring matter chlorophyll, and any iron shortage inevitably means that fewer green chloroplast cells are made, hence the pale colour. What chloroplast cells there are tend to concentrate near to the veins, so that the little carbohydrate that is elaborated is quickly moved into the nearby veins and carried to where it is needed, thus we get a characteristic green outline to the veins in an otherwise pale green, even yellowish, leaf. The indication is serious because, with leaves not able to work properly, the carbohydrate energy food supply is not being elaborated and the entire plant is only firing on one cylinder.

The remedy often suggested is to get iron into the system quickly by foliar feeding. This is fair enough when the proprietary foliar feed is made up and used correctly. When, however, another suggestion is followed – similar feeding through the leaves by spraying with iron sulphate – extreme care must be exercised. This is the main chemical ingredient of a method of lawn weed killing that literally sucks the sap out of leaves upon which it rests by reversing (plasmolysis) the principle (osmosis) by which plants absorb nutrient solutions from the soil. Spectacular cures for iron deficiency are possible with iron sulphate, but the safest way to use it is as a very weak solution – no more that can be heaped on a 1p coin in a full gallon of water – mist-sprayed on just enough to make the leaves glisten, not drench and drip.

Serious iron deficiency is most likely to occur in chalky soils where, although iron may well be present, lime locks on to it in a chemical combination that then makes it unavailable to plant uptake. The condition can also follow heavy applications of lime and is one of the risks that have to be taken when a heavy liming is needed to neutralize severe acidity quickly when it is causing problems like canker for example. It is not easy to distinguish between iron shortage as such and shortage induced by lime (chlorosis), and therefore the remedial action needed. The give-away is to watch carefully: chlorosis has the same yellowing between the veins, but it begins and becomes more advanced in the topmost leaflet, and is followed not by a pale green leaf continuing to struggle, but by its total collapse and withering as the iron becomes not just short, but wholly denied.

Manganese shortage is very similar to iron, but is less marked: the yellowing tendency is blotchy, margined and striped along the lesser veins. Magnesium shortage is more identifiable, with patches in the centre of the leaves that yellow, turn brown and die.

Leaves are one of the most important parts of any plant, and healthy hard-working leaves are crucial to the rose. They are the factory where carbohydrate is elaborated in the presence of light to provide the energy source for all living and growing processes. Anything at all that hinders or prevents the energy factory from doing its job throws a plant into a lower gear, and it has to work so much the harder to make progress.

Straight chemical fertilizers are for the most part designed to provide the three major elements nitrogen, phosphate and potash, and seldom if ever contain any of the minor elements. So little of the minor traces are required, that organic manures invariably contain enough of all that is needed. Deficiencies should not be allowed to occur, and they will not if you ensure steady organic input to the soil by mulching. For a concentrated nutrient source use an organic manure like Humber, which of course contains all the various elements from the materials that go into its composition.

# 9

# Propagation

It is all very well to say that the production of a new rose plant is a skilled job and best left to specialists, but that takes little account of the satisfaction to be derived and enjoyed by trying something difficult, and being successful. So if you feel inclined, why shouldn't you try your hand? It can be interesting and satisfying – even just to read about it! Having said that, one or two points need to be put and kept in perspective.

A lot of encouragement has been given in recent years to the idea of increasing one's roses by making cuttings – almost proposing it seems, that it is a way of avoiding the cost of buying new plants. It is not particularly difficult to get rose cuttings to sprout roots, and to suggest that that is all one needs to do to raise new plants of any and all roses is to mislead by disregarding why all the trouble is taken to propagate H.T.s, Floribundas and many more by budding and, less often, by grafting.

Currently, one of the rather loosely applied definitive differences between plant and animal life is that plants can be propagated in either of two ways, sexually by means of seed, which involves male and female contributions from different plants or from different parts of the same plant, or asexually (vegetatively) by means of cutting and layering, which is analogous to cutting off an arm or a leg and growing an entirely new individual from such a part into a whole new body. Propagating roses by seed is more involved, so we will begin by looking at the less complicated vegetative methods favoured by a majority of amateur gardeners.

# Asexual propagation

A **cutting** is simply a length of stem top growth – with some plants it is a soft-tissue tip, with others a more mature hard-wood section – which, when inserted into soil or a suitable growing medium, and sometimes helped and encouraged by the presence of artificial hormones, will fight for life by producing roots, and so grow into a new individual plant. By using our understanding of the nature of a node and the storage therein of energy, the development of callus healing tissue, and the development from that of adventitious tissue (see page 59 *et seq.*), we can greatly increase the chances of a cutting 'striking'.

Many roses are very ready to make root in this way. The ramblers, Rugosas, Musks, Gallicas and most of the Old and species roses make root easily, whereas *Rosa centifolia*, the 'Moss Rose', is reluctant, as are (for some reason not at all understood) roses that have yellow, or predominantly yellow, flowers. With roses that are normally grown on their own roots, propagating your own by cuttings is quite feasible, but with H.T.s, many Floribundas and those which are budded and grafted, apart from the fun it is not worth the trouble. In being bred intensively for colours and scents, so much vigour is often lost that in order to realize its full potential a plant needs to have the much more vigorous upthrust of a 'wild' rootstock pushed into it. When such top growth can be persuaded to produce its own roots as with a cutting, the best you can expect is an indifferent plant and a poor root system. By all means try it, but don't think that you are going to produce lots more of your favourite budded roses by this method.

Where the type is suitable this is how to set about propagating roses by cuttings. Towards the end of August or early September you will need wood of the current year's growth that is quite firm and mature. The easiest procedure is to leave a stem unpruned in early spring, so that a number of lateral side shoots are produced. These are ideal for our purpose and by late summer should be just about right. Prune out the stem and take it into the shed where you can sit down comfortably to prepare the cuttings – they will have to be made very carefully, and you will need a very sharp knife. Sever each side shoot by pulling away, or cutting if necessary, so that a heel is left attached. Remove the shoot tip to leave a cutting about 9 inches (23cm) long, and then trim away the lower leaves to leave only the top two. Remove the lower thorns to make the shoot easier to handle while you pare the heel clean and smooth to encourage the formation of callus tissue. Dip this end into hormone rooting powder while it is still moist from the cut so that some powder adheres, shake or tap off the surplus and lay it aside for a few minutes while the others are being prepared. This gives the shoots time to dry which, short as it may be, helps the formation of callus tissue and in fact inserting cuttings too quickly while the cutting tip is still moist and unhealed is one of the most common reasons for failure. This is more important with softer cutting like geraniums and fuchsias, but it also makes a lot of difference with roses.

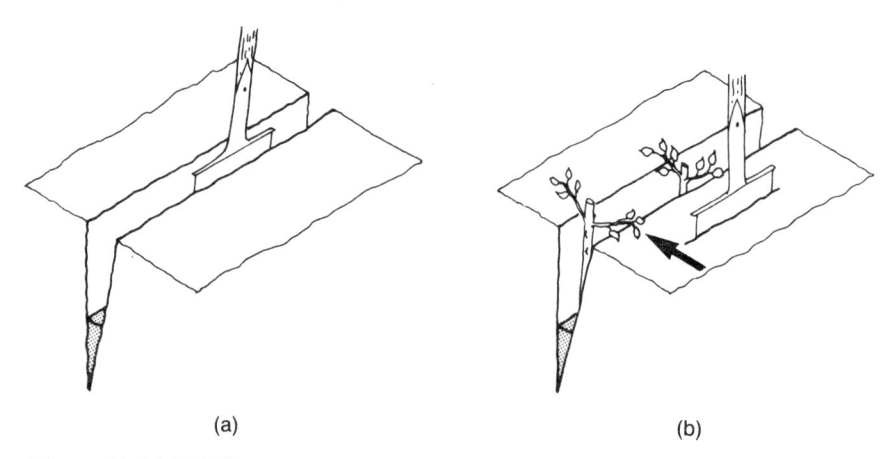

(a)   (b)

**Figure 14.** (a) Half fill the slit trench for your cuttings with sand. (b) With the cuttings in position in the sand, dig another slit 3 inches (7.5cm) away, take out the soil and firm it against the cuttings.

In a partially shaded part of the garden, not overhung by trees, shrubs or other plants that can lead to rain drip and where air movement will not be impeded and so encourage fungal attack, make a slit trench by driving in the spade full depth with the blade held vertically, and forcing open a narrow V-shaped slit, as shown in Figure 14. If there had been no rain and the soil become dry, we used to prepare these slit trenches the day before and fill them with water from a can, but carefully, so as not to wash the soil back into them. Sprinkle sharp sand along the slit – enough to fill in the bottom 4–5 inches (10–12cm) or so.

Systemics didn't exist in my nursery days, and we had to use contact pesticides. It is a lot easier these days, so make up a little cocktail of compatible systemic insecticide and fungicide, plus a drip or two of washing-up detergent to achieve a good wetting, in a small bowl, and swish the two leaves of each cutting in the solution so that they get a good wetting and protective coating. Insert the cuttings by pushing each one down into the sand about 4–5 inches (10–12cm) apart and with the leaves at right angles to the line of the slit, so that growth emanating from the axillary buds grows out into free space between the rows, not into the cutting next door.

The leaves will need to be clear of the soil surface, which means that you will have a row of cuttings protruding some 3–4 inches (8–10cm). Drive in the spade again, about 2–3 inches (5– 8cm) from the cuttings slit, and lever the soil over tight against the cuttings – check this by taking a few between thumb and finger, and try to lift them: they should be quite firm. Leave the second slit open, or fill it with compost or sand, and use it to water the cuttings with a can in dry weather, without splashing and wetting the foliage.

The cuttings will remain in this position until the following autumn – 12 months – during which period you will need to keep an eye on them for pest and disease and, of course, include them in your routine precautionary spraying and care. These are new-born babes facing a rough tough world: they need help, not neglect. After 12 months you should have nice young plants nearly ready for moving on to permanent quarters or, if the cuttings are of the rugosa type and intended for rootstocks on to which you are going to bud other varieties, they can be planted out ready for working. You will not be driven like the commercial nursery into getting as many as you can per acre (hectare), and can therefore afford to be a little more generous with spacing to give yourself room to move about more comfortably. If you have that many to deal with, spacing them 2ft (0.6m) apart and 3ft (0.9m) between the rows would be ideal.

The second method, **budding** is where vegetative propagation becomes distinctly more involved, difficult – and interesting. Some nurseries will supply rugosa rootstocks for those amateurs who want to try their hand, or you may raise them yourself by cuttings as described above. There are two main methods of budding – that which may be regarded as the traditional way, and another 'new' method that is more often used for other shrubs and trees – although we were using it 40 years ago on both bush and standard roses. The take was not quite so certain with some of the more 'reluctant' varieties, but the more vigorous types were quite successful, and the method is a little quicker to do.

First, the traditional method. It is usual to grow on the cuttings for a year so that the stock stems become somewhat thicker than a pencil but rather less so than your little finger. In about late July, with the scion foliage strong and healthy and the rootstock main stem still green with no sign of ageing, we are ready to think about the most backbreaking job in gardening! It is very easy to look at diagrams and read how it is done, but quite another matter when you have to get down to soil level with thousands to do and a foreman standing over you! A proper budding knife will be required – a penknife is no good at all – which is like a planting trowel in that both ends are used and the handle is not just for holding in the hand. The knife blade makes the cut, but the budding knife handle has a thin wedge-shaped end that is used, on turning the knife round, to open the cut.

Select a strong healthy stem that has borne a good bloom, or is still carrying one that has gone over the top, and look at the stem lower down – to see if you can find nice plump axillary buds or eyes in the leaf axils – these are latent growth buds, and they are going to become your new roses! You can either cut this stem away, as you would at pruning or after flowering, or, if you are only budding one or two, take a bud and leave the stem standing. The fresher the bud, the more likely it is to take without trouble. Cut away the leaflets from the leafstalk at the bud you are taking, but leave the stalk, which you will need as a handle. If you are cutting from a severed stem, take it with you to the stock to be budded, or if you are taking a number of buds, get the stem into a deep can of water at once and use it as soon as possible.

At this point, technique becomes personal preference: you can either make the cut in the stock first and then prepare the bud for insertion, or prepare the bud, put it into your mouth (handle protruding) to keep the cut surface wet, make the stock cut and slip the bud in straight away. Our hardwood propagator would do even better. Standing up to straighten his back, he would take as many as half a dozen buds, popping them all into his mouth, then down he'd go, snick, snick, bud in, and on to the next – he went so fast that it took two assistants following behind and tieing in to keep up with him!

With the stem in your left hand (if you are right handed) snip off the leaf and make a shallow curving scooping cut, with your thumb against the stem to steady your hand and control the cut, and take out the bud with about an inch (2.5cm) long scoop, as shown in Figure 15. According to which procedure you are following, the final preparation of the bud is done immediately before implanting, so into your mouth or implant now accordingly.

PROPAGATION

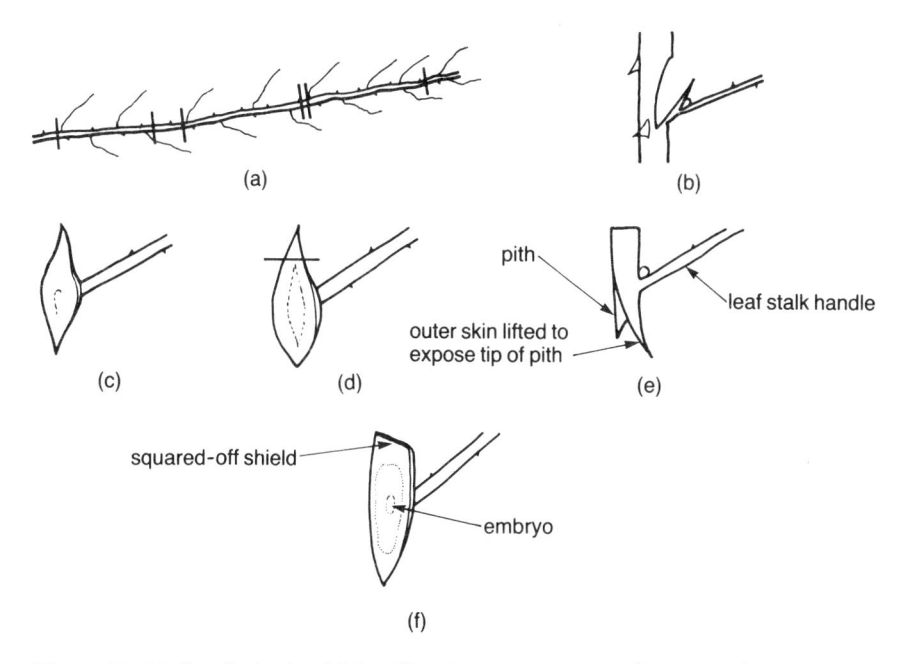

**Figure 15.** (a) Cut the buds which will make your new roses from a good strong stem that has borne healthy flowers.
(b) Strip the leaflets from the stalk, leaving the stalk as a handle. Cut away and down behind the bud in a gentle curve. Bend the 'handle' down to pull away the cutting with a heel.
(c) Pare the surface of the heel clean, straight and smooth.
(d) Square off the top of the heel.
(e) Bend back the lower end and use the knife to lift a sliver of pith to reveal the swelling of the embryo bud.
(f) The bud is now ready for insertion.

To make the implanting cut in the stock stem, drag a little soil away from the stem to give you a little more room in which to work, wipe away any mud splash with a wet rag and nick a T-shaped cut, ideally about an inch (2.5cm) or so above soil surface level. If you have any choice in the matter, try to do this on the south-facing side, and as the bud will grow out to the south, rows should lie east-west, so that the shoots grow out into the row space, and not into each other. The horizontal top bar should be scarcely ½ inch (15cm) long, and the vertical cut from it about ¾ inch (2cm) long. The cuts do not have to be deep, just enough to enable the two lapel corners to be lifted with the thin wedge end of the knife handle to reveal the green cambium layer beneath.

Final preparation of the bud consists of cutting square the top tip of the bud shield, and lightly bending back the other tongue end just enough for a tiny sliver of pith wood behind the eye to lift. Slip the blade tip under this, and carefully prise it out to reveal the back of the embryo bud as a tiny swollen area. If there is a hollow instead of the swelling, you have prised out the bud with the pith sliver and ruined it – start again with another.

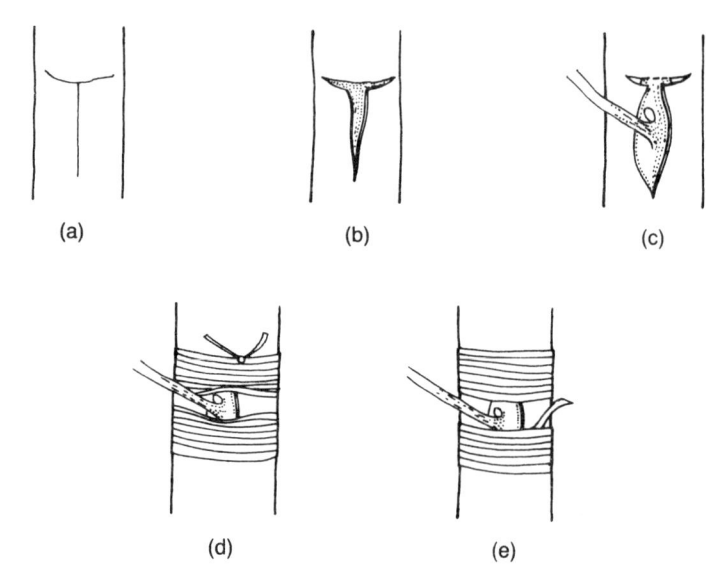

**Figure 16.** (a) The T-shaped cut in the stock stem, 1 inch (2.5cm) above soil level.
(b) Lift the two lapels to show the green cambium layer beneath.
(c) Insert the bud under the lapels with the squared-off top held tight under the cross cut.
(d) Tie in with raffia or (e) a cut length of elastic band.

Careful speed is the essence now. As soon as you can see that the embryo is unharmed, don't touch it (keep it virgin clean or you may infect it), but hold it by the handle and ease the shield shape into the T-shaped cut. If you have judged the T and the square trim well – this comes with experience – you will be able to press it down so that the squared-off tip sits firmly under the top of the T and is held there. Close the two lapels, and continuing the old traditional method, bind firmly but not too tightly with raffia – you can buy this as 'bass' from a sundries shop – that has been prepared previously into 18 inch (45cm) lengths and well soaked to make it soft and pliable. Don't cover the eye itself, as it will want to swell, and you will want to be able to see it. Tie off above the implant, push back the scooped-out soil and that part of the job is done.

A variation that we used to do, but which takes a little practice to get right, is to cut an elastic band, hold one end with your thumb or finger tip just below the implant, reach round the back with the other hand, stretch the elastic and, keeping it stretched, bring the end round and over the section under your thumb, grip it in the same way, pass round again and over the starting point. If you have kept the elastic stretched enough you should be able to now lift your restraining thumb and use two hands to wrap the elastic round and round, working up to the eye and past it, holding in the lapels firmly under the stretched elastic. When clear of the top of the T, finish off by passing the last but one wrap over your finger tip to form a loop, pass round again and slip the end through the loop and pull tight, and the elasticity will hold everything tight. Long in the telling, but as soon as you have the hang of it, very much quicker than bass. Thin plastic tape is also obtainable for this purpose, and I've seen narrow strips of cling film used very successfully! Both are used exactly in the same way as the elastic.

The second way of budding is a little easier, perhaps, but needs practice to get things just right. Again, it is a matter of personal preference whether you prepare the bud or rootstock stem first, but until you have had some practice and know just what is involved, I suggest that you start with the bud. About ½ inch (1.5cm) or a fraction more below the selected bud, make a cut about ⅛ inch (0.3cm) deep and sloping downwards a little as shown in Figure 17. Next, from about the same distance above the bud, begin a curving cut to pass behind the bud and clear of the embryo to meet the cut below – the bud shield should come away quite cleanly, still with its little handle.

Now comes the skilful part. You have to repeat the same size cut on the rootstock stem but, as it will probably be a slightly different thickness, you will not need to cut in quite so deeply (the object is to take out a shield shape that the bud will fit as perfectly as possible). This method is best suited to materials that are of approximately equal thickness, and it works quite well with 'maiden cuttings' (see page 99) used as rootstocks. The important thing to aim for is a good match; when the bud sits in its little step and is ready for binding in, you want to see scarcely any stem wood showing at the sides and top. This ensures that the cambium layers at the edges of the bud shield and the bared section of the stem are directly in contact for their entire length and there is no space between.

(a)        (b)        (c)

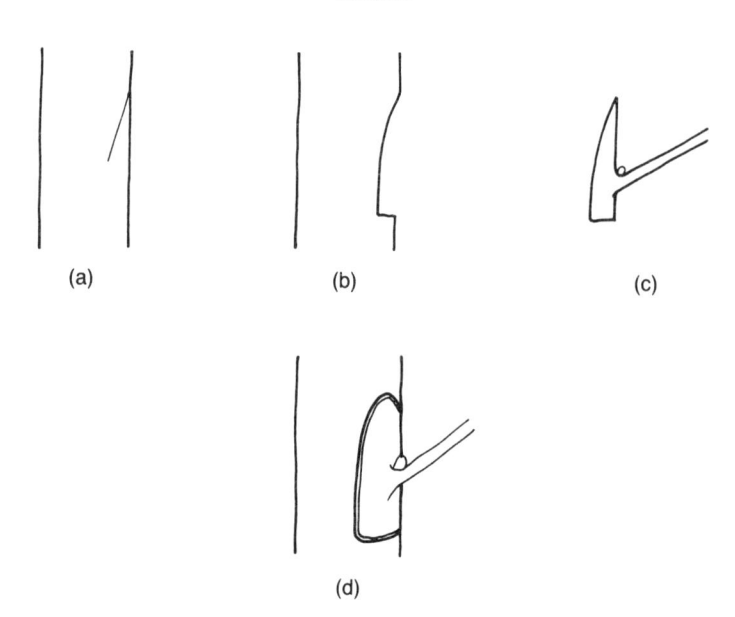

(d)

**Figure 17.** An alternative method of budding. Take a ledged inset out of the stock stem with two cuts, (a) and (b). Cut out your embryo bud as before, but this time squaring off the base rather than the top of the shield. Fit the shield into the stem, (c), and bind as before.

This sounds more difficult than it is – you'll be surprised how quickly you can become quite proficient at it. There is no top ledge as with the T-cut method to hold the bud in position while you bind it in, so you have to be careful how you handle the bass or the elastic band. We tried taking out the pith from behind the bud, and we tried leaving it in – it made little difference. Special elastic strips can be bought nowadays for this method, but I cannot see that they are any improvement on our elastic bands!

Three or four weeks later, you can take a close look. If the handle and what you can see of the bud are still green, the prospects are good. A fortnight later, bass binding can be very carefully snicked at the side to allow the bud to swell, whereas elastic binding will stretch and can be left a little longer.

If the bud turns brown, it is likely that the union has refused. Remove the failed bud, clean off any browning on the stem and paint over with a protective fungicidal paint such as Arbrex. There is still time to try again: insert a bud on the other side of the stock and cover all with the binding. If the second bud fails, don't waste any more time. Depending on how close it is to successful neighbours and the risk of root disturbance, grub the rootstock out. The unscrupulous growers sell these failures as 'hedging roses' (see page 35 and question number 32 on page 181).

Stems for standards can be raised, either by seed or cuttings from *Rosa canina* or *R. rugosa*, each run up as 'whips' (single main stems with all side shoots removed as they appear). It is fun to dig out a nice long briar stem from the hedgerow for this purpose, but how can you be sure about what you are getting or whether two identical buds will behave the same as each other when they are on different stock stems? Hedgerow briars are best left for walking sticks.

The implantation will have been carried out – hopefully, not too painfully! – with the thorny rootstock top growth still growing away merrily. I have seen and heard advice that it is easier to cut the top growth out of the way first before budding. No doubt it is easier, but it is quite wrong. The stock must be grown on as though nothing has happened – the top growth is needed to pull up the sap from the roots, past and into contact with the bud. A weekly routine of inspection has to begin at about the end of February. A new season of growth is about to start, and as little as possible of the rootstock's upthrust must be wasted on its own foliage. As soon as you can detect a slight swelling and reddening of the implanted bud, we have to think about diverting thrust into it – with care.

If you are a professional grower, this bud is merely one among thousands, and you will not have the time to fuss and mollycoddle it – the head comes off in one go, and the bud has to take it full blast. Either the union is strong enough and can stand it, or it can't, and hard luck. For the amateur, however, this is your creation, and you won't want it to fail at this stage for the want of a little time and thought. I have seen beheading done too early and too suddenly – with the result that the still not perfectly united bud is literally pushed out by the sudden flood having nowhere else to go. The way to avoid this disaster is to behead gradually – we took off about a third of the top growth every 7–10 days, so that the final beheading can be completed just above the implant by the end of March or mid April. Paint the final cut with Arbrex to seal the wound.

With the top finally off, leaving a sloping cut to make sure that rain and dew doesn't lie there, you can expect the bud to grow away fast. Do make sure that there is no crossing and crashing between neighbours; loop in with soft fillis string as necessary. You now have a maiden. Some will try to bloom during the first year, others will not; it is better not to let them. Remove any buds so that energy is concentrated into building up strength. In the autumn, it is ready either for planting into its permanent position or for sale in the nursery.

Standards are much easier to work on – the work is at eye level and your back doesn't have to break. It is usual in this case also to implant two buds, or even three with weepers, in order to get a nice full and evenly balanced head. A single budded standard, or a double where one has failed, can look distinctly lop-sided for the first few years until it has had time to develop – this is the sort of stuff you have to watch out for in the cheap 'end of season nursery clearance sales' and street markets.

Standard weepers are produced by budding and sometimes grafting, rambler types into stems a foot (30cm) or more higher than bush types in order to enhance the weeping effect. A further enhancement is to spread the top growth over a wire umbrella to get the hanging stems well away from the central support.

Frowned upon by the purist, the 'Irishman's weeping standard' is similar to the 'Irishman's cutting', in which a basal cutting is taken with roots already attached. Very much easier to produce, these weeping standards consist simply of an easily struck rambler cutting with only the one single strongest shoot allowed to develop into a whip and stopped off at the desired height – or you can throw all convention to the winds and simply use a short pillar, fix an umbrella into position, and let a normal growing rambler fall over it. A glorious garden belonging to a customer friend in Hampshire had an avenue of these leading to the dining room patio, and the effect from the house was no worse for not being puritanical. However, whatever form the 'standard' takes, you must realize that the lofted shape increases the sail effect and makes it prone to wind damage and greenstick fracture. A very firm stake is imperative.

The third method, grafting, is similar to budding and differs in that a short section of wood with more than one eye is enjoined instead of a single bud. It is seldom practised with roses now – there is so little advantage over what can be achieved by budding – and is really of superfluous interest to be included here.

# Sexual propagation

Raising more roses by seed can be a very frustrating business, or they can seed themselves with the efficiency and enthusiasm of weeds. Some species, *Rosa moyesii* for example, seed themselves with such abandon that it is not at all unusual to find self-sown seedlings growing freely underneath the shrub, and others are enough to tax the patience of a saint – that is all part of the challenge. The thrill, and perhaps the claim to posterity, is in being able to bestow a name on a rose that is different to anything seen before.

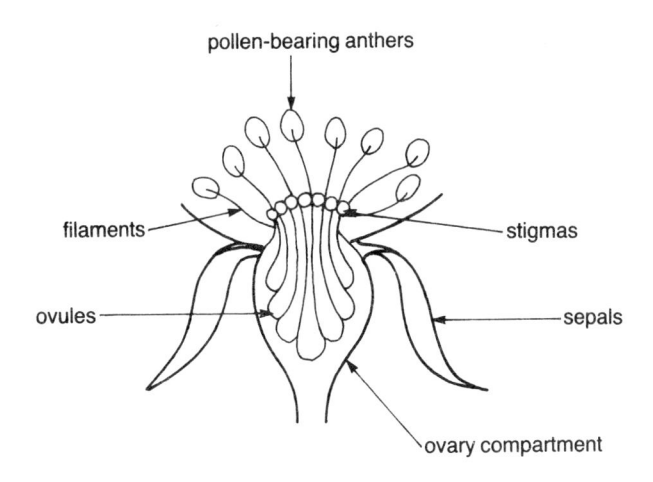

**Figure 18.** The simplified anatomy of a rose flower in cross section.

Some amateur rose-growers are not interested, but more than just a few regard hybridizing and crossing their roses to see what happens as the summit of the rose-grower's art, so here is a short discourse for them on this delightful aspect of rose growing. Hopes and anticipation you will have, but it is necessary to temper these feelings with a warning lest the expectation evaporate in a cloud of disappointment.

We all know the story of the two beautiful swans who brought forth what was regarded as an ugly duckling but which later surprised everyone by turning into a swan itself. Even the professional hybridist, with masses of detailed ancestral records and statistics at his disposal, invariably has to raise thousands of seedlings — all calculated and, theoretically, designed – before finding one that might, and only might, interest the rest of the world. That is only the beginning – there is then the budding on to vigorous rootstock to see if the bloom's promise and prospects are confirmed. Then follows the practical experience of time, resistance to pest and disease, a too-similar competitor nipping in and beating you to it – these are just some of the hurdles and obstacles to commercial profit.

However, roses are not swans, and all too often ugly ducklings remain ugly ducklings. The mathematical odds against you producing a new miracle are incalculable, and there can scarcely be a permutation that hasn't been tried before, but it has happened, and no doubt will again, that an amateur somewhere in a small garden with limited resources will beat the pants off the professionals. That is not the reason for trying however, nobody will deny that it would be very nice to achieve fame and fortune with a world-beater, but the amateur gardener seeks primarily the satisfaction of creation. In his eyes, all his chicks are swans, and anything else will be a bonus.

So, without any likelihood, and certainly no guarantee, let's talk about hybridizing. The mechanical processes involved are straightforward enough, albeit requiring no little patience, delicate handling and care which, all told, is a skill in itself. Many who take their hybridizing seriously prefer to have their roses growing in the controlled conditions of an unheated greenhouse, but with simple precautions, the beds outdoors are quite feasible.

The amateur is most unlikely to have, or want to be bothered with, all the nuances of hereditary dominance and recession – in any case, good old-fashioned luck of the draw is the biggest single factor. Select carefully the plants you want to cross – it is important to work with clean healthy plants with good vigour and constitution. Instead of allowing a natural and haphazard fertilization, we have to control it. Basically, therefore, the job consists of transferring male pollen from the anthers of the variety that is to be the male parent to the stigma of the variety that is to become the female or 'seed parent'. Of course, you can reverse the roles, make a cross both ways, and compare the results.

Modern botanical science knows a lot about dominant and recessive genes (which characteristics are dominant over others) but despite all the science, the one thing that you can be sure about is that there is no certainty about which characteristics of either male or female parent will show through in their progeny. Although you naturally hope to reproduce the desirable qualities, you are just as likely to reproduce the undesirable ones, and not only those of the parents, but those also of the ancestors from some way back. Some varieties do not produce good pollen, others are very good, but are poor receivers and not good seed-bearers. As we have already said, the whole process is an enormous game of chance.

Plants will normally come to bloom earlier in a greenhouse than outside, but in either case the most propitious time for the operation is during a spell, and after a couple of days, of bright sunny weather. It is usual to prepare the seed parent first. If the bloom is a double or semi-double, wait until the outer petals peel open but the inner petals remain closed and covering the stigma. With a single bloom, we have to work just before the petals open. As soon as the stigma is revealed and exposed, you cannot be sure that some keen and inquisitive insect won't beat you to it and carry in pollen from heaven knows where.

Some people like to remove all the petals to 'clear the decks', others will remove just enough from the centre to give enough space to work. Remove enough petals very gently and carefully then, using tweezers, remove all the male filaments with their pollen-bearing tips. Cover the bloom with a polythene bag – or better, if you can make them up, fine muslin bags that will let the air in but keep the insects out. Seal the bag with a wire 'twistit' to protect the female stigma which, in a day or two, will become sticky and thus ready to hold any pollen that touches. We have to be absolutely sure that only the pollen we want reaches the stigma. Look now for a bloom of the male parent. As soon as it is well open, and perhaps already dropping pollen grains on to its own stigma and petals, pick up a few grains with a small paint brush, and transfer them to the stigma of the female. Take the bag off, fertilize the stigma, and replace the bag again as quick as you can – interlopers still have to be kept out.

If you don't have a male flower with pollen dropping, take the most developed flower, open it carefully to expose the anthers, use tweezers carefully to take out some filaments and lay them on a clean dry plate or saucer. Place them in a warm dry position away from draughts or you'll lose the lot. In a few hours, you will find the pollen dropping and you can proceed as before.

If your experiments are blessed, the ovary will soon show signs of swelling and the unventilated plastic bag can come away as the stigma is no longer receptive. Tie on a label carefully to identify the cross or with a number or code to refer to your records book. By autumn, the seed pods or hips will be turning red and ripening, and you will need to follow the procedure outlined in the answer to question number 41 on page 193.

Naturally, when the seedlings are planted out, you will be all agog to see what the blooms will be like. Some will show you what they are made of early on, when only a few inches (centimetres) high, others will be more reluctant, and will make you wait. Now comes the hard part of scrapping those that are worthless, and that may be many or all! Those that you think are worth persevering with can be grown on for another year, getting a second chance to bloom. If that confirms your first fancy, use eyes from ripe wood to bud onto rootstocks as discussed earlier in the chapter.

You may find the first year's bloom on the rootstock pleasantly and surprisingly different to the original bloom on its own roots. If it disappoints, don't scrap it at once, but wait for a second year and give it another chance to redeem your hopes and optimism. At all stages, label everything, and keep a record of everything you do.

# 10

# Exhibiting

So, having bought or created your roses, planted, fed and nurtured them, held at bay the armies of nature, killed the bugs and defeated the diseases, then comes the time when you can savour the exquisite beauty of the rose. For many gardeners it is satisfaction enough to have won through, to take a rest and have time to stare, and what better place to do that than in your garden? Others follow the familiar pattern whenever enthusiasts meet, whatever the interest, of 'Mine is better than yours!', or 'I can grow roses better than you!' and put it to the test in competition. As with cats, dogs, cattle, leeks, gooseberries and a thousand other things that allow enthusiasts to pit their techniques and skills against each other, competitive exhibition can become obsessive and take over one's way of life. Once bitten by the bug, you are liable to become an embroiled victim for life.

Just as growing roses is the better for experience, so with exhibiting them, it also has 'tricks of the trade' to catch the eye of the judge, and even to deceive! It is a world of its own, and for those inclined, whether on a trestle table in the village hall or in the august arenas of the big shows, here are a few pointers to set you off in the right direction. Without doubt, the queen of the show bench is the Hybrid Tea, so we shall be talking in the main about that type, although much applies and adapts to classes and categories that you may find in the show schedules for other kinds, such as Floribundas.

Of course, a seemingly perfect and better-than-usual bloom can appear at any time, but timing for the show bench is another matter. Clearly, you are more likely to have blooms just right by trying to have a selection of buds coming along in succession rather than by leaving it to chance. The gardener with the biggest garden and most plants therefore has an advantage over the smaller fry with only a few, but that does not mean that the village postman cannot beat the lady of the manor! You will need to prune a little harder even than the usual advocated earlier in this book. The plant will be asked to work even harder and, like an athlete in training compared to a sedentary office worker, will need better and more careful feeding. A nice rose garden and a few blooms for the house may suffice and keep pace with your feeding and routine, but the extra demands of exhibiting will soon find out the flaws and show if you are sailing close to the wind.

Select the best and strongest of the stems that grow out following a hard prune the previous season, and spring prune to about half their length, to an outward-facing bud. This will mean that more buds are retained that can, and no doubt will, develop into stem shoots. This way, each pruned stem will bear more main shoots – the bigger demand has begun. As they develop and grow, rub off any inward-facing shoots to preserve the open shuttlecock form. Of course, precautionary spraying has to begin early – you cannot risk the possibility of pest or disease damage – and as soon as the first flower buds can be discerned, you will have to begin calculating against the calendar and the show date.

Unless you have hundreds of plants from which to choose, there is absolutely no substitute whatever for experience and judgement in deciding the next procedure, and the most valuable instrument you could possibly have to help you decide is a notebook – record everything. As a rough guide – and it can be nothing other than approximate because every year will be different to the previous one – it can take a month from early bud stage to the bloom just breaking. You will need to know the habit and past performances of each plant. Does it take 30 days, 32 or 35? Is the rate of growth faster this year? What has been the effect of weather and feeding? A notebook is essential because you cannot possibly keep it all in your head.

Ideally, you will try to concentrate on the main stem terminal bud, and to disbud all secondary and side buds as they become big enough to snap away, but you will have to make your mind up very early whether you will need to delay flowering a little by taking out the main terminal bud, or even if there is enough time to allow a secondary or a side shoot to develop and take its place. Timing is the tricky part of exhibiting, and you can only acquire the art by experimenting and keeping a detailed diary. How many weeks or days, what feed, how much and when, weather, temperature, sun and cloud, all go into the calculations and, finally, whether you hit the right day right on the button, or miss, and by how much.

Feeding should follow the rule 'little and often' to the extreme. Steady, gradual conditions are the essence, and anything out of line or unusual, like quickly assimilated liquid feeding, or even heavy watering, can result in a hasty response. Alright if you think that you are running late, and want to hurry things along, but it should always be by design, not accident. Hastening also results from even a slight drying at root level; the plant senses the possible consequences of a dry spell, and hastens towards flower and seed.

These can be deliberate hastening tactics. Those that delay are often a little crude. Some growers try to delay a bud opening by tying a turn of soft wool around it to physically hold the petals in close, even to the extent of only snipping the wool away on the show bench! The bud has to be quite dry and kept dry, with the wool not so tight as to cause a disfiguring bruise or mark. It is a risk, and needs considerable care to avoid disaster. Some growers erect little 'dunce caps' above the blooms to protect them from rain – another hazard – and too-bright sun. These caps are easily made or can be bought in different sizes to meet the needs of not only rose-growers but also for larger blooms such as dahlias and chrysanthemums. The shading can slow down a bud and make the difference of a day. Another effective trick is to slip a black plastic bag over a too-forward bud, so that it has an extra-long night or two.

Although we have all heard stories about the 'clever Dick' who bought a big cabbage at the greengrocers on his way to the show and won first prize with it, you'll be most unlikely to get away with anything like that at any really meaningful competition. Neither are you likely to be successful if you suddenly make up your mind to enter roses next day or next week. The show schedule has to be studied in advance, not only to decide what classes you will enter, but also to be quite clear about the rules that you will have to obey. If the class says: 'one red rose on a 10 inch (25cm) stem, displayed in a glass vase', you cannot complain if your much superior bloom on an 8 inch (20cm) stem in a china jug – comes nowhere! Show rules are not made to be tricky and difficult, or for the judging to be over-fussy. It is only fair that races are run in lanes, with everyone starting at the same time, and conform to certain prerequisites so that nobody gets an unfair advantage. Generally, the actual rules are the result of past experience, made to avoid just this sort of thing.

Chosen blooms are best cut early on the morning of showing. Cut the stem cleanly, and put it into water immediately to avoid the possibility of an air bubble entering the open cut which can act as an air lock later in the day, and prevent water rising up the stem. When you see what began as a perfect bloom dropping its petals before the end of the show, this is the most likely cause. Add a couple of ice cubes to keep the water cool; this slows the bloom and reduces the chances of it reacting to cutting by opening too quickly. If you are putting more than one stem into a container, remove enough leaves and thorns if the rules allow (if they do not say clearly, check with the show secretary), so that tearing and damage is avoided as more stems are slid in alongside. The container should be deep enough to accommodate at least half the stem length, and the blooms be dry and separated to avoid collision – crumpled tissue paper between each bloom is essential for even the shortest journey.

A long journey takes some organizing, with more careful attention to water, ice, temperature and protection. After your arrival at the show comes the 'dressing up'. Some show rules actually permit the 'fiddle' of pushing horticultural stub wire up from below into the swollen ovary part of heavy blooms that have a tendency to nod and flop over – 'weak neck' – and then to hold the bloom upright by twisting the wire around the stem. Personally, I don't like it – apart from encouragement to other such dodges, we should be judging roses and their cultivation, not crutches and artificial aids.

Another dodge which you may see being practised by your experienced competitors is 'thumbing', which consists of bending back the outer petals and curling them with gentle stroking by thumb or finger. This is to get the bloom to strike an attractive pose for the judge's eye. I think it is regrettable, and should not be allowed.

Showing to best advantage is one thing, but some of the fiddles and dodges go way over the top, and I feel appalled at times to see how judges allow 'old hands' to get away with quite obvious manhandling and doctoring. I've even seen them using 'leaf shine' to polish the leaves and make them shine! That is how much some competitors want to win prizes, and you will decide whether you want to get into that sort of race.

Among the more legitimate tricks of the show art is encouraging a bud that is only just on the point of opening to get a move on and concentrate another half a day's growth into the next hour or so, and so be opening nicely as the judges walk up. Ice cubes cool the water and hold the bloom back, tepid water speeds it up. If you see a thermos flask among the equipment at the dressing bench, that is what is going on. Get the water too warm, however, and the bloom that opens nicely for the judges arrival can 'blow' before their very eyes.

'Blowing' is caused not only by raising the water temperature; a hot stuffy marquee will have the same effect. Holding back a bloom is rather like holding a dog at the leash – as soon as the restraint is relaxed in the warm conditions, the bloom races away to catch up on itself. When this happens, leaf drop is further encouraged by the bloom and leaves evaporating water faster than the stem can absorb and replace it. You can reduce the chances of this happening by increasing the small area through which the stem can absorb by cutting a cross an inch (2.5cm) or so deep with a sharp knife into the cut end, and gently splaying open the four quarters.

Floribunda classes are a little different, and are not treated as such pampered prima donnas as are the H.T.s. All the same, you would be wise to check what is permitted and what is not allowed so that you don't get caught out on a technicality. The schedules generally call for a cluster or truss with the individual flowers nicely opening together. Most varieties tend to have a main bud in each group running ahead of the others around it. Normally, this should be disbudded before the show – how long before will depend upon your judgement. Its removal diverts energy into the other buds and this can hasten their opening by a day or two, as will the removal of side and minor buds that haven't a chance of making it by show day. However, before disbudding Floribundas, do check out the schedule – there may be a stipulation regarding the minimum number of blooms and how many can be disbudded.

Rambler classes seldom figure as such in schedules, but when they do, treat them generally as for Floribundas and H.T.s, except to bear in mind that, because the blooms are so much further from the soil and root system, the effects of dryness and restoration of moisture are delayed.

Finally, by all means test your skills against others – you'll learn far more from mistakes than by successes. Try, try and try again, and record everything you do.

# 11

# A Work Calendar

The month by month work calendar that follows is by no means exhaustive of all the myriad tasks that need to be done, and it would be quite wrong to regard it as a definitive and complete step-by-step list of instructions. If you have read this book intently, you will appreciate that rose-growing is an art, involving judgement amidst a sea of imponderables, not a slavish adherence to a list of how to do it instructions. That understood, and allowing for the variation of weather and geographical position, the following summary may be useful as a reminder of what should be occupying your mind as you turn up each new page on the calendar.

**September** Prepare heeling-in trenches to receive plants on order. Prepare any stakes that will be needed. Make sure that all planting and staking materials are ready to hand.

**October** This is where the year really begins, and is the last chance to complete the September preparations. Orders can be expected to arrive later in the month, and planting can begin as soon as practical. Check all stakes and renew all ties.

**November** Complete planting, including any planting out of seedlings and rootstocks. Shorten back any long growth exposed to wind to reduce the risk of wind rock. Give a thought to Christmas gifts to fellow rose gardeners.

**December** In areas where rust and black spot diseases have appeared, drench-spray plants and soil with Bordeaux mixture. Review the year's achievements and records in your notebook.

**January** This is an important month, not for work outside, but for armchair gardening.

**February** Keep a careful watch for newly implanted buds, and begin pruning back stock wood. Top up mulch.

**March** Scratch in first feed with Humber, and do any further cutting back of budded stocks. Hard prune H.T.s and Floribundas unless there is a hard frost, and half prune exhibition plants – this should be complete by the end of the month. Check all stakes by forcing, and renew all ties regardless.

**April** Give your roses a monthly feed, and begin routine protective spraying. Single any multiple-growth shoots. Cut back any frost-damaged shoots, and any that have not responded to pruning – suspect spur die-back. Rub out any inward-growing shoots on all bush types and keep watch for crossing stems. A busy month.

**May** Monthly feed and routine spray. Climbers will be making strong growth – tie in and bend reluctant bloomers. If it is a dry spring, water new plantings and seedlings by soaking. Be ready to begin disbudding on exhibition plants.

**June** A danger month for diseases: routine systemic fungicide spraying starts – continue at 2–3 week intervals until September. Monthly feed. Disbudding continues. Tie in ramblers and climbers. Send for catalogues.

**July** No feeding after the first week of the month. Dead-head ruthlessly, prune back early and once-only flowering types and clean up fallen debris meticulously. Tie in ramblers and climbers. Maintain mulch. Order new roses. Prepare materials ready for budding at the end of the month.

**August** Dead-heading continues. Prune back once-flowering types. Danger month for fungus diseases, especially in hot dry spells, so soak accordingly. Prepare for cuttings. Final budding.

**September** Back to square one! Meticulously clear up any debris, and continue fungicidal spraying.

# Questions and Answers

# 12

# Questions and Answers

## 1 Controlling greenfly

*This year my roses have been inundated with greenfly. I have used every spray I can find – most of them seem to work for a time because shortly after spraying the greenfly have gone, but in a day or two they are back again as bad as ever. I have read that aphids multiply very fast – but surely not as fast as this? Where do they all come from, and whatever can I do? They are spoiling the flowers, which do not open properly.*

Life can take some very extraordinary forms, and the aphid is just one, albeit familiar, example. The sight of the first one or two greenfly in spring and early summer does not evoke a recognition of impending serious plant destruction. It is only when the few become thousands and even millions, usually within the space of a few days, when buds and shoots disappear under a seething mass, that it occurs to many gardeners that they must remember to get something to deal with them – next time they go to the shops!

This is what has happened. In early spring, with warmer temperatures, eggs that have over-wintered on host plants hatch into female greenfly – there are no males at this stage – the vast majority of which have wings. These are very soon blown on the wind to other plants when they all quickly begin to give birth, repeatedly, to living young wingless females, which within a short time each begin to give birth repeatedly to wingless females, and so it goes on generation after generation, multiplication upon multiplication. Literally, millions of offspring are produced in a short time, and not a single male is involved – they do not exist!

This reproductive process, called parthenogenesis, is not at all uncommon in the insect world, and by a long, long way is nothing like as incredible or bizarre as some examples. It does, however, explain how a plague can appear almost overnight. The multiple birth continues through the summer months, encouraged by mild weather and suitable host plants like your roses.

Overcrowding is one condition – there are others – that triggers a hormone that leads to the production of more winged females which are soon blown away by wind. Nature tries to solve its overcrowding at home by equipping the next generation with the means to go away quickly and start colonies elsewhere. Of course, there are natural predators – birds, other insects, wasps, hover fly lavae, beetles like the ladybird, and so on – and, it is a good job the aphids don't all live otherwise the world would very soon be 6ft (2 metres) deep in greenfly!

Shortening hours of daylight, lower temperatures and changes within the host plants themselves at the onset of autumn and winter triggers another hormone which leads, not to winged females, but to a generation of males, the only time that they occur. Mating follows, which results not in live young, but in eggs, deposited deep into crevices and cracks to over-winter, and in due course to emerge and begin the process all over again. The adult parents die during the cold of winter, unless they can make their way to an obliging greenhouse, conservatory or shelf indoors with suitable host plants.

It is necessary to describe the aphid reproductive process so that you can 'know thine enemy', and understanding how the population explosion occurs explains why control measures have to be very thorough. A 95 per cent kill achieves little because the remaining 5 per cent quickly replace their lost sisters – with interest. It requires little imagination to appreciate the cumulative effect of so many creatures each sucking the life out of a plant, stunting and weakening it, making the plant suffer, struggle and become less able to resist fungal attack. You may have regarded the little greenfly as not particularly serious, but I hope that this changes your mind, it is an insidious dangerous beast.

Furthermore, as strange as we may find the reproductive process, the feeding procedure is also rather unusual. It consists of inserting a very slender tube into the plant cells, sucking out the liquid sap, absorbing the nutrients it needs, and 'spewing' or 'spitting' what is left back down the tube into the plant again. Again, this is not confined to the aphid – other insects and creatures do much the same thing, and some of them, the leaf-roll sawfly for example, secrete hormonal and similar growth-affecting substances that cause the leaves to curl and roll, which then makes it more difficult for predators to get at them.

This is bad enough, but the really serious aspect of greenfly is yet to come.

Many plants attacked by aphids are subject to virus diseases, and quite often, how they get into the plant is as incredible as the life story of the aphid itself. The virus is taken up by the aphid with the ingested sap from an infected plant. Within the body of the creature, the virus incubates and becomes capable of infecting other plants – many viruses have to pass through this incubation period within a predator to become infective. One of our experiments as students was to use a hypodermic needle to inject sap taken from an infected plant directly into healthy plants, sometimes repeatedly, and observe that nothing happened. The healthy plants remained healthy. However, as soon as they were exposed to greenfly from the infected plants, they quickly showed all the signs of virus infection.

So, with the direct effects of mass sucking, and side effects like susceptibility to fungus and introduction of viruses, aphids have a lot to answer for and have to be kept under control, but how? Being naked and soft-bodied, greenfly are easily killed by a contact poison. There are other members of the aphid family like the 'woolly aphid' that have extremely effective self-protective devices which make control very difficult, but this one is not in that class. There are several insecticides that will quickly polish off greenfly; preparations based on lindane and malathion have been available for several years and are quite reliable. Having regard to the method by which the tiny insect sucks out the sap, you would expect it to seek new and soft tissue into which to sink its tube, which explains why you find them concentrating on new soft shoots, buds and on the softer undersides of leaves. Clearly, it is absolutely vital to spray upwards from underneath as well as on the more obviously affected shoots and buds.

Frequently, in their search for soft tissue, greenfly work their way into the innermost crevices of buds, opening blooms and shoots – who hasn't found them right inside a lettuce? Contact sprays cannot reach them there, so we have to resort to other methods. Where it is practicable, we can introduce into the sap stream a chemical that diffuses throughout the plant and renders the entire sap system poisonous to greenfly and other creatures that suck and bite. Such plants then remain toxic and pest-free for some time until the toxin dissipates – from two or three weeks to longer, depending upon the nature of the plant – after which it has to be applied again.

With roses and ornamental plants, there is no problem, but with plants that are intended for food we have to be careful, and it is important to obey the makers' instructions to the letter. Most preparations indicate the safe period required to intervene between applying the systemic and human consumption – always make sure that the information is clearly stated on the bottle.

Finally, heavy infestations are always predictable following a mild winter because so many eggs and adults escape death in the cold. The lesson in this case is clear: don't wait for the plague to start, but be prepared, get a protective coating in place early and refresh it regularly, especially on the soft tips and buds that quickly grow out of the protective coat. Prevention is much better than trying to cure or repair this kind of damage. (See also question number 15 on page 160.)

## 2 Not so super 'Super Star'

*I have a bed of fifty 'Super Star' roses which I planted three years ago. Why are they covered with mildew each year when other neighbouring varieties are unaffected? I feed them well with various rose fertilizers, so it can't be that. [See page 129]*

On the contrary, it could have a lot to do with the fertilizers you are applying. Red roses have for long been regarded as particularly liable to mildew attack, a fault that is widely regarded as being passed on to some degree to those varieties, not necessarily red themselves, that have a red variety as one of the parents. There is enough evidence to support this idea for it to be considered seriously. However, I don't think that it is the whole story, and there is more to this problem than that.

In my opinion, and that of many rose fanciers, if it is grown hard and vigorously from good and properly ripened budding eyes implanted into good rootstocks and fed correctly, the vermilion coloured 'Super Star' is one of the most marvellous roses ever produced. It is not in the least surprising that, from the moment of its introduction and first showing, it achieved immense international popularity – more quickly, probably, than any other rose in history.

And that at once has been the cause of a lot of the trouble that so many have experienced. It is not only prone to mildew, but also to 'weak neck' – indeed, after all the acclamation, it was at one time widely called 'Super Flop' as the blooms fell about and flopped over. But it was not the fault of the variety at all! Too eager to cash in on its popularity while the early price was high, many so-called 'growers' were prepared to sell their souls and cut buds from anything they could lay their hands on, without worrying unduly about ripeness and condition.

Now, while there may be something in the genetic make-up of reds that lays them and their progeny open to mildew, the reputation that 'Super Star' also gained for not being able to hold its head up makes me question your source of supply – after all, you say that other varieties are not affected. Although you do not identify the rose fertilizers you have been using, the fact that you mention that you have used them and evidently place great store by them makes me suspicious! Most, if not all, fertilizers sold specifically for roses are largely, if not wholly, inorganic. They are mixtures of various straight chemicals, make no contribution whatever to the organic content of the soil and, indeed, it can be very well argued that their prolonged use has a deleterious effect upon soil structure, and therefore, far from being of benefit to the roses, actually do more harm than good in the long term.

At the Parks Dept. nursery where I worked for some time, we produced a vast number of roses every year for the London parks, and it was one of the reasons for some disparaging regard among the gardeners there of the standard of gardening 'outside in the parks' compared with the standards set in the nursery that there was always complaint about mildew, whereas it was seldom if ever seen on the roses before they left the nursery. It was simply put down to 'rotten looking after as soon as they leave here'. Years after, when I had learned a great deal more than I knew then, I realized that there was most likely another explanation.

Our hardwood propagator – a brilliant plantsman – was a fanatical believer in and user of a by-product of the fishing industry, available at that time, called 'Eclipse Fish Manure' – I later used it myself when it became my privilege and responsibility to decide what fertilizers and manures would be used, and I can only say that I never used anything better. However, the fishing industry changed, the fish content of the manure had to be modified, government decrees concerning the proportion of ingredients affected what could be called 'fish manure' and what had to leave out the word 'fish', so that nowadays the product has to be given a different name. In my opinion it is still the best manure, and although the organic base has changed from fish, it still has a very strong smell! I don't object to it, it is certainly no worse than pig and some other manures, and the smell very soon goes when it reaches the soil, but some people don't like it including, unfortunately, those misguided shopkeepers who think it will drive customers away! It is therefore not easy to find a retailer.

What was the connection – if there was one – between the use of Eclipse Fish and the absence of mildew? When I had learned more about my job, and was delving deeply into the botanical effects of nutrients on various plants I learned about the function of potash in the processes that go on within plants, how it affects ripening and colour in bloom and fruit, how vital it is to the vigour and health of plants, and how a shortage of it – or an inbalance in the other major elements – at the crucial time of maximum growth rate leaves a plant weak-kneed, soft and lush, unable to resist the constant attack of fungus and those forms of life that are ever ready for the soft option.

One of the features of the old Eclipse Fish was the balance between the three main nutrients nitrogen, phosphorous and potassium, and the fact that the potash was released for plant uptake steadily over a long period. Was that the explanation why there was seldom any mildew to be seen in the nursery? Certainly, very few of the outside parks used fish manure. It may all be very circumstantial, but there is no doubt that it makes sense. I use the modern product extensively, and I don't struggle with mildew, nor do my roses hang their heads.

Decomposition of the organic content begins slowly, and as the decomposition bacteria proliferate, nutrient availability increases gradually and reaches a peak about 80 days after being put into the soil. After this there is a gradual tailing off. This is a long sustained feeding action, and it indicates the best way to use this manure. The manure is concentrated and, as with any other, it is quite capable of causing scorch. The best policy, therefore, is 'little and often'. During the second half of March, sprinkle the dry powdery material either generally at about 1 ounce (28g) per square yard (square metre), or a level dessertspoonful – no more – around each rose at 8–12 inches (20–30cm) distance from the stem, and scratch-hoe into the soil or mulch surface.

Repeat this procedure each month until July, and then no more – no special 'autumn' feeds. The first application will reach a peak in June, followed by other peaks until the last towards the end of September, with the all-important hardening potash steadily available all the time. Anything later than that would encourage growth when the plants should be thinking of slowing down and getting ready for their long

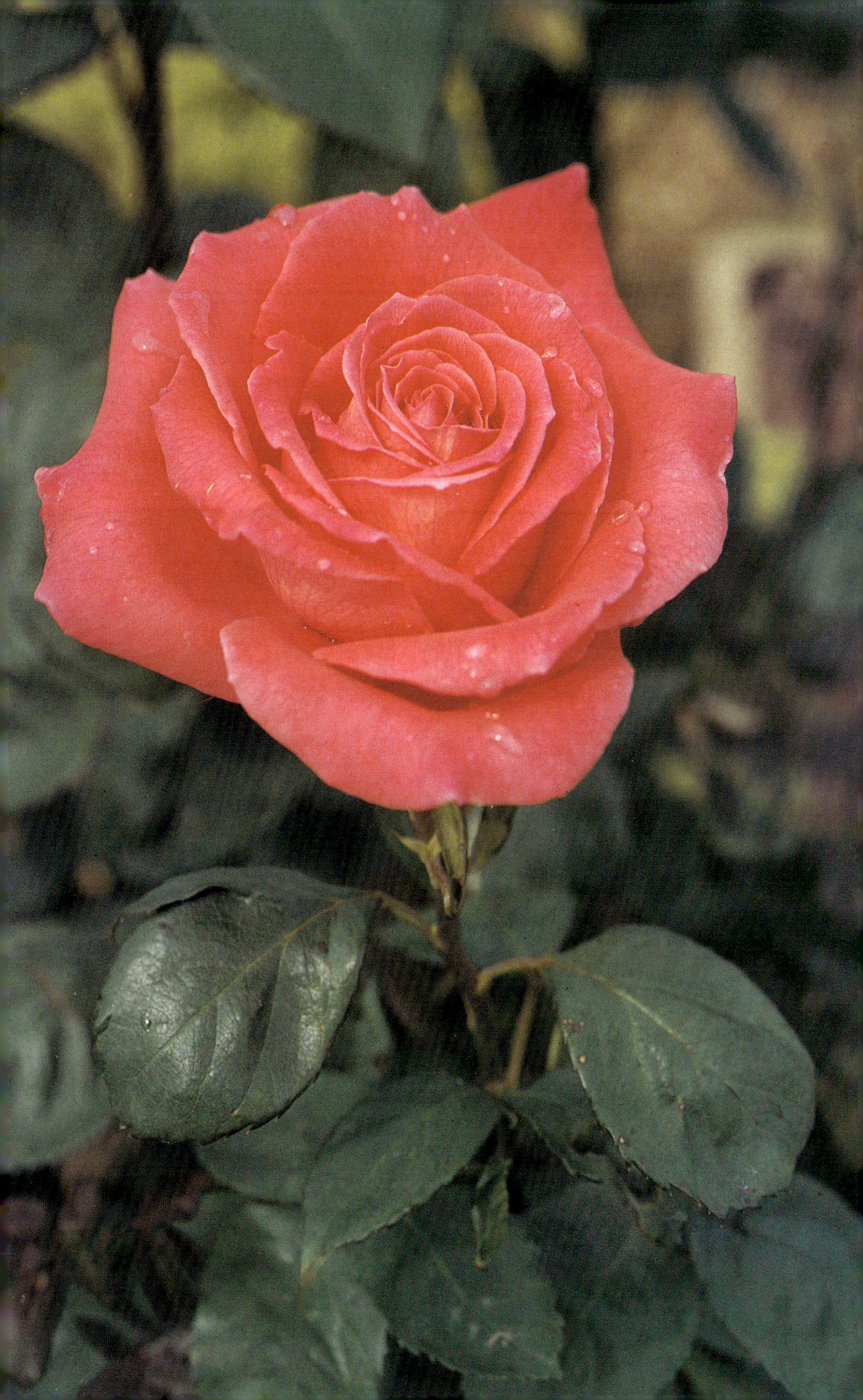

*(overleaf)* 'Super Star' (see pages 23 and 126), raised by Tantau in 1960, is one of the most brilliant of all modern H.T. types, and appears almost to glow when the light is poor. It needs to be grown well to avoid disappointment.

*(top left)* The strongly scented 'Paul Shirville' (see page 212), raised by Harkness in 1983, is ideal as a standard.

*(top right)* 'Peaudouce' epitomizes the sublime classic beauty of the modern H.T. Raised by Dickson in 1985.

*(above left)* The Floribunda 'Iceberg' (see pages 68 and 146), raised in 1958 by Kordes, is regarded by many as the whitest of all whites.

*(above right)* 'Sue Lawley' (see page 238) is a modern version of the old *Rosa mundi* bi-colour theme.

*(opposite)* 'Hannah Gordon' is another appropriately attractive example of a 'name' bloom.

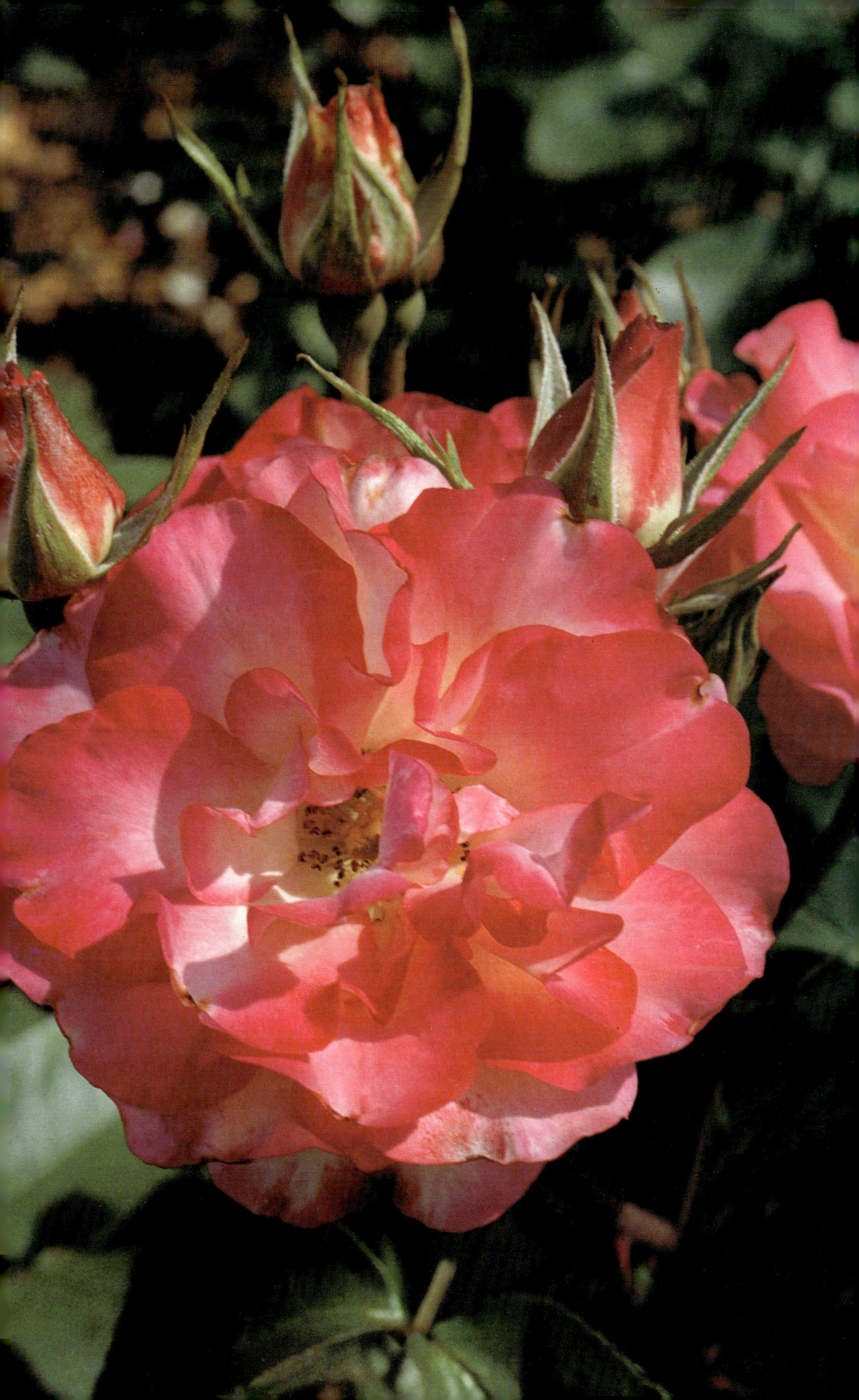

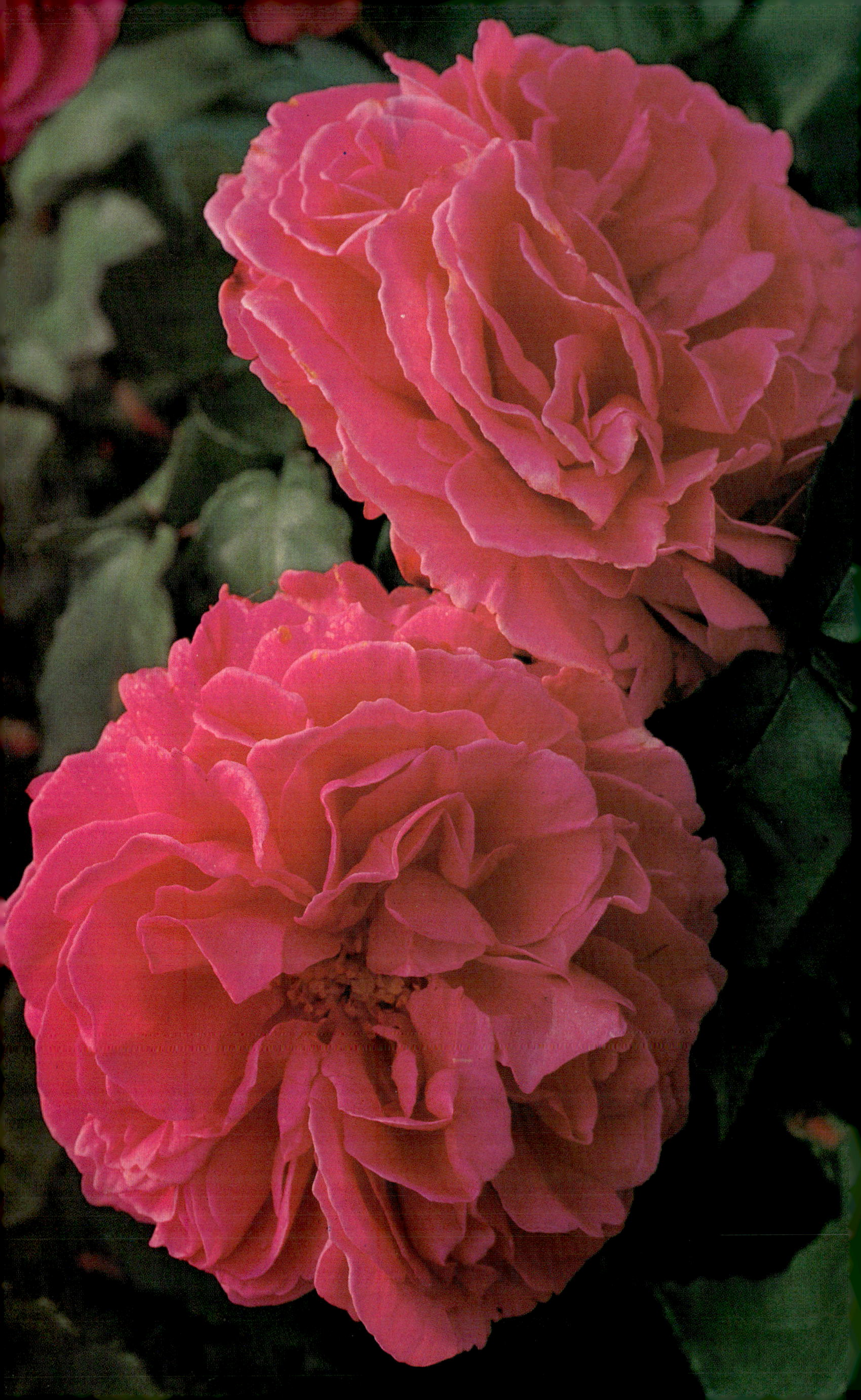

*(opposite)* 'Mme Isaac Pereire' (see page 26), a 100-year-old Bourbon favourite, still compares well with the moderns. It produces huge blooms and has a rich, strong fragrance. However, it needs a lot of space to flourish and is not for the small garden.

*(above) Rosa gallica* 'Versicolor', the renowned *Rosa mundi* beloved during Elizabethan and Tudor times, is still very popular.

*(top left)* Fully open, flat, quartered blooms and a couple of buds of 'Comte de Chambord'. One of the most popular of the Portland group, this is a fragrant rose and not too big for a smallish garden.

*(top right)* These are the enormous 4–5 in (10–12.5cm) diameter blooms of the vigorous and fragrant *rugosa* 'Roseraie de l'Hay' (see page 192).

*(above left)* The thornless rose 'Zéphirine Drouhin' (see pages 158, 212 and 225) flowers continuously through the summer. Its free flowering and strong fragrance have kept it ever popular since it was raised in 1868.

*(above right)* 'Emanuel' is a New English rose recently introduced by Austin as a tribute to the designers and makers of Princess Diana's wedding dress.

*(opposite)* The perpetual flowering modern hybrid Musk rose 'Ballerina' carries a wealth of hydrangea-like bloom clusters. A very pretty rose as a hedge or a standard.

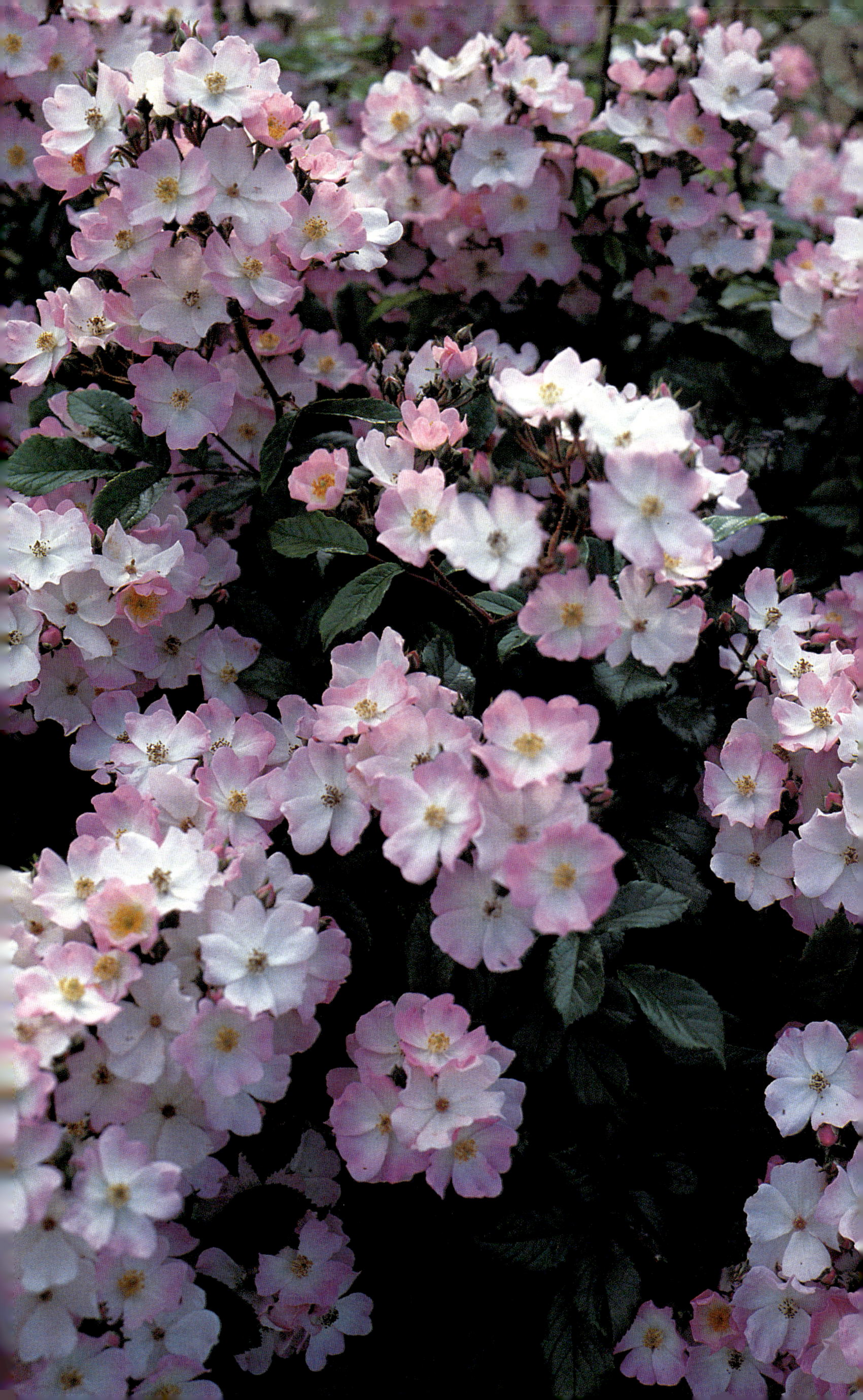

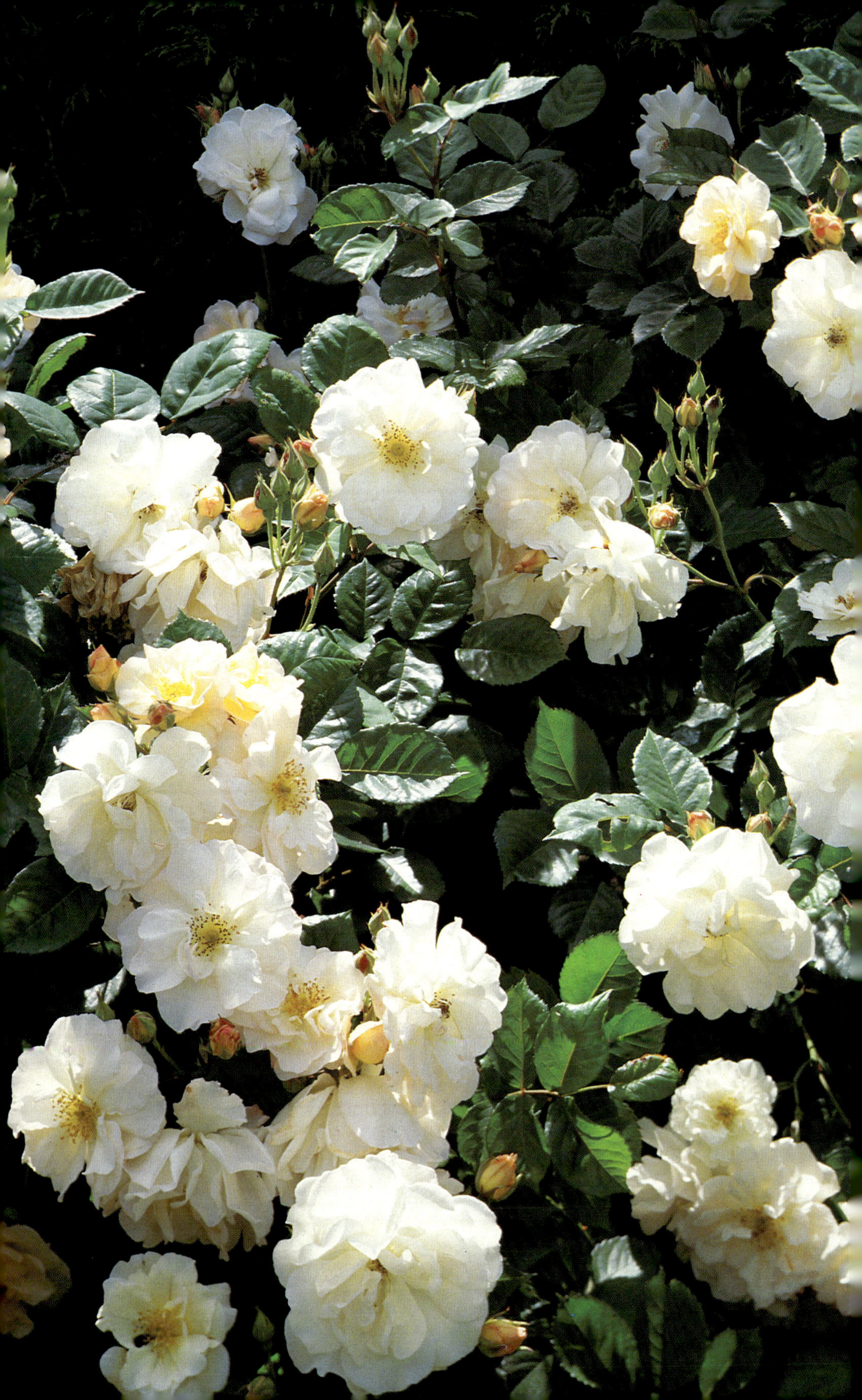

*(opposite)* One of the best of the Pemberton hybrid Musks, 'Penelope' flowers with almost exuberant freedom, as you can see by the buds still to develop in this picture. The blooms have the typical strong musk fragrance. However, growing 6ft (2m) high and wide, it needs plenty of space to develop.

*(above)* 'William Shakespeare' is a typical example of the 'English' group developed by David Austin. This picture illustrates very well how the lighter colour of the early bloom darkens with age. The bard would have been proud of his colourful and strongly fragrant namesake.

*(top left) Rosa moyesii* 'Geranium' produces spectacular autumn displays of orange red hips after equally beautiful vivid red summer blooms (see page 142).

*(top right)* Late blooms and early hips are frequently borne at the same time on *Rosa rugosa* 'Rubra'.

*(above left)* 'Graham Thomas', another fine rose raised by David Austin, combines the character of an old garden rose with strong yellow blooms, good fragrance and a repeat flowering habit.

*(above right)* The showy 4–5in (10–12.5cm) diameter blooms of the modern shrub 'Nevada' (see page 242) smother the bush in early summer. This is a vigorous 7ft (2.1m) dazzler, at its best in the bright sun.

*(opposite) Rosa xanthina* (see pages 30 and 185) is sometimes called *flore-pleno* to reflect the double/semi-double nature of the blooms. Native to northern China and Korea.

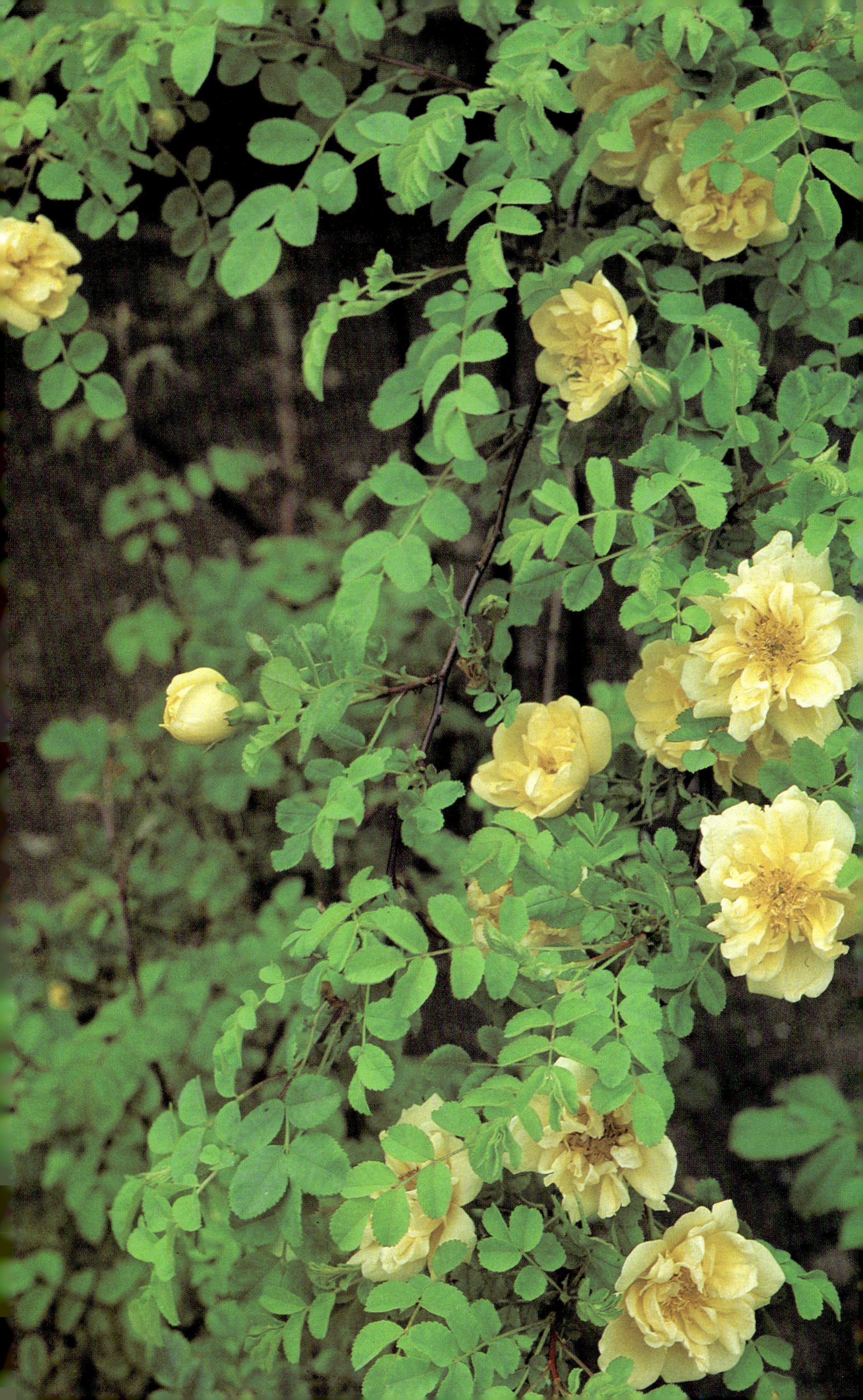

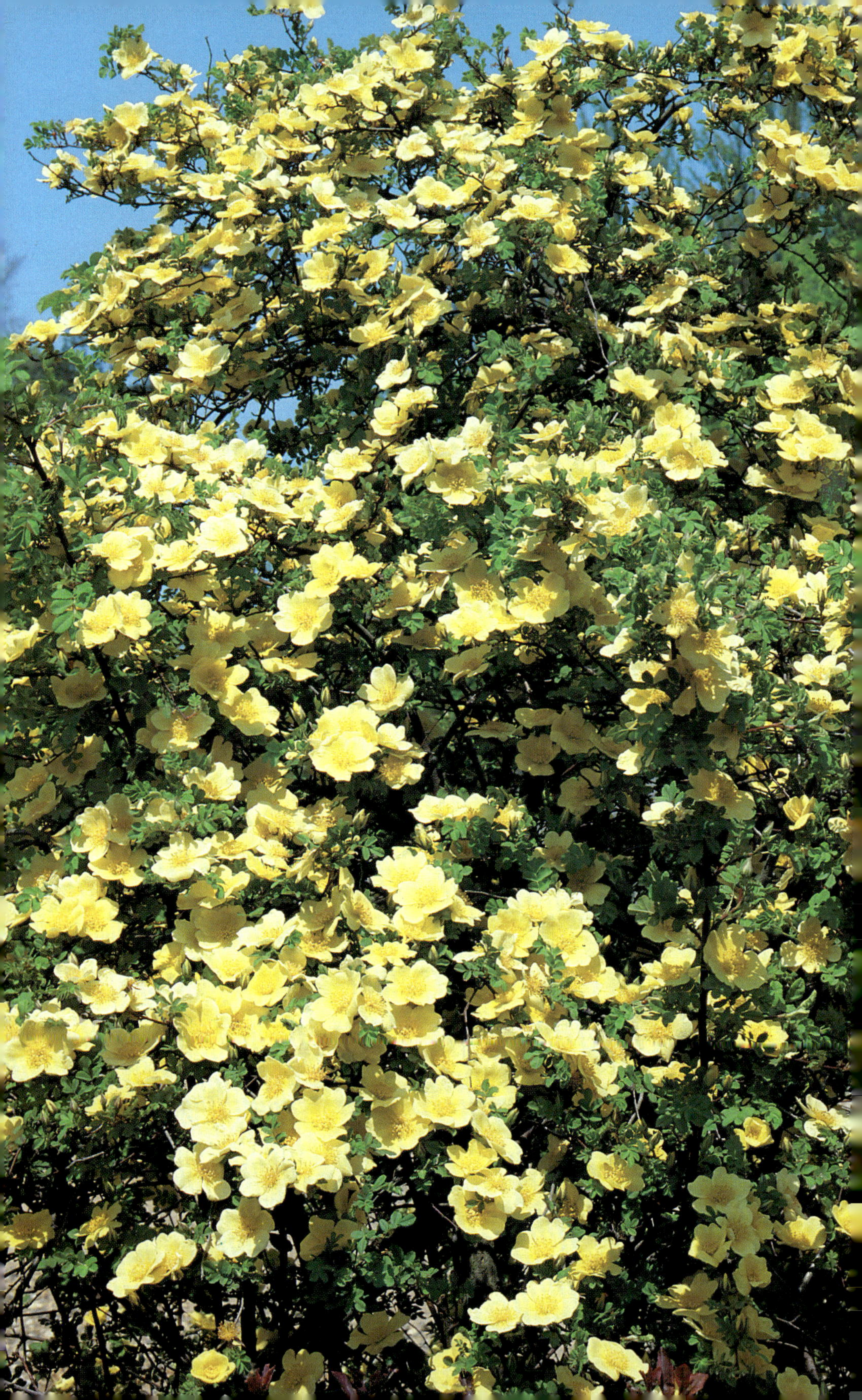

*(opposite) Rosa xanthina* 'Canary Bird' is not always as reliable and good as this fine example – the classic case for always seeing in bloom before you buy. When it is good, it fully lives up to its evocative name. See page 30, and the illustration on page 139.

*(above) Rosa banksiae* 'Lutea' (see pages 214 and 215) is generally considered the best of the banksian climbers. To see these long tresses hanging from high up in a supporting tree is breathtakingly lovely. Not bad on the house walls, either!

*(top left)* A rose for all seasons, this is *Rosa moyesii* 'Geranium' in its colourful summer livery – before the autumn hips come along (see page 138).

*(top right)* Strongly fragrant 'Maiden's Blush' was recorded as early as the 1400s, and is still widely grown.

*(opposite)* This illustration of the dwarf patio rose 'Stars and Stripes' (see page 238) is virtually actual size.

*(above left)* The huge flower clusters of 'Wedding Day' (see pages 212, 236 and 237) are apricot in the bud and open white. Fragrant and pretty, this is a marvellous rose for all who have space to grow it.

*(above right)* The hybrid perpetual 'Ferdinand Pichard' (see page 237) rivals *Rosa mundi* as the finest striped bloom of all. Richly fragrant.

*(overleaf)* 'Danse du Feu' (see pages 178 and 259). This French raised hardy climber has become one of the most popular of all for pergolas, pillars and walls.

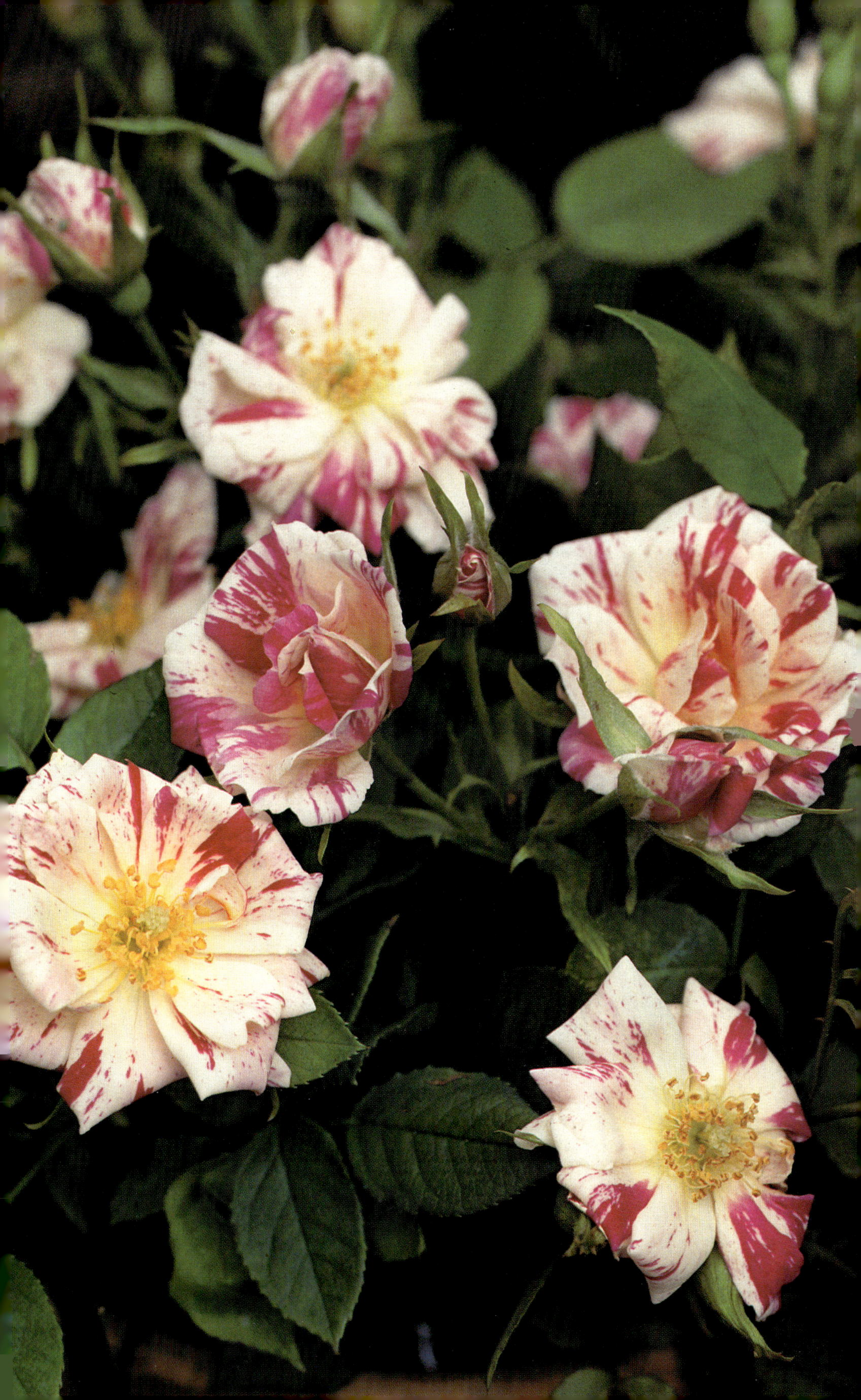

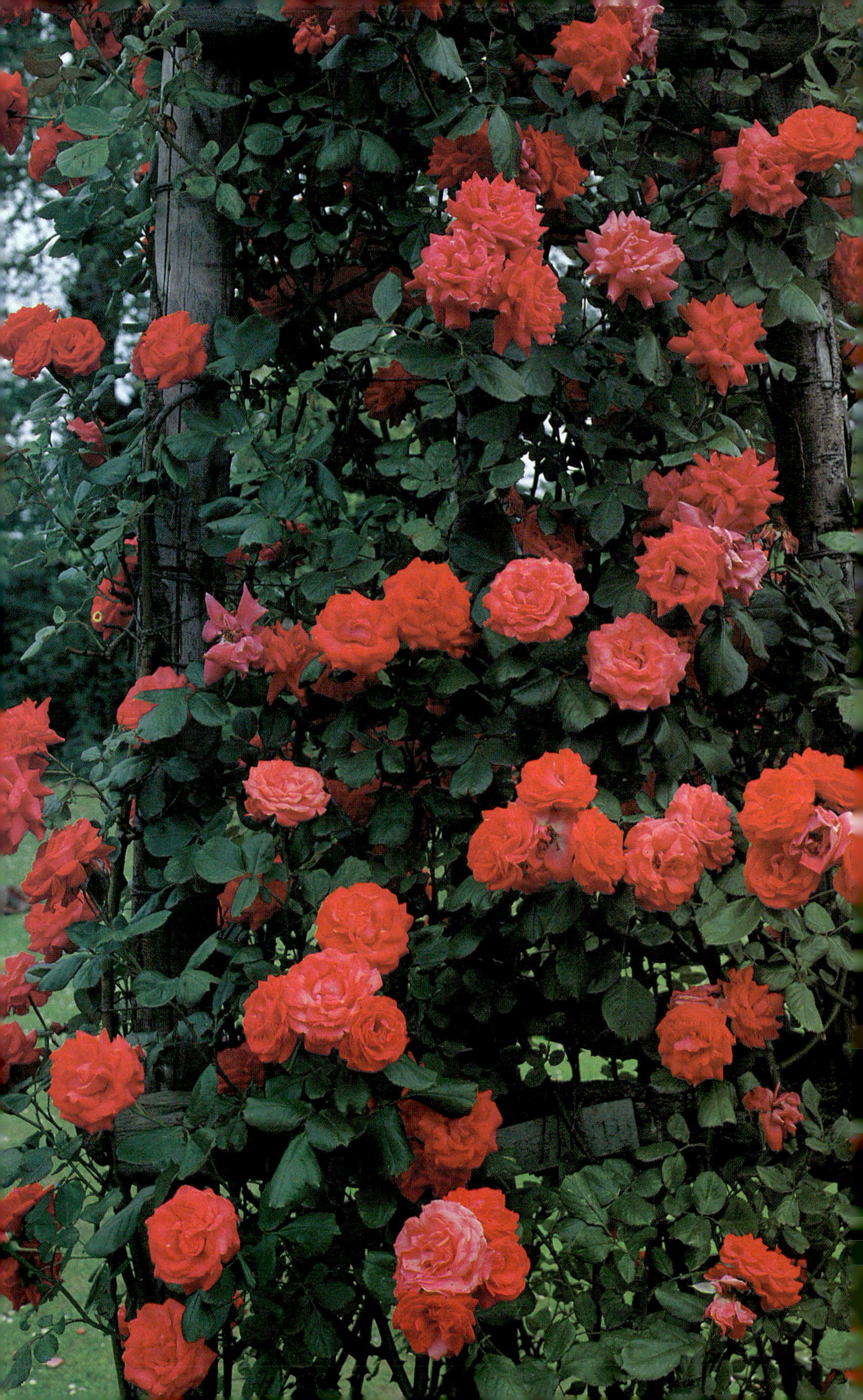

sleep. This is the best way to use this particular manure – other fertilizing materials will have different time scales and nutrient ratios, and the application rates will therefore vary.

Prevention by correct feeding is better than cure, but mildew is relatively easy to control with modern sprayed-on fungicides like Karathane and Benlate, provided you attack at the very first signs of it and don't allow the fungus time to get into the plant system and take hold. If this happens, it becomes a very serious debilitating disease and can wreak terrible destruction on shoots and young growth.

## 3 Where to find old favourites

*Although there are some fine red roses available, we do not think that we have ever seen anything as dark and magnificent as the deep crimson velvet of the variety 'Charles Mallerin' that we saw on the Wheatcroft stand at Chelsea many years ago. Our problem is that we cannot find a grower that still offers it any more – or for that matter several other varieties like the bronze foliage, dazzling orange 'Zambra'. Why is this, and is there any way that we can find out if any of these older treasures are still in cultivation?*

It is quite natural to yearn after old favourites, and a nice feeling when you find one still available. However, consider carefully before ordering and growing – there is more than one reason why varieties are offered and then withdrawn, sometimes after only a few years (as you will realize when reading the narrative sections of this book).

New introductions every year mean that just as many have to be left out to make space for them, and those that fall by the wayside are the varieties that are superseded by something better, healthier, more resistant to disease, more floriferous, or with better sales appeal! Despite the accolades that accompany each new introduction, time tells, it always does, and the flaws show out.

'Charles Mallerin' was a fantastic rose; a crimson so deep that it was like black velvet! It was so good it took the premier award at the Montreux Show in 1957, which is regarded as the world championship. However, it unfortunately proved to have a rather weak constitution – what the trade calls a 'poor doer' – and needed very careful cultivation and nursing for relatively few blooms.

Perhaps such difficulties make the perfect bloom that much more valuable in the eyes of the beholder, but that is not a commodity that sells, and it will be difficult to find the variety now. The best way I know to find out if it is still grown and offered is to write to the Rose Growers' Association, 303 Mile End Road, Colchester, Essex, CO4 5EA. The 1989 edition of their *Handbook* listed more than 2,400 varieties and 73 nurseries growing them, and cost £1.00 post free.

## 4 A fresh rose bloom for Christmas morning

*I remember my father always giving my mother a fresh rose bloom every Christmas morning from the garden. Now I have a garden I would like to do the same for my wife, and would be grateful for the names of any varieties that continue to bloom so late each year.*

What a nice thought! There is a peculiar form of one-upmanship in being able to pick a nice bunch of flowers in December, and presenting a fresh rose on Christmas morn – and could there be anything nicer? Of course, it will hardly be likely to compare with a bloom from early summer, December weather is all wrong for a start, and most roses have long decided to call it a day, but some varieties just don't know when to stop. By growing these, given a fair chance by the weather, and perhaps using a little ingenuity, you should be able to place a nice rose bud alongside the tea and biscuits.

If the last few days weather before Christmas look like being uncooperative, there are a couple of tricks you can try. Cut a bud when colour is showing, remove all but the two topmost leaves, and allow it to dry a little, but not wilt, in a cool place. On Christmas Eve morning, cut a couple of inches (5cm) from the stem and place it into water at once. Next morning the bud should be just on opening point and right on cue. The second method, which can be used with a bud that looks likely to open a day or two too early, is to cut the bloom, remove all but the top couple of leaves as before, and as quickly as possible get the cut end and the leaf scars under water in a tall vase to which ice cubes from the fridge have been added. Renew the ice night and morning to keep the water and the rose stem as cool as possible. This is an old showman's trick to hold back blooms that are reaching their peak too early for show. Conversely, moving it into tepid water and a warm room will open a bloom very quickly.

A very good variety for our purpose is the modern pure white 'Iceberg'. Buds in December sometimes show a slight touch of pink, but the above treatment either clears it or hides it under the opening petals to give a nice white bloom (see p.130). The vigorous 'Queen Elizabeth' also tends to run on late, and can be treated in the same way for a pink bloom, as can the strongly scented bright red 'Fragrant Cloud'.

If you can provide a well sheltered position – they don't like frost – you can try the China roses. They have somewhat smaller blooms but the group offers a range of colours, and one of them, 'Old Blush China', is also known as the 'Monthly Rose' because of the regularity with which it repeatedly blooms. Anything from 4–6ft (1.2–1.8m) tall, the silvery-pink, sweetly perfumed flowers continue to appear right through autumn into winter. Naturally, this attribute attracted a lot of attention when it was brought to English gardens from China in the latter part of the eighteenth century, and reputedly it is the variety that inspired a famous poet of the time, Thomas Moore, to pen words that have become immortal as 'The Last Rose of Summer'. If you can have an interesting story to tell your friends about the plants in your garden, so much the better. Add a little romance to the tea and biscuits.

Should 'Old Blush China' be too tall and large, you could try another China rose, 'Hermosa'. This is about 2½ft (0.8m) tall and wide, with pink blooms that are small but very fragrant, and keep coming until very late.

Finally, a couple which, although not strictly China roses, are very similar and are sometimes listed under that heading. 'Cécille Brunner', the so-called 'Sweetheart Rose' – an apt description because it is constantly in bloom – has very small blush-pink, H.T.-like blooms and strongly fragrant. 'Perle d'Or' is very similar but with rich apricot shading to cream when fully open, and a delicate scent.

The older and species roses are not listed by every rose-grower, and are seldom if ever seen in garden centres. Drop a line to David Austin Roses – you will find the address on page 265 – and kindly mention this book if you will! He makes a speciality of just this sort of thing, and his handbook and catalogue is an Aladdin's Cave of rose treasures (see the Bibliography on page 263).

## 5 Can blooms be kept in the deep freeze?

*How can I use my deep freeze to preserve flowers, especially roses, for Christmas? The instruction book says it can be done, and has a pretty picture, but gives no precise instructions.*

I have often heard it said and claimed, but have never seen it done. There is a vast difference between chilling a bud for a few days as described in the previous question, and going right down to the temperatures of deep freezing. You could try the vegetable drawer of the fridge, but if you do, wrap each bud securely in cling film or it will lose too much moisture and wilt beyond recovery.

As you probably realize, not all fruits can be frozen – strawberries and raspberries, for example, usually collapse into a soggy mess as they are thawed, and rose petals usually behave the same way. The expansion of freezing liquid in the tissue cells of many fruits and flowers bursts the walls, and like a frozen water pipe that bursts, you see no problem until the ice thaws and runs out. Many fruit and flower tissues, depending upon how quickly the freezing occurs, hold their shape while frozen, but the structure has been ruptured, and they collapse with the thaw.

By all means try – you may be lucky, but as I say, I have never seen it actually demonstrated. An idea that does work – sometimes – is to immerse an entire, tight, just-beginning-to-open bud and stem, with just a couple of leaves, in a narrow tray or dish of water. It is vital that all air bubbles are removed; they may try to cling around the petals, and it helps to add one drip, no more, of washing-up liquid to dispel these.

With the flower completely immersed, put it into the ice cube compartment of the fridge – this will freeze solid, but the cold is not as fierce and intense as the deep freeze. When you want the bloom for display, lay the tray in tepid water for a few moments just to free the ice block, and then lay this on a plate or shallow dish so that, as the frost clears from the surface, you have your rose embedded in a block of ice. The effect will last only while the ice melts, is a little messy on the dining table and, again, the beautiful rose becomes a soggy brown if you leave it there long enough for the air to get to it.

By far the most satisfactory method of having a rose at Christmas is to grow and prepare fresh blooms as described above in question number 4.

## 6 Are roses afraid of ghosts?

*I replaced some Hybrid Tea roses that had died for some reason, and the new plants died. Now I have been told that this always happens, and that roses will not grow where others have died. It sounds very far-fetched to me*

## QUESTIONS AND ANSWERS

*– surely there cannot possibly be anything in it? They have always been fed well, and we have no particular problems, other than moss.*

This reminds me of the scoffing that goes on at those folk who talk to their plants. They may be slightly crackers in thinking that their plants have an intelligence like us and can understand what we are saying, but what the scoffers fail to recognize is that such folk care about their plants and are expressing a feeling for them – the modern word is 'empathy'. People who care about their plants are therefore more likely to have happier plants than those who do not talk to them, that's all.

There is a body of opinion that says that when a rose dies, another will not grow in its place because it knows and dies in sympathy! You may think it just as crackers as the folk who have a chat with their plants, but the fact is that it happens, and a lot of gardeners write letters about it. The problem does cause concern, it is widespread, and it cannot be simply dismissed as a ghost story. No pest or disease is discernible, and yet perfectly healthy plants languish and die. Most gardeners from this school of thought – invariably they are amateurs – point to personal experience, often repeated (an important clue).

Modern scientific investigation has not isolated a virus, bacterium, fungus, or other mysterious foreign body that would explain what happens, and we can therefore regard the unknown disease theory as irrational as is the sympathetic heartbreak. We have to look for rational, sensible and similar factors.

It is the case that the problem invariably occurs in beds and positions where roses are grown exclusively and have been for several years, and that the first deaths are of old, well-established plants – that is the first clue. Complainants often protest that they have to hoe frequently to prevent the competition of weeds and moss – second clue, for it is evident that we are dealing with deteriorating soil fertility and structure. Repeated demands on the same plant nutrients by the same crop being grown repeatedly in the same position is of course a widely recognized cause of 'soil sickness', as is build-up of pest populations and diseases specific to the crop in question. The condition we are discussing here is frequently put down to 'rose sickness'.

Now, this questioner may well have been applying fertilizers – he doesn't say which – but he does refer to moss, and this is a sure indication of acidity and poor fertility. Frequently, as in a lawn also, it is a direct consequence of too much use of inorganic chemical fertilizers, and little or no, certainly insufficient and therefore diminishing, organic input. Even at a distance and solely on the evidence within the question, it is a pretty safe conclusion that the soil under these roses is extremely low in organic content. A further consequence of this is that the supply of the minor and trace elements is depleted.

Artificial fertilizers may supply the three majors – nitrogen, phosphorus and potassium – although, I would argue, scarcely ever in balance, but do nothing in respect of the minor elements. For these, you have to rely on organic matter and preparations. How long a soil can go on supporting plant life before minor element shortage presents problems is quite unpredictable; soils vary and their stored resources vary, depending on their formation and history, and some plants are more responsive and vulnerable than others to shortage of a particular element.

I referred to this being a problem that is virtually confined to amateur gardeners. Just consider: why is it not the serious problem one might expect it to be among the rose specialist nurserymen, most of whom do not have sufficient acreage to grow different crops and move them around to vary the nutrient demands? They grow roses repeatedly in the same soil, so where does 'rose sickness' come in? I suggest that it is more rational to explain this phenomenon as a serious shortage of one or more minors – who can say which with any certainty? – accentuated by a soil structure that has 'gone to pot'.

Read through Chapters 4, 5 and 7 dealing with preparation before planting, feeding with a balanced nutrient source that is organic and containing plenty of minors, and maintaining a steady organic input to the soil structure by mulching. You really must correct the high acidity of your soil – a test kit is inexpensive and easy to use – and put down lime or ground chalk as indicated. The soil under your roses is like your bank balance: if you make more withdrawals than deposits, the day comes when you cannot pay for anything, and the soil won't grow any more roses. Get a good wodge of organic matter under new plantings, feed with Humber or Growmore, and mulch, mulch, mulch – and forget about ghosts.

## 7 Improving clay soils for roses

*For several years we have tried to grow good roses in soil which is heavy clay. By spring, most stems become pale, even yellowish with brown patches and some die-back. New growth following pruning seems to start well enough but then tends to wilt and struggle into very poor foliage – there is hardly a bloom, poor at that, and the plants are extremely unhappy. We have followed lots of advice to no avail and now despair of growing decent roses. Can you please help?*

The first thing I suggest you do is to stop despairing, and secondly, to stop following advice until you understand why you are doing it. Good cultivation of roses, as with every other plant, has very little to do with following advice from other people, or knowing what to do, how to do it, when, and what with – but *why*! Understand why – and every other question becomes answerable by plain common sense.

Roses prefer a dense soil to a light sandy one with no body in it, but that doesn't mean that they will thrive in a heavy, sticky, badly drained, airless soil, which probably explains your clay exactly. You may have heard of the use of 'Nottingham marl' in the preparation of cricket pitches, and the excellence of Nottingham's Trent Bridge ground. Marl is a dense clay that does not settle into a wet, soggy mess like ordinary clay. Some of the finest rose growers in the world are to be found around Nottingham, and you would be right in thinking that there must be a connection between the two facts. Your clay is an excellent raw material for growing good roses. What you need to do is to turn your heavy sticky stuff into a little Nottingham by converting it into marl. How you can do this depends on understanding why clay behaves as it does – and then tackling the cause.

With the naked eye, most gardeners can see individual grains of sands, but the size of the particles that constitute clay are so small that a microscope is needed in order to see them. The remarkable fact is that these clay-sized particles only need to constitute some 30 per cent of a soil sample for that soil to have the characteristics of a clay – heavy, wet, poorly drained, sticky and difficult to work with. If you begin with a soil that is 100 per cent clay, or nearly so, just consider how much sand, grit or whatever else will need to be introduced to reduce the proportion of clay to less than 30 per cent of the whole. It doesn't take much to realize that 'brute force and ignorance' methods of trying to alter the nature of clay – which is what sand and grit amount to – are a waste of time. This may kill a few sacred cows, but there it is – sand and grit cannot change the nature of clay; the cause is very, very much more involved than that.

Clay stays wet and sticky, because water does not pass through between the tiny clay particles as the spaces between them are so small. Clearly, the problem is to make the spaces larger, and that is easier said than done. Over the years, in addition to sand and grit, there have been some ingenious ideas and products put on the market. None of them have lasted very long, and have proved to be more effective at getting money out of gardeners' pockets than they have at getting the wet stickiness out of clay!

There is a natural solution, that has stood the test of time, and it is not expensive – which is undoubtedy the best reason why it is not more commercially promoted and well known, there is so little profit in it. Where, in geological history, clay has become overlaid and permeated with rock gypsum, the clay does not resist the passage of water – and to explain why this is so, and therefore what you will have to do to the clay in your garden, we shall understand much better by considering a similar example, an analogy.

Most readers will know the old party trick of rubbing a comb or a pen with flannel, or a stick of sealing wax with silk, and making small pieces of paper leap up to attach themselves. This is caused by static electricity. Each clay particle has the same electrical charge and, if you remember school days in the physics lab. and the rule 'like charges repel, unlike charges attract', this means that the clay particles are pushing each other apart and preserving the tiny apertures through which water cannot pass. Gypsum particles have a strong opposite charge, which means that the tiny clay particles are attracted, cling to and group around the gypsum in the same way that the paper pieces cling to the comb and pen. The spaces between the groups are thus much larger than when the clay particles are not grouped (the correct word to describe this is 'flocculated') and water passes through more easily.

This is a very much simplified explanation of a very technical subject, but I hope can be followed sufficiently well for you to realize that it is a waste of time and money adopting remedies that do not treat causes, and that it is necessary to have confidence, through knowledge of what you are doing, to pursue a line of action perhaps through a lengthy period when no improvement may readily be apparent.

The maximum rate that a clay can assimilate gypsum, is 8 ounces (230g) per square yard (square metre), per annum, and this is best interpreted as 2 ounces (50g) per square yard (square metre) every 3 months – simply spread it on the surface and let the weather take it in from the mulch. The process may take a couple of years to show a marked improvement on heavy clays, and you will have to be both patient and persistent, hence the need for your understanding.

The above cultivations will gradually flocculate the clay, get air into it and make it more responsive to organic input, feeding and mulching. Until you do effect a structural change in the clay, it cannot behave like a soil. Your clay will remain as infertile as the road outside, and that is where you may as well put down your feeds for all the good they will do.

## 8 Why remove old flower heads?

*We are advised repeatedly to remove blooms as soon as they are past their best, but just why is it so important?*

Unless you are purposefully propagating by seed or want the hips, you should cut off flowers as soon as they fade – always paying attention to the rules of pruning – to concentrate the plant's energy into subsequent bloom or bloom-bearing growth. As soon as a plant, any plant, begins the process of ensuring the next generation and perpetuation of the species, it also begins to lose the need to put up more bloom because it has achieved its primary purpose of perpetuation of its species by going through the process of setting seed. By taking off fading blooms and any developing seed which will be in the swelling pod or seed capsule (the rose hip) the plant is thwarted and has to try again, if that is its nature (repeats, recurrents and remontants do this), or if it is a 'one-timer' to divert its energies into developing stem growth that will bear flowers for another try next year.

It is most important, however, to bear in mind that you should not simply dead-head and leave it at that. Read the chapter on pruning and the reasons why, and always regard dead-heading, with all plants, not only roses, as a form of pruning. Whatever the plant, and especially with your roses, never, ever, leave purposeless internodal spurs which, apart from looking unsightly, are a direct invitation to die-back.

## 9 Cutting blooms does no harm – unless . . .

*A colleague argues that it does harm to rose bushes to cut blooms for the house. Can you settle the matter for us, please?*

It is a question of degree. You won't do any harm provided that you don't overdo it, and that is a matter for your judgement. A bloom or two, or a few perhaps from a floriferous bush, is one thing, exhaustion is another.

The important point to bear in mind is that although you naturally want a nice bloom and stem to take away, you should give more attention to the still-growing bush. What you cut off doesn't matter, it is the condition of what is left that does. Cut the flower stems just above a leaf joint so that a growth bud can grow out quickly, but do not cut with scissors, because they will crush the tissue. Use scimitar-cut secateurs that are sharp and in good condition, so that they leave a clean fast-healing wound on the living plant.

## *10 Rejuvenating an old veteran*

*An old rose bush which has been a part of the family since it was planted to celebrate an anniversary 22 years ago has become so tall and thick with branches that something had to be done about it. The flowers were also becoming poor and less in number, so last year we cut out a lot of old gnarled wood, and only five stems remained. Should these be pruned hard this spring, or do you think that the bush has been hit hard enough already? We don't want to lose the bush if we can help it.*

In the normal course of events, one would be inclined to say that an old veteran of 22 years owes you nothing, and that a bush that has been allowed to get into this senile state would be better scrapped to make space for a new start. However, that doesn't take account of the sentimental attachment, does it? Can anything be done to help it rejuvenate and find a lost youth? No one can say: the answer can be no more than 'perhaps'.

In this case, and others like it, the cutting out of several old stems at once would have been better done gradually, one or two each year, to avoid too violent a shock. To remove any more of the remaining old growth by pruning this spring could very well prove disastrous because the rising sap would have little or nowhere to go, and as old as the rootstock is, it would have to find an outlet for itself by putting up suckers.

Rather than an almighty clout, and trying to put to rights in one go the consequences of prolonged mistreatment of this kind, it would have been wiser to have proceeded with more caution by exerting pressure gradually to encourage any dormant buds with any spark of life left in them to break through the very old woody bark from low down, not high up where all the top growth has become concentrated. More bush roses are spoiled and misshapen by fear to prune hard enough and low enough than any other single cause, with the result that, each successive year, new growth starts higher and higher, and we get the familiar example of a 'bush rose' several feet (metres) tall, with all the growth at the top, and the base as bare as a tree trunk!

Whether this old chap will be able to break out or have to resort to suckers, you will have to wait and see. I wouldn't hit it any harder this year. Come the following spring, if no new growth has broken from the base, you can increase the pressure by taking out a further stem of old wood, but not more than one each year. If you are lucky and new growth breaks out from below, you will have to use your judgement as to how much diverted energy it will be able to take, and whether you can hasten the removal of the old stuff. I would think that two or three summers from now will be enough to show whether the plant is going to respond. If it doesn't, I'm afraid there is no alternative: you will have to take leave of an old friend.

When the time comes, cutting back should be done early in March if the weather looks like remaining mild for a couple of weeks – any likelihood of frost means that you will have to delay till after the cold spell. Hard freezing can split open a freshly exposed cut, and that is the last thing you want. Keep a mulch in place by all means, but I would refrain from feeding and encouraging growth until you know whether it is going to come and where from. Until new growth arises, any extra root activity and intake is more likely to increase the risk of suckers.

If you are lucky and the plant does take on a new lease of life, try in future to prune as low as you can on green wood, to an outward-pointing bud. Read Chapter 6 which deals with the reasons for pruning, and take the principles on board – but gently does it, you are dealing with an aged citizen. Any more drastic action will put its last light well and truly out.

## *11 Moving old established plants*

*I have a very old 'Peace' bush rose – must be 20 years at least – that I am obliged to try to move to another part of the garden. It was given to us by an old friend, no longer with us, and we therefore want to make every effort not to lose it. What is the best way to tackle the job? It is still very healthy and gives fine blooms each year.*

You will have to accept from the outset that you are running a big risk in moving any shrub in an advanced state of maturity. Roses don't like root disturbance at the best of times, and when they have been settled as long as this, you have to be very careful indeed, and not a little crafty.

The job will have to be tackled during the dormant period; when all the leaves have fallen and the stems are quite bare. Begin by preparing the new position a few weeks in advance. Take out a planting hole about 3ft (1m) wide and two spits deep, keeping the two soil layers apart, and the two heaps positioned on the far side from where the plant will be dragged from. Tip in half a barrow-load of compost, or the contents of a spent growbag, sprinkle over a small handful of Humber Manure or Growmore, and fork it all into the bottom of the hole. This needs to be finished and ready before you think of lifting the plant. Two days before the actual move, fill the hole with water and let it drain away.

Even though the plant is in a dormant condition, it will be quite essential to keep root disturbance to the very minimum by lifting the rose with the roots contained within a soil ball. This will clearly be rather large and heavy. You will need some help in lifting and moving it – don't try doing it alone – and a special method is needed. You will need a sheet of heavy gauge plastic, a small tarpaulin, or something equally strong. You will be able to judge the size as you read on.

Starting some 2ft (0.6m) from the base of the plant, take out a semicircular trench, and throw the soil in a heap and well clear. If you meet any roots, sever them cleanly with secateurs, don't just bash through them with the spade. Take out a second spit from the bottom of the trench, but getting under the plant. If you meet many roots, you will have to go deeper. Try to leave as much root as undamaged as possible. This second spit of soil coming up will be sub-soil, and it must again be thrown well clear, but in a separate heap.

In order to get down yet another spit and under the rose, you will probably have to give yourself room to wield the spade by widening the top of the trench, which is why you had to begin by throwing the soil well clear. Your aim is to get under the plant and expose half a root ball with the other half still firmly rooted and supporting the whole. Roll up the sheet to halfway and pass the rolled edge down and under the plant, with the unrolled section coming out of the trench. Tie this up to the plant so that it doesn't get in the way while you refill the trench under the sheet, keeping the sub-soil at the bottom, and the top spit at the top. Now you are half way there.

Dig under the rose from the other side in the same way, and pull out the rolled up section of the sheet so that it now passes right under the plant, and you are ready to move. You will probably have had to remove enough soil to give yourself room to work, so that there is now an incline up which the root ball can be dragged. Depending upon how far you have to go, you may find a board or a tray helpful as a sled. This is the part where you will definitely need help. Compare the soil ball to the prepared hole – you will need to position the plant at exactly the same level, and there may be more soil to come out or go back. Determine which side of the plant will 'face to London' and drag-lift it into the hole. When you are happy with the position, lift and drag out the sheet – you may find it easier to roll and work the sheet under while you rock the ball to and fro, but do be careful not to damage the rose at this stage. Fill in firmly with top soil only, treading firm with your heel, cover with mulch and the job is done. Watering is not necessary, because it is already down deep under the plant where the roots will work to find it.

The hole from which the plant was lifted can now be filled in, taking care to use sub-soil in the bottom, and the more fertile top spit at the top. Soil from the second hole will need to be barrowed over to make up for that moved in the soil ball. With both holes filled and levelled off, you deserve a cup of tea for a job well done!

## *12 A rose without thorns is still a rose*

*When visiting friends in London, we went for a walk with them in Peckham Rye Park and there in a rose garden saw a large rose draped around the stone pillar of an arched walk, covered with pink flowers – but amazingly, there were no thorns! Thorns are the one thing we don't like about roses, and we would like to plant this one in our small garden, but we could not find a label to identify its name. Could you possibly tell us its name or which type of rose it is, and something about it – or is it some kind of freak?*

There are very many different kinds of rose from different parts of the world, the number of species alone runs to three figures, and the crosses and hybrids are countless. The ranges of variation include colour, growth habit, size, scent, and numbers or degree of thorns. Some are numerous and fine, almost like fur, while others have fewer but much bigger thorns that are hard and vicious. One variety has no thorns at all, which in fact, although it was raised as long ago as 1868, makes it a still popular and widely grown variety.

It is 'Zéphirine Drouhin' and you should be able to find it in catalogues under the headings 'climbers' or 'Bourbons'. It is a climber that will get up to 10ft (3m) high if allowed or, as is usually the case, will make the same length diverted over a pergola, fence, pillar or similar support. A not uncommon idea is to let it wander into small open trees like lilac and elder, where it neither smothers its host, nor is itself deprived of light, and where its bloom puts on a long-lasting display after the host has finished (see page 134).

The rose-pink flowers are not particularly fine individually, being ruffled and frilly, but are produced in great quantity over a long period and, characteristic of the Bourbon roses, are richly scented. Best seen lifted high on a pergola or similar structure where the bloom can be approached close to, this variety is also used for hedging, but the absence of thorns limits its use as a barrier, and its climbing habit imposes some difficulties when pruning and dead-heading.

Prune fairly hard a year after planting, when the roots have become established, to promote growth shoots from the base. After that, little pruning is needed for a few years until the first stems begin to show their age by becoming 'barky'. Then try to establish a routine of taking back one old stem each year so that new growth is encouraged and the shock of cutting back is kept to a minimum.

It is a very useful and attractive rose, but has one serious fault which you have to consider very carefully before planting it. Even when fed properly with careful attention to potash availability, its resistance to black spot and mildew is almost nil, and it is invariably the first variety to be affected by these fungal diseases. Unless you are prepared to carry out regular routine protective spraying with a systemic fungicide, you have to run the risk and danger to neighbouring roses of introducing such a susceptible rose into their midst. A thornless rose is all very well, but it has no defences – in more senses than one.

## *13 Coping with an enforced second move*

*Last February I had to move a bed of 15 two-year-old roses to a temporary position. They all flowered well, and in a few weeks time, in the New Year, I shall be ready to plant them permanently. Are there any special precautions I should follow to ensure that they survive the second move?*

Well, you evidently did a good job with the first move, and with care and attention to preparation beforehand and during replanting there is no reason why your roses should not make a second move successfully. In fact you would be imitating nursery practice – have you ever considered what happens, or what should happen, in a well-run nursery to those plants that are left unsold by springtime? Imagine, rows and rows of different varieties, with varying numbers sold and gone from each row. That then adds up to a lot of space that is going to be wasted – nurseries cannot afford to leave the ground vacant and idle, so they 'box up'. Plants required to make up orders are lifted from the back end of each row or 'run' so that the identity labels placed in front of the first plant of each variety remain undisturbed. When the orders have been completed, and while there is still time to replant before spring growth becomes too far advanced, those that are left in the first variety are lifted, roots trimmed, and replanted again – in the same position! The second variety is then lifted, roots trimmed, and replanted immediately following the end of the first to close the gap. The third then closes up – 'boxes up' – on the second, and on to the end so that all the individual vacant half and part rows are filled in and the space collected into one area, which can be put to use.

Now that may seem to be no more than making sure that space is utilized to the full, but there is more to it than that. Lifting and root trimming serves to prune the root systems so that what is called 'adventitious' fibrous root forms at the pruned root ends. This is feeding, assimilative root, and a plant with well-developed fibrous root is better able to withstand replanting. Many shrubs and trees will spend two, three, four or even more years in the nursery rows, being lifted each or every other year, to develop a good fibrous root system. It is skilled, labour-intensive work, and part of good nursery practice that goes on behind the scenes. This is one reason why first class plants cost more than inferior material.

Roses are normally sold and replanted during the first dormant period following the first year's growth and blooming from the implanted bud. Those that don't sell first time can be boxed up and sent out later as two-year-olds; indeed, we used to hold back the less vigorous kinds and 'poor doers' so that they would make better plants before being despatched. But after that, the plants are no longer youngsters, and no longer saleable. At one time, after they had provided budding material, they were burnt. Nowadays, many nurseries have retail 'garden centre' outlets attached, and those roses that don't sell bare root are often lifted and replanted in containers so that they can be sold all the year round.

Read the narrative chapters here dealing with preparation before planting. Fill the planting holes with water a day or two before planting to encourage root activity (this is important), and you should have no trouble this time – but don't make a habit of this sort of thing!

## *14 Don't bother to move it*

*I want to turn my front garden over to lawn, but at present it is dominated by an overgrown and sadly neglected 'Peace' rose – neighbours tell me that it is at least 25 years old! It still gives nice blooms and I wonder if it can be moved. If so, what is the best way to go about the job?*

When it has to be done, the job can be tackled as described in question number 12 (page 157). In this case, however, you might well consider that at this age and condition, the poor plant owes nobody anything, and it would be much more simple and labour-effective to scrap it and plant new. Apart from the sheer difficulty of handling a thorny plant of this size, there is the likelihood also of it failing to survive the shock.

Whenever the words 'old', 'overgrown', and 'sadly neglected' are expressed, the more we have to bear in mind that the plant is becoming liable to canker. This often starts from snags and damage caused by hoeing, chaffing where stems have crossed, bad pruning, and sheer neglect.

Even with the best managed roses, there comes a time when age takes its toll, and we have to make a rational answer to the question: Is it worth going on any longer? This sounds like a classic case of 'no, it isn't'. I would not hesitate to get it out and, in the interests of hygiene, to the fire.

## *15 Underplanting roses*

*I have several rose borders and beds which I think would look much better by being underplanted with short growing plants. I am told that it is not easy or satisfactory, but I would like to try. Can you please suggest some suitable plants?*

The most common reason for wanting to underplant is to enhance the colour and effect by blending or contrast, and very attractive are the effects that can be had with all manner of plants. However, the rose likes to live alone, and has a poise and character that defies cohabitation. It has a beauty that is singular, and doesn't need the presence of others to bring out the best.

During my time in the parks, I remember there was a lot of experiment with underplanting roses, using all manner of ideas and colours. The only combination that didn't disappoint was a pale blue viola under pink and pale reds, and that didn't get one excited. No, the rose is queen, she stands alone, and does not improve in a throng, and those who suggest to you that the rose doesn't take kindly to underplanting are expressing a well-known fact.

Furthermore, there is the cultivation problem posed by underplanting. Roses respond to a steady moisture level and a steady nutrient level, both encouraged by a steady organic input to the soil derived from a steadily maintained mulch cover to the soil surface. This needs frequent prodding and scratching to keep it open and prevent it from packing into a crust that sheds rain and hinders the access of air. Underplanting and mulching get in the way of each other – you cannot do both.

If you can modify underplanting a little to planting nearby, perhaps along the edge of a border, there is a plant association that may not have a lot to offer colourwise, but which has an astonishing effect on greenfly! Beneficial plant associations have been known for a long time, and for the renewed interest in this recently, we have to thank the Henry Doubleday Research Association and the many gardeners who object to the use of chemicals in the garden, and who prefer to enlist the assistance of natural predators.

The plant in question here is *Limnanthes douglasii*, commonly known as the poached egg plant, and so called because of the fanciful similarity of the colours of each little flower to those of a poached egg. An annual that in favourable conditions readily seeds itself each year, the bright yellow and white flowers, attractive in themselves, are more likely to start a fight with roses than to blend with them. However, the flowers are particularly attractive to hover flies, the larvae of which have a voracious appetite for aphids. The number of gardeners who report wholesale clearance of greenfly by this method is such as to suggest that greenfly control can be guaranteed. Perhaps you will find this plant association more acceptable than underplanting.

## 16 Drought and roses

*I have two plants of* Rosa moyesii *'Geranium', one three years old and the other planted last year. The new one has made no growth at all, has lost most of its leaves early in the season and looks very poorly. The older one has grown very little since planting, and is tending to die back at the ends each year, but bears some flowers and hips. How can I encourage new growth to break on these roses? It seems as though they are suffering from a perpetual drought.*

I wonder what your preparation before planting was like – *Rosa moyesii* is a species that can make a large plant 10 ft (3m) tall and as wide. Its variety 'Geranium' although a little more compact, perhaps 8ft (2.5m) tall and wide, is still an entirely different proposition to an H.T. bush. Not that a bush rose can grow away and become established without adequate preparation and good planting, but the potential dimensions merely emphasize the need to do the job properly (see pages 138 and 142).

The first task any new planting, not only roses, has to do is to make root into the soil and develop a system that can absorb nutrients sufficient to support top growth and foliage. To do this, the first and therefore the most important requirement is adequate moisture. Nutrients have to be in solution before a plant can absorb them, that is the first priorty. Second, even without leaves, a living plant is evaporating moisture – that is part of its living process – and it has to be replaced, through that part of the plant that does the absorbing, and which, by the sound of it, has not been very active. New foliage and bloom increases the evaporation rate, and the demand on the roots is therefore greater – what precautions did you take before planting to make sure they would be able to do their job? Did you simply dig a hole and plonk the plant in it?

I suggest that you read Chapter 4 dealing with preparation before planting because, if you really want to give your roses a fair deal, you will have to chance the risk in lifting them during the dormant period next winter and planting them again, properly this time. Otherwise, by the time anything you do from the soil surface can get down and affect the roots, it is doubtful if they will still be around.

Put a couple of bucketfuls of compost, peat, spent growbags, anything that will hold moisture, deep into the planting hole. Mix in a small handful of Humber Manure or Growmore, and fill the hole with water so that the soil under the plant is well soaked and the roots have to go down to look for it, make new root and become established. After replanting, cover the soil surface with a mulch cover to keep soil evaporation down, and to encourage worms to get busy. For both plants to be struggling in the same way, there seems little doubt that your planting preparation was seriously at fault and you are now going to have to work hard to put matters right.

## *17 Moving an established standard*

*I have a fine standard rose over 6ft (2m) high in my garden, and I am forced to move it. Can you tell me the best way to do so?*

What we don't know from this question is how old and established the tree is, although 6ft (2m) high suggests that it may have been growing in the same place for some time and is well 'dug in'. In addition to the problems associated with moving an established plant, an established standard presents us with two special problems.

The first is that a standard rose is basically a bush (unless it is a weeper, when it will be a rambler type) separated from its root system by a long stem up which sap and nutrients have to rise and down which carbohydrates from the leaves have to travel, like traffic belting two ways on a long narrow road with no passing places. The effect of this is that when something like limp wilting foliage occurs, due to dryness at the roots, it is going to take longer to put right, as the sap pressure has a lot further to go than in a bush.

Secondly, there is the physical problem of moving not only the tree but also its stake. I suggest that you read question number 11 (page 155). You will have to move the standard with a root ball and although this may not be as big as with an overgrown 'Peace', you will have to get down sufficiently to free the stake holding the tree so that both can be moved together. You will need to replace the stake during the move, so read up the chapter dealing with staking and the preparation of the stake beforehand. You will need a stout pole at least 8½ft (2.5m) long if it is to support properly a 6ft (2m) standard with an already developed head.

Have the new position prepared as described in question number 11, and the hole filled with water two days before. Lift the tree by the 'half and half' method, and try to plant it with the soil ball and stake intact. When you have firmed up, cut through the ties and, as carefully as you can, twist and rock the stake so that it can be pulled free. Insert the new stake into the hole and drive it firm. It is quite likely that you will need to get up on steps to do this, so get somebody to steady them. When you drive the stake in, don't use a hammer or similar tool but a block of wood, which you will find easier and safer to handle, and less likely to damage the stake. Alternatively, use a crowbar carefully to enlarge the hole, without breaking and damaging the roots, and treading firm afterwards.

Make your ties as described in Chapter 5, and loop in the top branches to prevent rock and neck-break. Finally, especially after wind, keep an eye on the standard and its new stake to make sure that they are quite firm, and that wind-rock does not develop a water hole around the base of either stake or plant stem.

## *18 Can rhododendrons kill roses?*

*Roses grow well in my garden, except near a large rhododendron. It has been suggested at our allotment club that the rhododendron is killing the roses. Do you think this is likely, and why does it not affect other plants?*

Laburnum, all parts of which are poisonous if eaten, is often accused of poisoning the soil for other plants, so it is not surprising that rhododendron and yew, which are also poisonous, should also have the finger pointed at them. There has never been any scientific proof of this and, having regard to the botanical principles that govern plant growth, there is no rational postulation as to how there could be such proof. I suggest that you will have to look elsewhere for a logical explanation, and quite likely to your preparation before planting.

If you look at rhododendrons in the wild, you will seldom, if ever, see anything growing under them. This is not due to poison but to the very subdued light intensity under the canopy of ground-hugging evergreen foliage, and to the smothering effect of the leathery leaves as they fall and form a carpet that is very slow to decompose. A further effect, likely from a large and therefore long-established rhododendron, is the exhaustion of plant nutrients from the soil by a spreading root system, and this means that other plants, especially newly planted roses, don't get a fair share of moisture or nutrients.

You have to take even more care and attention with your preparation before planting, with organic input, soaking before planting, and feeding with a slow-release, balanced, long lasting, organic nutrient source. There is no intrinsic problem with your

## 19 Buds will not open

*A rose bush I bought cheaply two years ago from a local garden centre to replace a dead bush bloomed quite well the first year, but this summer all the buds formed until they became big and then failed to open and rotted, falling over in their stalks. Could you tell me the reason for this please? I have 80 other roses and if it is a disease I wouldn't want to put the others at risk.*

Presumably this trouble hasn't happened with the other roses, and for it to have occurred two years after a new planting suggests to me that it is not pest or disease, but an example of 'balling', a physiological problem often regarded as inimical to reds, but not confined to them only. The flower buds do not develop properly, the petals fail to expand and then turn brown and collapse. Wet weather is a common factor, but usually it is the culmination of other contributory causes that lead up to the final refusal to open, such as alternate dry and wet periods, mild temperatures and cold spells, an unbalanced nutrient supply with a low potash availability, and perhaps also too much nitrogen leading to soft, lush growth and the use of immature implantation buds at budding time.

Short of moving it into a more protected position or screening it – which is rather like turning your garden into a hospital ward – there is little you can do to protect your plant from the weather. So you should do everything you can to improve the growing conditions. If you will read the chapters in this book concerning preparation before planting, you will appreciate the need for adequate moisture and balanced feeding.

Never, never be tempted to buy roses 'on the cheap'. A good grower will have put a lot of experience, knowledge and practical skill into producing a plant that he is prepared to put his name to, and you should pay him accordingly. You cannot get a good rose, if you don't start right.

## 20 Suckers

**1** *One of my roses last year made foliage of a different colour from the rest of the bush, and also bore blooms like 'Queen Alexander' rose day flags. I* wonder if this is called a 'sport' because several more of my other roses are doing the same thing this year.

**2** *Some of my roses have shoots with the leaves arranged in sevens instead of fives like the rest of the foliage. Do I remove these shoots completely or is it only necessary to remove individual leaves?*

**3** *When I planted a dozen roses two years ago, I made sure that the part where the budded growth comes from the stock was just below the soil surface. I have had a lot of trouble with these roses making suckers and now I have found that several of the budded parts are making their own roots. Is this right, and is there any connection with the appearance of the suckers?*

Three questions that are all part of the same basic problem. First, the single rose is not a 'sport' but the bloom of the rootstock, which is ignoring the bud of the choice variety and putting up its own growth, also characterized by the seven leaves instead of five. Why suckers occur, and what to do about them, is best explained by in turn explaining why we bud and graft.

Budding (implanting a growth bud under the bark of another plant and in contact with the sap flow of the cambium layer) and grafting (joining on a shoot tip or short piece of young wood to replace the removed tip of another plant), are done for many reasons, but mainly because most choice varieties of roses and fruits do not develop a vigorous enough root system of their own to allow the variety to grow and perform to full potential. Be it bloom or fruit production, quantity or quality, bearing when the plant is young or much later, a small tree or large, the stock has a profound influence on the kind of plant that develops, and quite different to what would grow if the choice variety were left to grow on its own roots.

Almost all bush roses are propagated by budding just above soil level, and standards by implanting the bud high up on a briar stem. As soon as the nurseryman can see that the bud has 'taken' he removes the original 'wild' stock foliage and growth above the bud so that sap and energy is diverted and concentrated into the choice bud.

Quite often, especially in the first year or two of growth, and when a root stock is getting away strongly, it has more energy and vigour to push up than the bud or grafted scion can take, and it simply resorts to making an outlet for the excess energy by putting out shoots and growth of its own, called suckers and briars. These can arise from a dormant bud on the stock portion or from the callus tissue that arises from a wound, which explains why you should always be careful when hoeing or digging deeply enough to reach and snag the roots.

The invariable risk that follows is that, having found an escape hatch, the stock then pours in its energy – the sucker growth is its own natural tissue after all – and at once begins to ignore the bud or graft implanted in its side. This bud therefore begins to suffer from neglect and, if you don't interfere to keep the growth growing the way you want, will suffer and may even wither and die.

Whether arising above ground or below from the root, suckers should not be cut away because, whether secateurs or knife, a clean cut allows the development of healing callus tissue from which adventitious shoots all too easily arise, and you are merely pruning in a way that promotes more shoot growth. Instead, remove suckers by pulling them away with a securely gloved hand or prise them away with pincers or pliers, and then seal the wound by painting it with Arbrex. A clean cut makes healing tissue and repairs quickly, whereas a jagged wound doesn't make healing tissue so readily, and the adventitious growth won't form.

The tall stems of standard roses and fruit trees will often throw off sucker shoots. These should be removed while they are still infantile and brittle enough to be rubbed away by thumb or fingers. If you neglect them and thus allow stem shoots to become established, there is the risk that pulling away can break or seriously harm the stem. In this case, cut the shoot away, but then roughen the wound with a rasp so that the callus tissue does not form so readily. Treat the wound with Arbrex protective paint or grafting wax to prevent disease spores getting in.

As for planting deep with the bud in or near the soil, the argument seems to be that this encourages the bud wood to put out root growth, and this helps by increasing uptake. I have heard quite eminent growers advocate this deep planting. All I can say is that I was taught – and it makes much more sense to me – to plant with the bud or graft well clear of the soil, so that adventitious rooting is not encouraged, What is the point of budding and grafting onto more vigorous stock, if you are then to encourage the bud to do its own thing? Far from increasing uptake, it can be argued – as the question testifies – that 'own roots' limits the scion's ability to take all that the stock has to give. It is not as hungry as it should be and thereby actually increases the tendency for the stock to find relief by suckering. As always, you must consider which way makes most sense to you, and make your own common-sense judgement.

## 21 Use of horse manure

*Could you please tell me what time of year is best to apply rotted horse manure to bush and standard rose trees?*

Before we come to the best time to use horse manure, two important points need to be made. First, the manure should be 'well rotted', and that means that it should have been composted, turned and aerated sufficiently to enable the decomposition processes to have progressed to a point where it is no longer possible to identify what it was to start with. By this time, it will have the consistency and colour of peat.

It may be that the horses have been fed a lot of hay, and in that case it is quite likely that some seed of the plants comprising the hay will have passed unharmed through the digestive tract of the animals and be ready to germinate as soon as conditions become suitable. Correct composting involves sustained heating to 'cook' and destroy any viable seed. Therefore, unless the manure has been 'hot composted' in order to become well rotted, you must expect to see grass and other weed germinating.

The second reason for 'well rotted' is basically to have reduced the nitrogenous urine content which would assuredly encourage leaf and shoot growth, but this, because of the induced imbalance in relation to the hardening potash, will become soft, flabby and more susceptible to mildew and other fungus attack. By the time it is well rotted, the respective nitrogen, phosphorus and potassium contents will have dispersed and reduced to very low and safe proportions. Thus the most beneficial use of animal manures like this is not for the nutrient content, but for the physical effect upon soil structure.

Under no circumstances should manure be forked or dug into roses, because this inevitably must snag and lift roots, encouraging the development of suckers. The best way to utilize the manure is as a mulch covering of the soil surface. Used in this way, evaporation of moisture from the soil is reduced or prevented, and hoeing to prevent the surface caking and packing hard can then be carried out clear of the soil and roots by light scratching in this mulch layer.

Moisture retention is a most obvious benefit, so ensuring that a good layer exists before summer and warm weather accelerates drying is an obvious good indication of the best time to put it down. Worms will gradually take the material down into the soil, and continuing decomposition also gradually reduces the layer. Topping up addition will be a steady requirement, and this can be done at any time because with the nutrient content reduced to virtually nil, there is no risk of encouraging unseasonal growth.

## 22 Use of seaweed

*I am proposing to make extensive planting of roses in my new garden, and as I would be able to collect seaweed, I wonder if this could be used to make compost. What nutrients would it need to have added to it, and what would be the best way to use it?*

You are particularly fortunate in being able to collect seaweed. It is rich in potash, contains several trace elements, rots down fairly quickly and inputs organic bulk into the soil without the risk of containing weed seed as is the case with most garden compost. It also has a high degree of moisture absorption, and with the substantial potash content, is particularly valuable for mulching roses.

You may find the salt a problem – on clay soils, this could increase the stickiness – and unless you are using it on crops like asparagus, onions and potatoes, which can tolerate a little salt – it is best not to apply it to the soil fresh as gathered, but to spread it out on a path, driveway or other hard surface, and wash it with the hose or let rain do the job. It is quite unsuitable for use in large lumps, and will need breaking or chopping to make it friable. A tool that I find very useful for this job is called a 'rotochop', rather like a large coarse mincer. I have not seen it advertised for some time, and perhaps it has gone the way of a lot of good ideas that do not get as much attention as they should. Keep your eyes open at agricultural shows and car boot sales. There is a growing interest in buying and selling old farm and gardening tools, and I have seen the rotochop several times among the miscellaneous bits and pieces.

The nitrogen and phosphorus content is so low as to be negligible, so don't dig the seaweed into the soil when it is fresh because the decomposition bacteria are likely to take too much nitrogen and induce a shortage. This problem doesn't occur when the seaweed is on the surface as mulch. If you put it through the compost heap, mix it well with other coarse matter because it can become very wet and soggy by itself, which is precisely the condition to be avoided when composting.

The type of seaweed commonly found and known as bladderwrack – the kind with the little air bladders that children love to pop – is much the best, and its potash content makes it very valuable for those garden plants that bear large colourful blooms, and for all fruits at ripening time.

## 23 Use of peat and pulverized bark

*From time to time I am able to acquire peat tailings and pulverized bark in loads of about 5 cubic yards (5 cubic metres). They are mixed, clean and dry and, as this is all organic matter, I guess that it has a use in the garden. I have a collection of over 400 roses of all kinds. Is there a direct use for this material, and what is the best way to use it?*

Four hundred roses! This material is tailor-made for the job, but it will have to be used with care and understanding or you could be in trouble. The first point to realize is that, in dry conditions, both peat tailings – usually taken to mean the more coarse pieces that do not pass through a sieve when granulated peat is being prepared from the raw 'as dug' – and bark have a quite prodigious ability to absorb moisture. Even more than they soak it up from whatever surrounds them, they will attract and draw it up and sideways through the soil from some distance away. You can imagine, therefore, that if this material is dry when put into the soil, it will very quickly soak up all the available moisture, and your plants will go short.

Secondly, both tailings and bark are in the early stages of decomposition ('short'), when the bacteria involved require plenty of oxygen and nitrogen for their own body processes. Dug into the soil, the bacteria quickly exhaust the soil atmosphere, and then turn their attention to the nitrogen in the plant nutrients in the soil solution. The plants are robbed, and thus we get the paradoxical situation that organic matter like peat, farmyard and other manures, when not sufficiently decomposed (well rotted), and put into the soil ostensibly to increase fertility and feed the plants, can actually cause a nitrogen shortage – the very opposite to what is intended.

Both above points are sheer hard fact, and you will therefore use your own common sense judgement concerning the advice, often seen and heard, to use peat when planting and digging through the plot. Make no mistake, this peat and bark mixture is invaluable, but you must make sure that it is well soaked before applying to the soil – it has to give moisture, not take it – and that means that it first goes through a period of further decomposition in the compost heap to get it beyond the dangerous denitrification stage.

By far the best place for it is not in the soil but on it, in the form of a 2-inch (5-cm) thick layer of mulch that hinders too quick evaporation of moisture, where its texture enables the surface to be scratched open to help the ingress of air to the soil and to hoe off weed growth. As it decomposes, worms can take it down. Keeping the mulch surface open is important, and its composition will determine how often you have to attend to it. Fine materials like peat and sawdust can pack and form a crust that then hinders air penetration and also sheds rain. This is why the best mulch is composed of more coarse texture like leaf mould and compost. Bear these provisions in mind and and you should be able to make very good use of a peat/bark mix.

## 24 Limited usefulness of bone meal

*I have a very large ornamental garden and, through the connection of friends, can obtain as much bone meal as I want from a factory that manufactures it. Could you tell me the best way to use this benefit?*

I am not sure what you mean by 'a factory that manufactures bone meal' and I wonder if you realize that you could be running a terrible risk. The products made from bones – bone meal and bone flour, according to how fine the particles are ground – and intended for horticultural use, have to be quite clear of a dreadful disease called anthrax. Regulations are in force that stipulate that all such products intended for sale should be inspected and certified as clear, and that the retailer should be able to provide evidence (a certificate) to this effect and that it is safe to handle. I am not sure in these days of packaging and supermarkets, with packets of the stuff on the shelves, that such evidence is always available or that you would be exactly welcomed for asking to see it, but I do remember, when I was in the trade, a neighbouring competitor getting into very hot water when an inspector called, and he could not produce the certificate for the sack from which he was weighing out and selling. Does the bone meal available to you comply with the regulations? If this frightens you, I'm sorry, but anthrax is a deadly disease about which we cannot be too careful. You must judge the wisdom of what you propose.

As for the plant nutrient usefulness of bone meal, its value is so out of step with reality that its widespread advocacy to the point virtually of 'chips with everything' is almost a gigantic hoax. It is supposed to provide phosphate and, as phosphates are essential for root growth, bone meal at planting time is supposed to help a new planting to make root and become established. The facts are rather different.

All plant and animal matter is comprised of chemical compounds that are much more complex and elaborated than the simple chemicals which, dissolved in water, were first absorbed by a plant, worked up into the structure of the plant and perhaps eaten and further worked up into the even more complicated compounds of animal body structure. Some animal structure is concentrated and contains plenty of the same elements that are essential for plant growth. Bone contains a lot of phosphorus and plants need phosphorus in their roots so, logically, putting bones into the soil is a good nutrient source. However, bone is a very long way from the phosphorus solutions that plants can absorb. It has to be decomposed and broken down by soil bacteria, and that is a long process, involving very many stages and different bacteria at each stage in what is called a bacterial chain. Whatever the raw organic material, each has its own bacterial chain, different to all others, between the original condition in which it reaches the soil and the final soil solution when it becomes available for uptake by another living plant. Bones have a long chain, and the decomposition process takes many months – much too long, in fact, for the bone in the planting hole to become available and be of any benefit to the plant during the period when it is making the new root to become established!

The number of bacteria which can get to work will be limited at first by the superficial surface area of bone that is exposed, and the only way in which the decomposition can be speeded up is to increase the surface area. So, instead of leaving big bones all over the place, they are ground into small pieces, and ground to the size of sawdust are called meal. The bulk is the same but the total surface area is much greater and more bacteria can get to work. Grinding even smaller to the consistency of flour further increases the area exposed, but it still takes months to complete the journey.

So you come to another problem. Plants need a balanced diet just as much as you do yourself, and it doesn't help much in the short term at least to use a mix of materials that all have differing breakdown periods. This difficulty is overcome by taking the bone, fish, or other source material some way along the decomposition track, arresting the decomposition when the remaining journey is much shorter, drying the material so that it is easy to handle and spread, and blending the ingredients so that the nitrogen, phosphorus and potassium fractions become available together. Humber manure does it in about 80 days and is by far the best nutrient source I know, much better by far than bone meal alone, even if it is free.

## 25 Tell-tale signs of potash deficiency

*I have several standard roses which have been looking poorly for some time, and this year a fair number of bush roses have also been affected by the same problem. The blooms have been poor, have not developed as they should, the colour is not as good as it used to be, the leaves turn yellow around the edges, then brown, and finally shrivel, dry and fall. Can you please suggest what is wrong, and what I can do to correct things? I feed well and put down a good coating of horse manure each year.*

Apart from keeping a diary of when you do this and that, and recording failures and successes for future references, every good gardener should build up a scrap-book of cuttings from journals, advertising, leaflets and so on and, especially pictures of diseases and nutrient shortages. You may already have these in a reference book or encyclopaedia, but a scrap-book is much more valuable. There is something about looking for information, cutting out, sticking in, and filing – the actions help you to memorize much better than something you merely look up in a reference book and reel off 'what to do' instructions like a mindless parrot. This does nothing for you, whereas something that you create and build up, with your own observations and experience, is much better. I have several files like this, and they are much more valuable to me than a fair library of gardening books!

Becoming familiar with and recognizing signs and what they mean is the stuff of real experience, and this doesn't mean how many years you have been at the job but how you have used your time, brains and common sense. Nearly all nutritional shortages, main elements and the trace or minor elements, show up with characteristic effects such as foliage, flower and fruit colour, blemishes, margins and damage. Foliage signs are the most important because they are there all the time, longer than bloom or fruit. The good gardener doesn't just spot something on a page, and think 'that looks like what is happening to my roses, I must remember that'. He cuts it out, puts it in the scrap-book, gets it out on wet evenings and looks through it, making darned sure he recognizes it on sight.

The four steps that follow discovery of a blemish are:

**1** Diagnosis – what is it?
**2** What is the cause?
**3** Correct the cause.
**4** Modify your management so that it doesn't happen again.

A dry spell with strong drying winds will sometimes cause leaf edges to scorch, but your browning is a long-standing trouble so it isn't wind. Late frost is more likely to scorch the tips. If we weigh up the evidence, the onset first in your standards and now in your bushes, poor colour, a worsening situation, the annual use of horse manure. Could the manure be fresh each year and bumping up the nitrogen? To me it all points to potash deficiency. Draw a picture of the signs, or take a photo, put it in the scrap-book for future reference.

A shortage of potash, can be caused by incorrect and unbalanced feeding or highly nitrogenous mulch. Whether actually short or induced by a chronic inbalance, you have to get some potash into the leaves and the plants as quickly as you can. Make up a weak solution of Condy's fluid (permanganate of potash), obtainable from the chemist. Very few crystals will be required to colour the solution blood-red; they are very strong. Wait 20 minutes for them to dissolve completely, add a couple of drips only of washing-up detergent so that a good wetting is achieved, and mist spray all foliage every other day. If any drops to the soil, never mind – the roots will pick it up – but the quickest way into the plant is through the leaves. You may have to keep this up for several weeks until you see new growth growing well without edge scorching.

That is the cure. Preventing it happening again does not mean more spraying, but making quite sure that the deficiency doesn't occur. Change your feeding to a balanced ratio such as Humber manure or Growmore. Cut out the fresh horse manure mulch unless it is well rotted.

## *26 Purple spot*

*Many of my roses planted four years ago look distinctly poorly, and I notice that nearly all the old leaves have developed purple spots and areas on them. Is this a disease? If so, what is it and what can I do to cure it?*

This trouble is called purple spot, which is somewhat misleading as the name almost suggests a disease, whereas the cause is quite different. The discolouration arises from the consequence of poor soil conditions and is accentuated by a marked deficiency of one of the more important of the trace elements: magnesium.

Roses like a dense soil, but that is not to say heavy, airless and poor draining like clay. After the soil disturbance of planting only four years ago, we might expect the soil to be settling back again, and the roses are telling you that they don't like it, it is probably too dense and airless. Short of digging them up and preparing the soil deeply underneath, all that you can do is to try to alter the soil nature from above, which cannot be done in five minutes.

You can open up the clay, improve porosity and help air penetration by spreading agricultural gypsum on the surface at a rate of 2 ounces (60g) per square yard (square metre) every three months, but do not exceed this rate, (see also question number 7 on page 150). If the soil surface allows – it is doubtful in these circumstances that you are mulching, as this is one of the symptoms of not doing so – the gypsum can be hoed in, but be careful to scratch just the surface to avoid any possibility of snagging roots and encouraging suckers. It is a slow process, but gradually the soil condition will improve.

The magnesium deficiency can be corrected quite quickly by making up a solution of Epsom Salts and mist spraying the foliage every other day, just enough to wet the leaf surface. I have found that a level dessertspoonful in a gallon of water is quite strong enough; the important point is the frequency. A drip or two of washing up detergent in the spray ensures a good wetting, and if it drips off into the soil it will do no harm.

Read Chapter 7 dealing with feeding and mulching, making sure that you appreciate the importance of and reason for balanced nutrient availability. Your roses are not suffering from a disease – yet – but this condition leaves them wide open to trouble.

## *27 Roses and acidity*

*I give my three rose beds a dressing of Top Rose fertilizer every month during the growing season and a spray of Murphy FF each week. I mulch with well-rotted manure, but many of the leaves are small and misshapen. On testing the soil I find it is very acid. What do you think has caused this? The soil is well drained and not at all heavy to dig and hoe.*

Roses prefer the soil to be a little on the alkaline side of neutral, so you have some correcting to do. There is an old saying about taking a horse to water and not being able to make it drink. Perhaps it ought to continue: 'and if you do force it to drink, you will only make it sick', for this is what you are doing. Plants should not go short of food, but it does not follow that you can grow better plants by forcing them to accept a super-abundance of food down their throats, and you are grossly overdoing it with this rate of fertilizer and foliage feeding.

I would cut out *all* feeding for at least an entire season and give the surplus a chance to weather and disperse. You will have to get the acidity reversed, but you should not try to do this quickly because a heavy application of lime, for example, will cause an even heavier short-term release of plant nutrients and lush growth that will be prone to attack by diseases. If you put down a light dressing of hydrated lime – 1 ounce (30g) to the square yard (square metre) is quite enough – every three months or so, the alkaline effect will be quite fast enough. Keep track of what is happening with a soil testing kit, and keep the mulching going – that is good.

If by describing your soil as well drained you mean sandy, you should realize that this increases the likelihood of acid conditions, especially if, as I suspect, the rapid washing out of fertilizers is the reason for your overfeeding. Very many artificial fertilizers of all kinds are based on sulphur compounds, and their breakdown to plant availability has a marked acidic side effect. You will do very much better in your soil type to use only organic manures with a balanced nitrogen, phosphorus and potassium ratio, and by keeping an eye on the acidity position with your soil test kit, make corrections with lime only very slowly. There is no such thing as an overnight cure in nature.

## 28 Roses in tubs

*I have two wooden tubs measuring 12 inches (30cm) high and the same in diameter. I would like to grow a miniature weeping rose of the variety 'Baby Jayne' in each. Could you tell me if this size tub would be suitable, and what, if anything, I need to add to garden soil to plant them in?*

The tub size would suffice for a miniature bush type, but is a little small for a weeper. However, it is worth trying if you bear in mind that the small tub size emphasizes the risks of drying out and rapid exhaustion of nutrients due to the frequent watering required, inherent with all plant containers like tubs, troughs and window boxes.

Therefore, you will need to provide a growing medium with better ability to absorb and retain moisture than can be derived from ordinary garden soil. Crock the bottom with a little plaster rubble if you can get it, crushed brick or broken pot, and plant into a compost made up of three parts John Innes No. 2 potting compost, and one part moss peat which has been well moistened. The peat has to absorb and give moisture, and you don't want to start with dry peat absorbing moisture from the soil. Frequent watering can cause settling and packing, so you will have to guard against that. Mix in a third to one half part crushed plaster rubble – this is to be preferred for the gypsum content, but failing that, settle for coarse sand.

Assuming that you will be planting at the optimum time, November, mix into this compost mix a level teaspoonful of Humber manure, or the organic nutrient feed that you intend to use. This quantity is very little as it is not to provide a nutrient residue at this stage – the John Innes content will do that – but to encourage a build-up in the bacteria strains that will later be involved in the decomposition of the organic manure you are going to use. Frequent watering to avoid drying out must also be expected to wash out soluble nutrient so much faster, hence the wisdom of using slow-release, long-lasting organic manures rather than chemical fertilizers.

Watering is going to be critical with a small tub. Dryness and wilting must be avoided at all costs because a standard weeper is going to be slower to respond than a bush type. Overwatering is the danger therefore, hence the ingredient of sand and rubble to keep the growing medium porous and open. Nutrient supply has to be little and often – a pinch once a fortnight teased into the soil surface should be ample.

The management of these tubs will be difficult enough with just a rose in each, and will be exacerbated by adding anything like other dwarf plants around the rim. Apart from the virtual impossibility of finding any plant that will enhance and blend with a rose, the extra moisture and nutrient absorption is just not worth it. Finally, bear in mind that tub-grown roses are subject to the same pests and diseases as those grown in the open ground, more especially if you let them suffer wilting and drying. Because of the relative size, a greenfly attack on a miniature could be devastating, so guard against this by starting a routine of precautionary spraying with a systemic insecticide every two or three weeks as soon as growth commences in spring.

## 29 Climbers in containers

*I want to grow a 'Danse du Feu' climbing rose around my door, but this opens direct on to a courtyard and there is no soil. Could I grow one in a container, and if so, how big would it have to be? Are there any special precautions I would have to take? [See page 144]*

If you will read the previous question and answer, there is much there that is applicable here – the basic difference, of course, is one of size. Bush and miniature types do not present much difficulty, but in order to accommodate a climbing rose that can easily make 10ft (3m) tall in open ground, you have more than difficulty. First, the container will have to be large in order to take the root run without undue restriction – I would suggest something of the order of 20–24 inches (50–60cm) deep and as wide. It will need to be well provided with drainage holes, and the growing medium will have to be capable of retaining moisture without holding it unduly and becoming a soggy mess. The compost mix suggested for the miniature tubs above would be suitable, except that I would reduce the nutrient content by using John Innes No. 1, because it will be necessary not to encourage this climber to grow too well. The quantity involved is not small, and without access to garden soil, there presumably is no alternative to buying it in, which will not be cheap. In addition, the 10ft (3m) average height for this variety will be growing from soil already 2ft (0.6m) above ground level, and you should therefore be prepared to see some stems reaching beyond 'round the door'.

A frequent cause for disappointment with containers exposed as this one will be is due to direct sunlight on the container sides, which heat up and become hot – you cannot expect roses, or any other plants, to grow with baked roots. One solution may be to use a metal or fibreglass container inside a timber or other attractive outer casing, in which case make sure there is an inch (2.5cm) or so clearance for ventilation and for heat to disperse.

Roses do not like root disturbance, and while it may be possible during the dormant season to turn out and replant a miniature rose in a small container, you are hardly likely to be able to do this with a container of this size. The gradual build-up of nutrient and trace element deficiency therefore is a distinct possibility. This is a very big argument in favour of using an organic source like Humber and, because it is practical on a soil surface area of this dimension, maintaining a mulch cover. Evidently you will have to buy this in as well, so a good idea would be to use granulated moss peat, and to take extra care of the trace element situation by spraying it or sprinkling seaweed extract into it every few months.

Finally, other than to repeat the similarities with the previous question, a climber growing in these conditions provides one of the exceptions to general rules. Dead-heading is good and usual practice in order to prevent a plant dissipating its energies into seed production and to concentrate on new growth for the following season. Size, however, is one of the problems here, and there is something to be said therefore for allowing this plant to divert some of its energy into producing a hip display for the autumn and winter.

## 30 Schumacher was right – small is beautiful

*I am very fond of roses, but as I only have a very small garden I would like to try my hand with some of the miniatures. Can you tell me a little about them, and are they as easy to establish as bush roses?*

Many gardeners are inclined to look rather askance at the miniature roses and regard them as some kind of modern freak. How such an opinion equates with accepting climbing 30ft (9m) monsters I'm not sure, and it is very unfair because many people with insufficient space for conventional bushes who only have small gardens, patios, terrace pots and tubs, are thereby enabled to grow and enjoy roses.

Apart from size and height, the important difference that affects cultivation is the necessarily shallow depth of the root system and the susceptibility therefore to drying out. With their suitability to pot and container growing, the risk is greater, and so is the need to be careful to see that it does not happen. Moisture-retentive organic content in the growing medium is therefore more important than it is with the bigger types that can search down more deeply. Perhaps the most frequent cause of trouble with all pot and container grown plants is that it is not generally realized that, as soon as a root ball becomes dry, it thinks it has become a duck's back, and water poured on from the top runs off in just the same way, down the sides and out through the drainage holes, leaving the soil and roots as dry as ever.

Grown in open ground, this problem is not so likely to occur, and if you follow the reasoning contained in the chapters dealing with feeding and mulching, there is no reason why you should not derive a lot of enjoyment and satisfaction from growing miniatures. One salient fact you should always bear in mind is that these little roses may be reduced in size, but the pests and diseases are not and, relative to the tiny tots, it is like having greenfly as big as bumble bees! The need to protect with insecticides and fungicides is therefore all the greater. Otherwise treat them as conventional bushes.

### 31 'Queen Elizabeth' as a hedge

*I planted a row of 'Queen Elizabeth' roses as a dividing barrier. Last year they reached 6ft (2m) tall and I pruned then down to half this height. This season, the bloom has been very poor, and the growth rather spindly, but some of them are now well over 6ft (2m) again! Can you tell me the best thing to do with them – should I prune them harder, or what?*

Although it is invariably listed with Hybrid Teas, this variety is so vigorous that it would be better and more appropriately transferred to the shrub types. It has been grown widely as a windbreak hedge, and some years ago, when visiting a customer at Angmering in Sussex, I found a hedge backing directly on to the beach that was every bit of 10ft (3m) high, covered in bloom, and obviously cocking a snook at the salt-laden breezes!

As you are asking for a barrier, this is how I suggest that you deal with this hedge from now on. As soon as the growth buds begin to swell next spring, I would prune back all the older stems very hard to sideways-pointing buds, ideally no more than 1ft (0.3m) from ground level, leaving no more than three or four stems, and these reduce by about a half. The result of this will be most vigorous reaction, with strong stems being thrown up from low down. What you do with them depends on the kind and height of hedge you are looking for. You want a barrier, and presumably one with lots of blooms, so, as the vigorous stems grow tall and while they are still soft and pliable, bend them down and tie them together with stems from the adjacent plant so that they lay horizontal and looped. You will probably have enough stems to make three or more loops between each pair. Arrange these at different heights about 1ft (0.3m) apart, and as the stems grow on keep them tied down to maintain a level height. Of course, if you have a fence to tie to so much the easier, or you can run some wire along rather like fruit training wires, but this is not essential. The effect of the bending down will be to induce the plant to fight back and produce bloom, and as side shoots form, these should be bent back and looped under in the same way. Very soon your hedge will be thick and quite impassable.

Next spring, prune back the stems that were left last time, and from then on, pruning will consist basically of taking out the one oldest main stem each year. This is easier said than done, especially when some side shoots have shot up through the lacing. The way I always tackled the job was to look carefully at each base, decide which old and perhaps barky stem was for the chop – then reach under and cut it through with long handled loppers. That may take some courage, as there is then no going back – but it is the best way. Obviously, we cannot remove the redundant stems in one piece, they have to be traced out from the first cut and removed piecemeal. Almost inevitably, you will be bound to miss pieces here and there, but not to worry, they will show out in a day or two as they wilt. Every piece must come out because leaving bits to die and remain is to ask for coral spot fungus to put in an appearance.

Every single piece has to go on the fire. Clear out fallen leaf with the rake, and burn the lot. Finally, bear in mind that this hedge could become an ideal over-wintering rest home for aphids and all the other pests of the rose. Most of the wood will be green, and in order to avoid damage from the corrosive effect of winter spraying, use a half strength spray of one of the less harsh sprays like Ova-mort or Mortegg. A mist sprayer is no good for this job – you will need a 'stirrup pump' type action sprayer fitted with a lance and an angle nozzle so that you can direct the spray up underneath from ground level.

With all this pruning and cutting going on, do remember that this is not any old hedge. You are pruning roses, and the rules have to be observed at every cut, especially with regard to leaving spurs and the danger of dieback. Read Chapter 6 on pruning.

## *32 Roses as a subject for hedges*

*I would appreciate your comments please on the suitability of roses for growing hedges. The variety* Rosa rugosa *is advertised quite cheaply and I wonder if it would be as good as it sounds in the advert.*

Two or three points here – and a warning! First, you need to be clear what you have in mind in a rose hedge. An open loose informal hedge as a demarcation, perhaps as a deterrent but not a positive barrier to cats and dogs, is quite easy and the choice of types and varieties that would be suitable is very wide. A more positive barrier can be grown by training climbers and ramblers along a support fence or wires, or by looping and entwining the stems of a vigorous shrub type as described in the previous question and answer. However, if you have in mind a thick clipped hedge, something like a clipped privet hedge but smothered in blooms as suggested by the misleading advertisements still to be seen in the press, then no way! Roses do not grow and bloom like that.

Genuine *R. rugosa* can be set 2ft (0.6m) apart and will provide an informal thorny screen with a few flowers that may vary between deep rose and white up to around 4ft (1.2m) high. For the first couple of years, no pruning is required other than cutting back over long and awkwardly growing stems, or these can be bent, threaded and worked back into line as in question number 31 above. From then on, with the plants well established, the aim should be to encourage a steady supply of new growth from the base by cutting out old wood as it becomes barky and dark in colour.

*R. rugosa* will follow on its display of single flowers with conspicuous showy seed pods, but if you really want blooms and hips, don't treat this kind of hedge to a diet of neglect. Constant replacement of stems and good flowering needs good feeding – and a rose hedge is no different in this respect to the other roses in your garden.

Now the warning! *R. rugosa* stocks are very widely used for budding H.T., Floribunda and other choice varieties. In the field, especially when the budders are on piece work at so much a hundred, they don't hang about and not every bud takes and grows away. Those that fail should be grubbed out – they are more nuisance than worth because the wood is a year older and tougher by the next time buds can be implanted, and are then even less likely to take. The none-too-careful grower, working on the cheap with not the best budders, will have a fair number of misses, and it is not surprising that, instead of grubbing out and burning, this chap looks to make an easy bob or two if he can. He bundles up the failures and sells them to a gullible public as 'rose hedging'.

The further trouble is that such growers are not too particular about the source of supply of the stocks, and the one thing that you can rely upon is a diversity in growth, size, vigour and bloom colour. If you want a uniform hedge, buy your plants from a reputable nursery, pay a good and fair price, and make it clear you don't want a polyglot lot of budding misses. In gardening, the only thing you get by buying cheap is regrets.

## 33 More on rose hedges: do they sucker?

*I am considering planting a hedge of* Rosa rugosa *roses, but wonder if they will sucker like H.T.s and Floribundas do. Also, will I have to remove dead heads or can I just let the hips form?*

By and large, the reason why budded roses sucker – from the roots below ground when they are usually referred to as 'suckers', or from above ground shoots when they are called 'briars' – is basically because the top growth, the scion, cannot take all the sap and energy that the root wants to send up, and the rootstock has to find relief for itself by putting up its own growth. In this case, the vigorous *R. rugosa* roots are going to push their energy into their own natural top growth, which is quite able to take it, and so there is not the pressure and need for the root energy to find a way out. Any suckers and briars that do arise will be the same natural top growth of the plant. It is not so likely, but that is not to say that it will not occur; indeed, in some species and types, suckers are a quite normal method by which the plant spreads and propagates itself.

There are two ways of dealing with them: either treat them as any other sucker and pull them away, or dig down and cut them from the parent plant with their own root section attached, and use them to extend the hedge, to fill in gaps, or even for budding on choice varieties.

As for the seed pods, some rose species have large or spectacular coloured hips and are grown mainly for this attraction. Undoubtedly it can tax the plant's strength to develop and carry a lot of hips instead of conserving the energy for next year's growth and bloom, however, *R. rugosa* is a vigorous species and this is its natural habit, so if you feed them and don't just neglect this part of their cultivation, they should be able to cope without trouble.

## 34 No flowers on a climber

*In February the year before last, I planted a fine and large container-grown specimen of the climbing rose 'Korona Red'. It carried a fair display of bloom in that first season, and made more growth, but last summer there wasn't a single bloom! I gave it some rose fertilizer in case that was what was needed, and pruned it lightly in October. But this has made no difference – there has been a lot of growth but no flowers this year either.*

It is not unusual for the turnover and sale of climbers to be a little slower than the popular bush types, and for ramblers and climbers to have been in the garden centre or nursery plunge beds for a year or two before somebody comes along and buys them, attracted somewhat naturally to the 'fine large specimens' rather than the smaller and younger ones. This inevitably means that the root system will be restricted within the container. Released from the restriction, a vigorous plant like this often responds to the chance to stretch out and spread its wings, and climb. No doubt the fertilizer that you put down helped it do this, and it got on with the job of becoming established, being too busy to pay much attention to making bloom. It has not felt threatened, so why bother? Pruning it lightly was more likely to have removed any bloom-bearing wood – leave it alone and let it settle down in its own time. Bloom will come when it's ready and feels like it, but not before.

The question does not explain how and where the plant is growing, and whether therefore it would be possible to try the old trick of frightening the plant, and causing it to react by endeavouring to perpetuate its own species by setting seed. To do this, of course, it has to make flower, which is precisely what you want. The best way to do this – if it is convenient, as on a fence or pergola – is to bend the soft and supple parts of the stems, at right angles if you can get them round that far without breaking them, every 18in (45cm) or so. This causes a restriction in the sap flow, the plant experiences difficulty and feels threatened, and it fights back by making bloom. Try it if you can.

What you should be concerned about at this stage of making lots of new, and therefore soft and lush foliage, is the risk of mildew. This variety is already rather notorious, and you should be careful not to increase the danger by applying nutrients that 'up' the nitrogen unduly. Read the analysis on the packet of the stuff you used – if the potash or 'K' percentage is not at least in equal proportion to the other two main ingredients, don't use it for this purpose again. Make every effort to obtain Humber manure, which is balanced, or Growmore. In view of what has happened so far, you would be very well advised to keep a careful close watch on the young growth and shoot tips for any

QUESTIONS AND ANSWERS

sign of mildew, and at the very first suspicion, spray with a systemic fungicide like Benlate.

This fungus can have a devastating effect on bloom production, and once it gets a hold on a susceptible variety like this, you must accept that it will attack each year and spread to others. Protective spraying with systemic, commencing early each spring, then becomes routine and vital. Neglect this at the peril of all your roses.

## 35 Pruning 'Canary Bird'

**1** *I have just planted a* Rosa xanthina *'Canary Bird'. This is referred to as a 'species rose'. Is the pruning any different to H.T.s and other roses?*

**2** *Last November I planted a standard 'Canary Bird' rose. A fortnight after planting, the trailers were pruned back to three eyes. This spring it bore two large single flowers only. It has grown well since, but alas, no further blooms. The planting hole was manured and bone meal lightly dug in after planting. What mistakes have I made – did I prune at the correct time?*

I wonder what the first questioner means in this context by 'H.T.s and other roses', and where this 'Canary Bird' is planted because it is capable ultimately of reaching 7ft (2.1m) or so high and wide, which makes it much too large for planting among the smaller bush types. Planted as a solo specimen or among other shrub types, it can be left to develop its natural arching habit so that, in late May and June, the long shoots can bear the masses of rich canary yellow blooms.

Removing them or partially cutting back, as I suspect is what has happened in the second question, is most likely to have removed bloom-bearing wood. The best bloom is borne on stems that have not yet become old; those that have borne bloom will throw out side shoots to bloom the following year, and so the shrub gradually 'fills in' and becomes well clothed. As soon as the older wood darkens and begins to develop a brownish bark in place of clear green, you have to make a decision involving a nice degree of judgement. The aim is to take out no more than one old stem each year and so gently to encourage a steady emergence of new growth from the base. It may take three or four years to settle into this routine.

Treatment of this rose as a standard is quite rare, which is a pity but understandable as it takes considerable time and care to develop a mature tree. The rather lax habit tends towards a weeping habit more than a 'mop-head', and the aim therefore is to prune out the older wood somewhat earlier in order to encourage longer arching stems that bend over and 'fall'. A magnificent example I knew in a garden at Bramdean in Hampshire had to be helped in this way by pulling down and holding the stems to a weeping position. Possibly the bending had an effect on blooming because in full flower it was, and I hope still is, an astonishing sight. The 'head' of stems that develops is very large and heavy. Staking therefore has to be correspondingly massive and secure (see also question number 36 below).

## 36 Pruning a standard 'Ballerina'

*We followed up your suggestion on where we might find a standard 'Ballerina' rose, and have been lucky to have just planted one as a centrepiece to our lawn. Could you please advise how it should be pruned to get those large balls of bloom? [See page 135]*

As the question suggests, it is not easy to find this rose offered as a standard, which is a great pity, because it is a rather unusual but magnificent sight. Sometimes listed under the Hybrid Musk heading, 'Ballerina' is a medium-sized shrub of some 4ft (1.2m) tall and wide, so clearly, put on a standard stem, it is going to be somewhat larger than most other standards, and will require special staking. The individual flowers are small, single, soft pink with a paler coloured eye and lightly fragrant, but borne in large hydrangea-like clusters. A well-grown plant has many of these and commands attention wherever seen.

To form a really good head virtually requires the sacrifice of bloom at the outset by pruning fairly hard the first year – like a Floribunda and not quite so hard as an H.T. – to encourage plenty of growth shoots that will not then need further attention from the secateurs, merely thinning out weak and spindly and crossing branches and stems that are in danger of rubbing and chaffing.

A bigger head than usual with large mop-heads of bloom spells danger in positions exposed to the slightest wind. Read Chapter 5 on staking and the advisability of planting to a stake that is long enough to pass up into the head. A top tie under this large head is absolutely asking for a tragedy. A new planting is the time to put in a stout and correctly prepared stake, not after planting, and if this has not been done, I would seriously consider lifting a recently planted tree and doing the job properly. You just cannot risk root damage by trying to get a stout stake close to the tree now. A 'Ballerina' standard is not an easy proposition, but what a performance!

## 37 Pruning China roses

*Would you kindly let me know how to prune my old 'Cécile Brunner' rose? It has reached over 10ft (3m) tall, and is a tangled mass of twiggy growth. The blooms it bears are very small and I think it would be better for a good pruning and thinning out. I would like to keep it down to 5ft (1.5m) maximum. Do you think this is possible?*

Roses are divided into many groups and classifications, and as the distinguishing differences are sometimes very small and narrow, it is often difficult to decide exactly where a particular variety should fit. The well-known variety 'Cécile Brunner' is a case in point – listed by some as a China rose, by others as Hybrid China, and by yet others that merely put it into the A.N. Others!

As a matter of fact, it was bred in France in 1881 – but who cares about such things when we are talking about beautiful roses? The questioner's homework is a little awry too, however, because the blooms of this variety are small normally – indeed, no larger than a thimble – but they have an exqusite H.T. type form, are blush-pink and sweetly fragrant. Attractive enough, but its strongest claim to fame – and I doubt if it has been able to display its ability in a plant in this overgrown condition – is its persistent continuity of flowering. Beginning so early and persisting so late – it is one of the best roses for ensuring a fresh bloom on Christmas morning – it has the nickname of 'Sweetheart Rose' because it is so constantly in flower (see also question numbers 4 (page 146) and 5 (page 147).

So, how are you going to get this mess to live up to its reputation? Grown as a free-standing shrub, it has a short jointed habit that would normally make between 3–4ft (0.8–1.2m) tall and wide, in a sheltered position 1–2ft (0.3–0.6m) more, and against a protecting wall maybe even 7–8ft (2.1–2.4m), so 'over 10ft (3m)' is exceptional and a measure of the overgrown condition.

First, you will have to follow the primary rules of pruning and take out all dead, diseased and weak spindly growth. There will be a lot of this, and you will need long-handled loppers and, very likely, a pad saw. That will clear the air and let in a little daylight. Next I would take out no more than one third of the oldest stems, those that have lost their green colour and become grey-brown and barky. Look at each candidate first, and try to follow it out through the twigs and foliage in order to assess what the effect will be after it has come out – you will still be living with the rose and will not want it to look as though it has been half slaughtered. Try to take out the old wood without leaving an ugly hole, but if needs must, then that is how it has to be, you are having to be drastic. Next, select the strongest-growing younger stems, still showing green, and reduce these by up to a third if you can, and the remainder weaker stems to just below the maximum height you want.

Without doubt, this will provoke growth of strong stems from the base, and the aim thenceforth is to get into a routine of taking out one major old barky stem each year, so that over two or three years you are able to complete the replacement of an old tangled thicket with younger greenwood. Don't be too drastic, removing no more than one old stem each, or every other, year. Apart from this gradual replacement pruning, confine the cutting back to light thinning as needed, and the removal of dead and weak growth.

## 38 Rose die-back

*Several roses in my garden are dying back from where they were pruned in March, and in a few cases the browning has extended down into the main stem. The rose beds were top-dressed with horse manure shortly after pruning and the die-back has appeared since. Do you think there can be any connection?*

This is a common and very serious matter, and we must risk repetition of much of what is contained in the chapter dealing with pruning in order to emphasize the seriousness. The most frequent cause of die-back, it has to be said, is rank bad pruning, and it can happen to all manner of plants, in addition to roses.

Whenever you prune or cut back, and for whatever reason, the most important consideration in your mind should concern not what you cut off, choice bloom though that may be, but the condition of and what is going to happen to the still-living plant. A clean cut without crushing or bruising and in the right place heals much more quickly and reduces the time available for disease spores and bacteria to enter the plant tissue. A damaged and slow-to-callus wound is one cause of die-back – we'll see why in a moment. However, the most frequent cause is that the living plant stem is left with the cut made in quite the wrong place, just below, midway between, or anywhere other than just above, a leaf joint.

Most plants, roses certainly, form embryo growth shoots in the angle between leaves and the stem from which they arise. This angle is called the 'leaf axil', and the embryonic shoot is an axillary bud. Look closely at your roses and you will see that there is a slight swelling in the stem where leaves and buds form which is due to the presence of special cells which store the carbohydrates that are elaborated in the leaf during daylight. This swollen leaf joint is called a node, and when we make a cut, it is this stored energy that we rely upon to form the layer of healing callus, much as a wound in your own flesh also forms a layer to stop bleeding, seal the entry, and then a much stronger scab. When we make a cutting, we utilize the fact that in many plants, some much more easily than others, the healing callus cells move on to form 'adventitious cells' which can absorb nutrient solution from the soil or medium surrounding them – that is, roots. The cutting is better able to do this if the energy store is close at hand than if at some distance away, hence cuttings are normally made just below a node.

But what of the living plant? A cutting taken in the above manner leaves an open cut on an internodal section of stem without an energy store closer than the next nodal leaf joint. This may be short or quite long, but it is a length of stem in which the energy required to form healing cells is not close at hand and has to be moved up. Callus is therefore much slower to form, the wound remains open to infection, and a cutting made ending with such tissue instead of a node would therefore be that much less able to form adventitious rooting cells, and would not take root and grow.

On the other hand, such stems that are trimmed back to a cut just above the next nodal storage area are able to heal quickly, and the rising sap is diverted into the embryo bud or already developing shoot, which is what is intended when we prune and disbud. When we prune badly and leave a length of stem exposed without an energy store close at hand, we bring one of nature's rules into action: 'what nature has no further use for it discards and gets rid of '. A length of stem without a node or axillary bud has no future; it has no purpose, it cannot grow on without a bud, and it cannot heal itself. The plant has no further use for this remaining stem tissue, and so ignores it. Even if it is not invaded by disease, it withers and begins to decompose. Now comes the serious danger.

As soon as they realize that there is trouble up ahead, some plants are able to react quickly and set up a layer of special cells across the next node which then acts as a barrier to the progress of decomposing or infected tissue. Plants are very clever at this – they know that, sooner or later, parts of their structure like leaves and fruit will ripen or otherwise come to the end of their useful life and become ready to be discarded. So they form a double layer of cells called the 'abscission layer', right across the base of the leaf or fruit stalk. These cells do not interfere with the passage to and fro of sap and carbohydrate during the growing period, but as the time approaches for parting, as in ripening, the abscission cells begin to change, hinder any further passage through, and become corky and brittle along the line between the two layers. Thus, when wind removes the autumn leaves, and the fruit falls, the severance is through the brittle abscission layer, with one layer of healed corky tissue on the leaf or fruit, and the other layer already healing the living plant! It is perhaps interesting to note that, when you lift a fruit gently to see if it will part easily and thus indicate that it is ripe, you are in fact stressing this very same abscission layer to see if it has become corky and brittle enough to break apart easily.

If you look very carefully at the nodes on the stems of your roses, you will see the scar from where the leaf fell. The scar is in fact the single layer of abscission cells. In some plants, even before they become corky, the abscission layer is more brittle than other parts of the leaf or fruit stalk. A familiar example is the leaf and flower stalk of the garden geranium, which snaps away quite easily near to the stem.

However, although the abscission layer is fairly evident in leaves and fruit, it is nothing like so evident or developed across stems and across the junctions of stems and shoots. Nevertheless, it is a similar layer of cells that a plant tries to activate when a useless spur has been left by damage or bad pruning as a barrier to the progress of decomposition or infection. When the plant is successful and quick enough, the spur is limited to a dried and withered section of stem, and the progress of die-back is halted.

Herbaceous plants are generally able to isolate spurs more quickly than shrubs, and roses are one of the least able to get a barrier up in time to stop die-back progressing through the first node, and sometimes several more, before it is halted. In severe cases, the dieback can run through into main stems and even the rootstock – and, of course, that is fatal. Even when die-back has been halted and only a short dead spur remains, there is still the risk of coral spot fungus, which starts off saprophytic (living on dead tissue), but which can turn parasitic (living on living tissue). This explains why the removal of all dead wood is one of the three prerequisite and primary purposes of pruning.

That is the physiological explanation of die-back. Add to it poor growing conditions like bad soil drainage, wet, stagnant or sour soil, inefficient and unbalanced feeding, unrotted nitrogen-high horse manure, low potash and poor vigour, and you can see how careless pruning or flower cutting is the last straw that breaks a camel's back, and can turn the risk of die-back into a raging certainty. In gardening, one thing always leads to another.

## 39 Help for crash victims

*My two small grandchildren recently broke down some rose bushes in our garden. After I calmed down, I trimmed back the broken and ragged branches with secateurs to try to prevent die-back. Is there anything else that I could have done? And what are the chances of saving the bushes?*

It depends on the extent of the damage. If a bush has its neck broken at or near where the original implanted bud emerges from the rootstock, its fate is in the lap of the gods. New growth of the choice top variety may emerge, but only may, depending on the age of the wood, or quite possibly the rootstock may have to find an outlet for its energy by putting up suckers. In either case, when damage is that serious, you would do best to replace the bushes and start again.

On the other hand, if damage has been confined to the superstructure, treat the damage as you would pruning. You have done exactly right in pruning to avoid die-back. Prune hard next spring, not in the autumn, feed with Humber manure or Growmore, and mulch to conserve moisture and get organic matter into the soil. If the damage has not been too serious, your bushes should then respond and, in a couple of years, look as though nothing untoward has happened.

## 40 Propagating shrub types by cuttings

**1** *I have tried several times to take cuttings from an old-fashioned scented white rose growing in our village churchyard, but without success. Can you tell me how to do this? I am sure I am doing something wrong somewhere.*

**2** *I have a hedge of the rose 'Roseraie de l'Hay', in which there are several gaps that I need to fill in to make the barrier complete. I cannot find this rose at any garden centre near us, in fact none of them have heard of it! Can you tell me if it is possible to propagate some more by cuttings, and how I should go about it? [See page 134]*

**3** *I have a long rose hedge which I only know as 'sweet briar' – the foliage is very strongly scented – and I do not know its correct name. It separates me from a lane alongside which is going to have a lot more passers-by from a housing development, and I would like to fill in some gaps and make it thicker to add to my security. Can you suggest how this could be done, please?*

Some interesting questions here, on the same basic theme. First question first. It is not possible from the question to even suggest what variety or type this could be. There are dozens that answer to such a general description, and we can do no better than follow a general principle.

About the backend of August, or a little later if the summer has been wet and the growth is a little soft, make cuttings about 9 inches (23cm) long from semi-ripe wood. A lot of readers ask what semi-ripe wood is, and the best general guide I have found is to suggest that you look at the growing ends of the stems, which are soft and supple, and not yet ripe wood. Trace the stem back to where you can tell, by the change in the colour of the green, that it is where this year's growth grew on from last year's. This earlier wood will by now be over-ripened for our purpose and too hard. The ideal is to take side lateral shoots with a heel attached, but unless you have deliberately allowed a stem of last year's growth to remain unpruned for this purpose, you are not likely to find side shoots of this kind. Therefore you are looking for something in between last year's over-ripe and this year's soft growth, perhaps some centre section wood which is the older of this year's growth.

From this semi-ripe section, cut lengths about 9 inches (23cm) long, with a horizontal cut straight across the stem below the lower node, and a sloping cut, as in pruning, above the top node of each cutting. If the length of stem permits, you may be able to make two or three such cuttings from the one length of stem. The advantage here is that the degree of ripeness will vary, and if you are not too sure of the semi-ripe wood, you stand a better chance of getting one about right. Additionally, you can pull away side shoots with a heel attached, as described in Chapter 9. Remove by cutting or snapping away – don't leave any snags – all but the two top leaves, and dip the freshly cut and still moist bottom tip into hormone rooting powder, such as Strike or Seradix Hardwood. Shake off the surplus and lay aside for half an hour for the wounds to dry and callus over. Insert to a depth of half their length with the tips hard on the sandy bottom of a sand-lined slit trench as in the sketch in Chapter 9 on page 100. They will need to be about 4–6 inches (10–15cm) apart, and shielded from direct sunshine. In about a year it will be obvious which cuttings have formed roots and are away – the top two or three growth buds will have grown out and made foliage. Lift them carefully, without disturbing the cuttings next door if they haven't started yet (leave them for another year) trim the top growth back by no more than a third, and plant the cuttings into a permanent position. When the growth buds begin to swell in spring, prune back the stems to about 5–6 inches (12–15cm), and away they go.

The second question concerns a *Rosa rugosa* variety, which can be treated in exactly the same way, as can the third, which I would think is *Rosa rubiginosa*. As they are already forming a hedge, you may like to try another method of filling in the gaps. Simply, take the longest stem or two end-on to the gap and bend them down to the soil. Where stem and soil meet take out a shallow hole, half a spit deep. Wound the stem either by nicking it half way through just on a node with a sharp knife, or grasp it in two hands – you will need stout gloves – and twist it enough to break the green bark. Bend and bury the stem at this point, and hold it down with a peg or lay a brick over it, leaving the top growth sticking up to begin the job of filling in the gap. This is simple layering and a surprisingly quick way of filling short gaps. Longer spaces take more time by this method, and the quickest way then is to plant out cuttings.

## *41 Propagation by seed*

*For several years I have saved seed pods from some of my rose bushes and planted the seeds in the spring, but never have I seen a seedling – they just refuse to germinate. I have tried heat as well, but still no luck. Can you please tell me how it is done?*

The germination of rose seed is not as simple and straightforward as might be supposed. The germination of the seeds of plants has evolved and become dependent upon very varied conditions and circumstances. Sometimes, a precondition can be allied to the means by which plants ensure that their seeds are carried away from the parent, both to avoid competition with the parent plant, and to spread the species afar. Parachutes that blow on the wind – like the dandelion – are a simple example, while others are more complicated and even bizarre.

Consider the tomato, and the jelly-like matter that surrounds each seed. Why do you think it is there? It serves two main purposes. The intention is that the fruit, either as a whole or just the seeds perhaps from a fallen fruit, will be eaten by an animal or bird, and be deposited far away. The slippery jelly entices the creature to eat the seed, and then assists the seed to pass through the digestive tract and resist destruction by the digestive juices. Of course, we can remove the jelly, dry the seed, sow it and achieve germination, but anyone who has seen tomatoes growing 'wild' on a sewage farm, their prolific growth and the unusual speed with which they bear ripe fruit, may correctly conclude that something has happened to the seed that makes it germinate and grow much quicker.

Some seeds have to pass through exposure to fire before the seed case will release them to germinate – with all the competition burned to cinders they get an unopposed start. Others require not heat, but cold. The natural precaution that has worked into the evolution of such seeds is that germination shall not be too early or delayed, and that the seedlings will have the most favourable conditions for growing successfully. Therefore, to get such seeds to germinate we have first to imitate the natural conditions of frosting.

Seeds of plants like hawthorn, holly and roses, need a period of winter cold and frosting, and we imitate this in a method called 'stratification', which refers not to the cold but to the layers of seed that are arranged in a suitable receptacle. Put 2 inches (5cm) of sand in an earthenware flower pot, then a layer of fully ripe rose hips – don't break out the seed – then another layer of sand, more hips, and sand and hips in layers, finishing off with sand. Wrap the pot in wire netting to prevent mice, squirrels or other pests getting a cheap meal, and bury the whole thing 2 inches (5cm) deep in an open border where rain, snow and frost can lie and have their full effect.

By the following spring, the husk and pith surrounding the seed will have rotted and the seed been subjected to a good winter chilling. Lift the pot, retrieve what is left of the hips – you may be able to wash the seed clean wrapped in a piece of muslin, but it isn't all that important and we never used to bother – and scatter the seed thinly in trays or shallow drills. Placed in a cool position, and not allowed to dry out, germination can follow during the same summer, or it can take a few years, just as it does in nature, as when such seed is self-sown and you find young seedlings growing under a holly or hawthorn, or a rose hedge where the soil has been undisturbed. You will have to be very patient.

As and when seedlings reach 2 inches (5cm) in height, they can be very carefully teased apart – you may find it helpful to do this in a bowl of water and 'wash' them apart – don't disturb their still sleeping neighbours any more than you can help – and pot them singly into 3 inch (7.5cm) pots. If you are a fan of John Innes composts, use no stronger than No. 1 potting – the seedlings do not want a rich feed at this stage and should be grown on 'hard'. Grow them on in the same cool position, or other position where they will be protected from wind drying and from direct sunlight.

Rose seedlings are new-born infants, and particularly vulnerable to attack by greenfly. You will find that protective measures have to begin at once. If you rely on the contact poison method, you will have to spray every few days in order to keep the growing tips covered by insecticide. Systemics are a much safer precaution, and less time-consuming – a spray every other week should suffice to keep the sap of each seedling toxic to biting and sucking pests.

## 42 Dealing with mare's tail weed

*My rose beds are full of a weed called mare's tail. I hoe and hand weed but I cannot keep pace with it. Last year I tried a selective weedkiller, but although I was very careful this caused damage to the roses where the spray drifted. Is there a safe weedkiller and method for dealing with my problem?*

Hoeing and hand weeding only makes matters worse because you are stimulating the plant to produce more and more underground stems and side shoots. Hormone weedkillers will kill it, but the problem, as you have found, is how to get the hormone into the weed and not into the roses as well.

You will need a long rubber glove that will come well up your forearm, like those sold for household cleaning. Over this, pull an old woollen glove or an old sock. Make up a solution of SBK brushwood killer – a fluid ounce in half a gallon of paraffin – if you look at the label on the bottle it will state the total contents and enable you to estimate the proportion needed for 1 ounce (28g). Mix the solution in a plastic bucket, and make absolutely sure that you do not use the bucket in the garden for any other purpose – even scouring in hot water will leave a minute trace and that is quite enough to knock over susceptible plants. By the same token, as you move around the rose beds, for Heaven's sake be careful not to kick or knock it over.

Put your gloved hand in the solution – the rubber glove will prevent your hand from becoming oily and smelly with the weedkiller – wait a moment for any surplus to drip, and wipe the main stem and foliage of each weed by grasping at the bottom and with a soft gentle pull, letting the foliage slip through your hand. If you think there is a risk of the larger weeds blowing against the rose and thus conveying the hormone to them, grasp only the lower parts, and make sure that your wet fingers wipe the stem itself. Gradually, the weed will wither and collapse. Don't cut or remove it until it is quite brown and dead, as all the time there is the slightest vestige of life it has to carry on translocating the hormone to the root system so that it too is killed. When it is quite dead, remove it as carefully as you can without brushing the roses and take it straight to the fire. Don't put it down, or even lay it in a wheelbarrow; the hormone in this form is very potent and can remain so for some time, and it is very easy to contaminate tools and equipment that then pass it on to other plants.

Young emerging growth is very easy to deal with. Before it becomes big enough to brush against the roses, simply wipe a wet hand over it, as they are quite vulnerable to the hormone at this soft stage. This is the easiest, safest and most effective way of dealing with this and other persistent weeds in cultivated ground, but do be careful at all times. Keep the gloves where they will not touch or contaminate anything else – even the 'smell' (which in actual fact consists of minute vapour droplets in aerial suspension) is quite enough seriously to affect susceptible plants like tomatoes. Under no circumstances use the gloves or the bucket for any other purpose but this.

## 43 Buttercups and other persistent weeds

*My rose border is infested with buttercups that get worse every year. How can I deal with them?*

There are several forms of buttercup, and for a rose bed to be 'infested and getting worse' suggests that we are dealing with either creeping buttercup, which spreads at an alarming rate by means of creeping stems that sprawl all over the place, dropping off new plantlets every few inches (centimetres), or bulbous rooted buttercup, the 'bulbs' of which are storehouses of energy that enable the plant to make new growth and grow again even after all the top growth has been removed, as in hoeing. Or you could be faced with both!

There is an old saying that you have to meet persistence with even more persistence, but this doesn't mean that the only way to knock a wall down is to bang your head against it harder and more persistently. Hormone weedkillers will have an effect, but the problem is to keep them in contact with the plants long enough for them to work. Buttercups take in the hormone only very slowly, and therefore, if it is to reach all the parts of a plant that is well spread out and endowed with plenty of reserves to come again and again, the hormone has to be kept in contact for a long time. The most persistent way of doing this is not to use a spray or brush, which can easily wash off, but to put the hormone in a soft wax that will stick and resist rain and watering.

Get yourself a 'Touchweeder' from the garden centre. This is like a shaving stick or short candle with which you dab the crown of each weed. They don't like this treatment, and although it is easy to say be persistent, I have in mind that we are dealing with a rose border that may be too large and demanding for this method of attack. You could adapt and try the method described in the previous question and answer – that would be very effective – or if you are not confident that you can cope with the safety precautions, you could try the modern 'emergent' weedkillers that take out soft green growth like seedlings and new shoots but leave more established plant tissue unharmed. This method will take longer to cope with these weeds, but you should be able to wear them down in time. Use Casoron G, Murphy Ramrod or Herbazin – there are several such products on the market.

Two final comments. Evidently you are not maintaining a good mulch cover on the soil surface. If you were, or now get one on, you would find that the buttercups will love it, and set about moving up into it! Mulch is much more friable than the soil, and that means that weeds with matted root systems like this are much more easily pulled out. Secondly, I wonder what this rose border backs on to – a fence? Is this where the infestation is coming from, or are you exporting it to next door? You could have a fair-sized job in hand here!

## 44 Safe weedkillers for rose beds

*Is there a safe weedkiller I can use around my roses to keep them free from grass and other weeds? I used to spread cuttings from the lawn at one time until I was advised that this was causing grass to grow in the roses – I haven't done so for some years now, but it hasn't made any difference, the grass is still there and I cannot stop it.*

If you were maintaining a good mulch cover of weed-seed-free material you would not be suffering from weeds, at least to the extent that a stab with a dutch hoe could not control them. Your roses would also benefit directly from the steady addition of humus to the soil and the better retention of moisture and nutrients.

There is no doubt that the grass growing in the rose beds emanates from the earlier practice of scattering lawn mowings. There is scarcely an amateur lawn in existence that does not contain an annual meadow grass, *Poa annua*, which, as the name suggests, is an annual. It is so successful with its annual production of seed that mowings thrown by the machine into the grass box will contain seed that is still capable of ripening and germinating. In fact, it can produce viable seed so quickly that, by the time it has become big enough for you to grasp with your fingers to pull it out, it has already shed seed and ensured another generation.

By now, your soil will be full of seed waiting for favourable conditions in which to germinate, and every disturbance like pulling out one grass seedling, brings other seed to a level where they in turn will germinate. There is an old saying 'one year's weed and seven-year seed', and you began by sowing weeds when you scattered the cuttings!

Your best chance of getting on top of this problem is to use an emergent weed-killer like Casoron G or Herbazin that affects seedling leaves as they emerge from the soil. You may well have to be persistent with this treatment and spray the surface every time you hoe and disturb the surface, at least until you have reduced the seed count to the point where the hoe can take over the responsibility.

## 45 Moss and what it indicates

*Could you suggest a way of getting rid of moss which keeps growing on the soil in my rose beds? Until last year I always scraped it off, but that involved losing a lot of top soil, so I used some of the moss killer that I use on the lawn to see if that would work. I was successful for a while, but it is now back worse than ever.*

Of course the moss has returned! It is amazing how many gardeners want to get rid of moss, and how much advice is given on how to get rid of it, for no better reason than a vague idea that it is unsightly and somehow does harm, whilst completely missing the point of what it means. It is not harmful in itself, but does indicate a harmful situation. It has to be eradicated, yes, but the sensible way to do that is not to put down a moss killer, either on your lawn or the rose beds, without doing anything about the conditions that cause it. When you use moss killer and the moss persists or gets worse, clearly there is something radically wrong, and you had better understand what it is.

In the same way that human beings regard themselves as being at the top of the animal evolutionary ladder – questionable at times, you may feel – plants also can be allotted appropriate rungs according to how far they have evolved from primitive life forms. Algae and single-cell plants are at the bottom, then lichens and mosses, then the ferns and tree ferns, and up rung by rung to the top, near to where, you may be surprised to find, are the grasses. The rungs that plants occupy on this ladder are determined by certain botanical and evolutionary principles with which we need not get involved here other than to recognize the important fact that, generally speaking, the nearer a plant is to the top, the more evolved and developed has to be the fertility of the soil to sustain it.

Only a very primitive degree of fertility is necessary to sustain the bottom rung life forms, whereas the higher plants require more and have only been able to evolve as the degree of fertility has also evolved with geological time. Roses are also near the top and, like the grasses, need a fair degree of fertility. However, there is a marked difference in their toleration and ability to hang on to life when fertility decreases. Mosses are very near the bottom rung, and can live in a poor degree of fertility that higher plant forms cannot tolerate, and indeed they are not sufficiently evolved and cannot adapt to thrive in conditions where the fertility has advanced beyond them.

As difficult as it may be to accept, in view of fertilizers and feeds that are supposed to make plants grow better, the simple fact is that the presence of moss is an indication of low and declining fertility. Here, it is vital that you appreciate that fertility is not dependent solely upon plant nutrients, but crucially upon the soil's physical structure, its organic content – humus, air penetration and its population of aerobic bateria – and upon its moisture content.

Moss thrives in acid conditions, and its presence in a rose bed is an indication that the top ½–1 inch (1.2–2.5 cm) at least of the soil is far more acid than your roses can tolerate – I would say that they are living on a knife-edge. In a lawn, comprised of shallow rooted grasses, moss is an indication of an already serious soil condition in the top 2–3 inches (5–7.5cm). Roses are deeper rooted of course, but the moss indication shows that infertility is already well advanced at the surface and, because this is caused by bad cultivation and mismanagement, it is working its way down to a level where the roses will suffer and succumb.

That is the cause of the moss. What do you do about it? The first thing to do is to leave it alone! It is nature's indicator to your soil condition. The way to eradicate it is not to burn the signpost or scratch it out, but to raise the fertility level so that the moss can no longer live. All the time the moss is there, you have an indication as to what is happening. You can obtain a simple and inexpensive soil-testing kit if you like; it will only confirm what the moss is already telling you.

Read the chapter and other sections relating to feeding, and change your cultivation accordingly. Get on a mulch cover as soon as you can, and as you have a chronic acidity situation to correct, I would scratch into the mulch 1 ounce (28g) of hydrated lime or ground limestone every four or six weeks, for at least six applications. If you do obtain a soil-testing kit, you can use it to check and observe the acid:alkaline ratio as it gradually moves to a slight alkaline bias. Take the soil test sample from at least 8 inches (20cm) down and be careful not to harm or disturb the roots.

From now on, chemical fertilizers are absolutely out. Invariably they are acidic and they contribute nothing whatever to the soil's organic content. Make every effort to obtain Humber manure, or as a second best, rely upon Growmore and – more important – mulch to provide organic input. Remember to keep the surface open with a long-handled fork or scratch hoe.

## 46 *The causes of mildew*

*Last autumn we planted a row of 'Crimson Glory' at the front of our house. They have grown well but have had mildew very badly – the blooms have been quite spoiled. Could you please say if this variety is particularly liable to this trouble, and if there is anything that we can do? I would rather replace the roses than have this trouble again.*

It is often asserted that red roses are more liable to mildew than other colours, and a possible explanation is suggested in Chapter 7 that deals with feeding. Whether or not the assertion is true, it is a fact that fungal diseases like mildews and botrytis are prevalent. The spores are about all the time, ready to invade and take advantage of any opportunity that suits them. Damp muggy weather, stagnant air conditions, impeded air movement and poor ventilation (often caused by overcrowding), and dryness at root causing limp wilting leaves are each well-known conditions that favour these diseases, and, that being so, it is direct incitement to them to encourage soft flabby growth with poor vigour and resistance by not feeding correctly.

Particularly with the red's alleged susceptibility, it is all the more important to ensure an adequate supply of potash, and to avoid any feeding or mulching with short manure that is likely to increase the nitrogen ratio. Prevalent at the best of times, and now well established on the premises, you must expect further attack as a matter of course, and help your bushes to ward off attack by providing them either with a fungicidal protective coating, or by injecting antibodies into their bloodstreams.

There are several fungicidal products available, both specific to mildew, and designed also to keep black spot at bay. Whichever you use, make up the spray strength strictly according to the directions on the bottle, repeating as advised as the coating wears or washes off, and additionally, get into the habit of sparing a few minutes each evening to walk around your roses, sprayer in hand to 'puff' all the new shoot ends and buds which grow so quickly that each day's growth is quite enough to expose a fair area of young, soft and vulnerable leaf tissue beyond yesterday's spray cover. You may have to be doing the same routine for greenfly, in which case try to make sure that the fungicide and the insecticide are compatible with each other. This is more likely if they are both prepared by the same manufacturer, and if it doesn't say so on the bottle, the retailer should have a chart or similar guide with this information. Bear in mind also when using contact fungicides and insecticides, that the easiest point of entry for pest and disease is the softer undersides of leaves. It is more important, therefore, to spray up underneath than to spray down. Always add a drip or two of washing up detergent to the spray to achieve a good all-over wetting.

Systemics in both cases avoid the need for daily 'topping out', but whether you use these or the contact materials, the old rule applies – you don't solve much by shutting stable doors after the horses have bolted. No matter how much you spray and protect, you are not going to do a lot of good after mildew has already got into the plant tissue. It starts early in the spring, just as the growth buds are beginning to break out, and this is when you have to start.

## 47 Black spot

*Are there any Hybrid Tea roses that don't get black spot? I replaced all my roses last year with 'resistant varieties' because of repeated attacks, but now every one of my new roses has been affected this year.*

Resistant doesn't mean that a variety will not be affected by black spot, and looking for a list of resistant varieties is not the best way to fight this trouble. Popularity, by its own definition, must involve wax and wane – and being an extremely popular, if not the most popular flower, the many different varieties and forms of roses raised every year have to weather the slings and arrows of outrageous fortune. Fashion is fickle, the pace of demand and trying to keep up with the competition so hectic and relentless that the headlong rush has led the rose into the troubled waters of sacrificing vigour and resistance to pest and disease in favour of flamboyance.

Nevertheless, in the helter-skelter scramble of coming, going and short-lived popularity, it has been remarkable how some of the older names have continued to hold their own. All too often, the ritzy strawberry blondes were willowy and fragile, and there has remained a place for reliability and not being so ready to succumb to wet weather, pest and disease. Today, rose breeders pay very much more attention to breeding for resistant qualities, and a couple of points become clear.

First, in view of the annually changing lists, it would be invidious and misleading to quote names of varieties for you because, like the earlier fashion and search for colour, development of new and more resistant varieties would soon make today's list out of date. The best policy is to obtain the latest catalogues from nationally known and reputable growers, compare them for the hard information provided, and judge accordingly. A good grower produces a good catalogue that is frank and honest when it comes to indicating the weaknesses as well as the strengths, including the susceptibility to black spot. You will find the list of nurseries on page 264–5 helpful in this respect.

Secondly, the field work involved in breeding and raising new varieties, budding good material into clean stocks and growing to a saleable product is a highly skilled job. Experience and skill costs money – you would not want to work 'on the cheap', and you cannot expect a rose-grower to do so. If you want good roses, you will have to pay a fair price – there is no such thing as a cheap rose, only rubbish. Sow's ear roses do not grow into silk purses.

Finally, resistant or susceptible, roses are liable to attack by pest and disease every day of their lives, just as human beings are. To remain healthy, they need feeding properly just as much as you do. That doesn't mean a super abundance of pep pills, tonics and easy-to-spread chemicals. It does mean slow and steady release of an NPK-balanced diet into a good soil structure containing a good moisture-retaining organic content.

Incorrect feeding and adverse soil conditions means an ailing plant, and an ailing plant, irrespective of its breeding and inbuilt resistance, is more vulnerable to attack. By all means select disease-resistant varieties, but do realize that there is little point in so doing unless you pay attention to feeding and good cultivation.

## 48 Can black spot spread to other plants?

*I am waging war on black spot on my roses, and appear to be winning because there is much less this year. However, there is still enough of it about to worry me that it could spread to other plants. Can you please tell me which are most at risk?*

Black spot only affects the rose family, but other plants can be involved to the extent that in and around them can be harboured rose leaves, petals and suchlike rose debris that can be carrying spores of the disease. Routine thorough spraying is a vital precaution, of course, but completely negative if you allow leaves and debris that harbour the spores – most likely already infested – to lie around and ensure another attack next year. Hygiene is absolutely imperative to control – every single morsel, whether prunings, dead flower heads, or fallen petals and leaves, everything must go to the fire as quickly as possible. That doesn't mean thrown on to the fire heap waiting for a convenient time to have a bonfire. If you cannot burn at once, at least put all such matter in a plastic bag to isolate any possible source of spreading the infection and see that it goes with the house refuse.

Cleaning up can be difficult from a mulch surface, but it must be done. Under no circumstances should debris be hoed or scratched into the mulch. Give black spot an inch, and it will take a yard – nothing is more certain.

## 49 Fungicide deposit

*I have a predicament. After spraying my roses with Benomyl fungicide, although I followed the instructions to the letter, I have a white powdery-looking deposit all over the leaves that is very unsightly. Rain doesn't wash it off, and I wonder what to do about it – it shouldn't do this, should it?*

What is your predicament? Isn't this exactly what a protective coating should do? It is a feather in the cap of the product and your spraying that rain does not wash it off. It may look a little unsightly to see a deposit left behind as the liquid of the spray dries, but that is a small price to pay for the safeguard. The alternative to precautionary measures like this is to leave your roses wide open to attack by pest and disease – they like roses just as much as you do, but not just to look at!

I wonder if you have been a little heavy with the amount actually applied to have left a deposit that is unsightly, but the fact that it is there shows that it is doing its job. Don't let new buds and shoots grow out of the cover – get a cover on them as well.

## 50 Rose canker

*What can be done about my dear old rose bushes which have dark and wrinkled markings on the stems? Most of these marks reach right down to the roots and the plants seem very unhappy.*

I hope that you can clear a space in your garden where you can have a good bonfire, because I am afraid that is what you are going to have to do with your old friends, but it will be the kindest thing for them. This sounds very much like canker, and perhaps a little more detailed description may help to confirm it. Normally, it starts with a yellow crinkly area with a reddish tinge at the edge, invariably at the site of physical damage. This can be bad pruning that tears and bruises, it may be caused by a carelessly handled hoe, or it may be the result of twigs and branches rubbing and chaffing. Badly made ties that allow movement and twisting is a common cause. As soon as the green cambium layer is breached, the trouble can start. The affected area turns yellow, then brown, and extends and cracks along the line of the stem exposing the wood tissue underneath, by which time you should be very well aware of what is going on, as it is hardly unnoticeable.

As can be imagined, rose canker is a terribly weakening disorder, and it is likely to show in other roses because it is encouraged by sour, acid and badly structured soils. As all the roses are in the same bed or garden it is likely that they are all subject to the same soil conditions, and an outbreak in one must be seen as an indication that all are at risk. The primary cause is poor-draining soil, wet, sickly, sour and acidic, a condition not helped by the use of fertilizers and feeds comprised wholly or largely of sulphatic chemicals. Clearly you have a considerable remedial job to do.

Immediate action is to cut out all affected wood far enough back to show clean wood without any sign of discolouration, and thus ahead of the spread of affected tissue. Where the canker has reached down to the root area, as described in the question, there is no point in cutting out affected growth, it has gone too far. Dig the plants right out, and burn all diseased material. Where plants can remain, you will need to put down a heavy dressing of lime, as much as 8 ounces (230g) to the square yard (square metre). The acidity has to be countered as quickly as possible. Follow it up a couple of months later by carrying out an acidity soil test with a kit that you can obtain quite inexpensively at the garden centre, and repeat with 2 ounces (57g) dressings every other month until the testing shows a slight alkaline reaction. Of course, you must make a test at the end of an intervening period with soil from 6–9 inches (15–23cm) down, and before you put down more.

Where plants are removed, I would play safe and not replant for at least one full year, using the time to dig in organic roughage, and putting down a very light dusting – ½ ounce (14g) to the square yard (square metre), no more – of an NPK-balanced organic manure that you will continue with. The purpose of the light dressing at this time is not to input plant nutrient, but to develop the bacteria population that will be involved later when you feed in earnest. Make every effort to obtain Humber manure, or failing that use Maskells Blood, Bone and Fish, but whichever you use, it is very important to continue with the one material and its attendant bacterial chain. It is pointless and wasteful to switch from one nutrient source to another, because the bacterial chains will be wrong.

If you are working with heavy clay, of course you start at a disadvantage, and the clay has to be made more porous and friable. You can do this by putting down agricultural gypsum at the rate of 2 ounces (57g) to the square yard (square metre), no more than this, every three months, and allowing the weather to take it in. It is a long process, and you will have to be patient. There is no quicker way to change the nature of clay.

Better structural conditions, better nutrient balance, and a better acid:alkaline ratio will make for better prospects for replanting, but before doing so, read Chapter 4 on the subject of preparation for planting. Canker is best regarded not so much as a contagious disease, but as something that results from very poor soil structure and conditions, and the only way to control it is to correct the cause.

## 51 Rose rust

*During early July I thought that young growth shoots looked unusually red and were shrivelling. Many of the older leaves developed orange-brown swellings, and in August I found that the underside leaf surfaces of these swellings had turned black. This does not answer to any of the diseases described in my gardening encyclopedia. Could you possibly say what it is and what I should do?*

This is a fair description of a disease that is rather uncommon, so it is not surprising that you have not been able to find a reference to it. No reference book could possibly contain every pest and disease to which the rose is subject, there are far too many, and the line has to be drawn somewhere between the more common afflictions and the rare and obscure.

The trouble described here is usually called rose rust, although it has to be said that except for the early reddish tinge of the young growth, there is not a lot that one would associate with the appearance of rust. It is not a disease to be expected in the northern half of UK (this question came from Lancaster) but this shows that it can appear on the odd occasion, and when weather conditions are favourable it can occur almost anywhere.

The most frequent reports invariably follow the sequence of a dry summer, a cold hard winter, and a cold spring. Now when you think about it, this is a long time for the plant to be under different kinds of pressure, so that when new growth appears after that it can hardly be expected to be the most robust. In fact it is a good example that shows how roses need the vigour and toughening effect of potash not only during summer and autumn. A nutrient imbalance that encourages a soft lush growth in spring only has to meet a testing weather sequence for your roses to be wide open to a punch. In so many ways, and so often, it is potash that is the most important nutrient for roses.

The immediate course of action is to try to remove affected leaves and sources of spreading the disease. Pick off all affected leaves and drop them into a paper sack. Carefully pick up all fallen leaves and debris – hygiene is important – into the sack as well, and burn the lot on a fierce consuming fire, not a slow smoker that will send it all round the neighbourhood. The remaining leaves and plant can be helped by a potash injection, and you will have to do this quickly. Make up a weak solution of permangante of potash, commonly known as Condy's fluid. This is easily obtained from the chemists and you will need only a few crystals to turn water blood red – it is very strong, and not very quick to dissolve, so give it half an hour or so before adding more. When completely dissolved, add a little systemic fungicide such as Benlate, just enough for a quarter strength or even less of the recommended dilution rate on the bottle, and finally two drips only of washing-up detergent to achieve a good wetting cover, for each pint of the mix. Use this spray mix to fine mist-spray the foliage every other day, and keep it up for at least a couple of weeks. That is the best you can do as far as curative measures are concerned, but prevention is always better than cure, and you must try to see that it doesn't happen again.

Anything that contributes towards poor soil structure and imbalanced feeding has to be suspect. If you are on heavy clay type soil, a 2 ounces (57g) per square yard (square metre) dressing of agricultural gypsum every three months – do not exceed this rate – will gradually make it more porous and friable. Get the soil surface covered with a good thick mulch of well-decayed compost, leaf mould, peat, or pulverized bark. Don't use horse or farmyard manure unless it is old, well rotted and quite unidentifiable as to its origin; there must be no suggestion whatever of a nitrogen-residual content from the urine to encourage softness. Don't prune hard in November as so much mistaken advice advocates, just a little shortening back of over-tall growth to guard against wind rock. Take off all seed pods and late flowers to conserve energy.

Read Chapter 7 dealing with feeding, and in early spring start a gentle feeding programme with Humber manure which will provide a good potash supply. Next spring keep a careful watch – you know what the early signs look like – and if there should be any sign of recurrence, take the precaution of spraying with the systemic fungicide/potash mix, and repeat every couple of weeks.

It is not a common problem, but when it happens it is very weakening, and that can often be the prelude to other nasties. They always kick a rose when it is down.

## 52 *Leaf-roll sawfly*

*Several leaves of my roses are curling up lengthwise. I opened some and found what appears to be tiny eggs. What is it and how do I deal with them? I don't see how insecticide spray can reach them.*

A fair enough description to identify attack by a clever little varmint called the 'leaf-roll sawfly'. Adults lay eggs in May and early June along the main rib of young and still developing leaves, which at once begin to react by curling, hence the name of the pest. As the larvae hatch to start feeding on the leaves, they are nicely holed up where nothing can reach them, neither predatory birds nor your contact killing sprays. When they have had their fill, the destroyed and shrivelled leaf remains fall to the gound and the larvae emerge into the soil where they pupate just below the surface. Here they remain until the next spring, when the adults emerge and begin the performance again.

Well, that is the life cycle, but where are the weak spots that enable you to get at them? Their rolled up air-raid shelter is very efficient. For a long time, the weak spot in the cycle was confined to the exposed adults before the eggs are laid and the leaves curl. DDT gave some measure of control because the poison was able to get into the flies through their feet as they alighted to lay their eggs, and they didn't last long after that to carry on, but in practice, and with time, that particular chemical group was found to have serious knock-on effects and is now banned. The story of DDT, like that of many another toxin, is solid testament to the argument that too many chemicals are put on to the market too quickly for any side and knock-on effects to have become apparent. For this reason, I am loathe to suggest, and you would be very wise to regard with some circumspection, the very latest insecticides offered to us. Give them time for the unforeseen effects to show out.

Spray or dust malathion, which will also take care of aphids, will deal with them if you can get enough of it into physical contact with the flies. Because they go for the young leaves, it is clearly vital that spraying or dusting should be repetitive and frequent — intervals longer than two or three days are quite enough for new foliage to grow out of the protective toxin deposit and be exposed.

Having had a serious attack, you must expect to have a fair number of pupae in your soil waiting to get going again next spring, and they could well be coming from neighbouring gardens. It will be prudent, therefore, to begin spraying early to catch the early risers. Spraying the soil with malathion also helps to catch the adults emerging from the pupae stage, but this will involve soaking and a fair amount of expensive insecticide.

You will have to watch very carefully for any sign of curl indicating that they have found a hole in your defences. Provided that there are not so many as to distress the plant, picking off each affected leaf will put those eggs out of action – get them straight on to the fire. The rolled-up leaves are not going to be able to perform their function properly, so their removal is no great extra loss anyway, but if there are too many leaves affected, you will have to fall back on the pest's second weak spot. The larvae will be chewing the rolled up leaves from the inside, so you have to use the period between the first indication of egg-laying and curl and hatching to render the sap stream of the plant toxic to anything that bites or sucks.

If you haven't applied systemics as part of your routine, and wait until the curling starts before doing anything about it, there will not be much time left in which to work, so you will have to make up systemic spray at the full strength as directed on the bottle, add a couple of drips of washing-up detergent in order to achieve a good wetting cover, and spray every other day for two or three times to try to get the poison into the plant tissues as quickly as possible.

Squeezing the leaf between thumb and finger to crush the larvae inside, is often suggested, but really this is a game of chance. It is better to take off the rolled-up leaf and burn it.

## 53 *Capsid bug*

*We have some 40-odd roses, planted the year before last. These seemed healthy until they began to make bud this year, and now we notice some irregularities. The stems seem too weak to hold up the growing buds, and some of these have turned brown and are clearly not going to open. Those flowers that have opened are misshapen and distorted, as are many of the leaves.*

The weak bud stems could be confused with more than one other cause, especially a lack of potash leading to 'weak-neck' or 'topple' (see question number 2 on page 126), but the clue to the real trouble is in the misshapen and distorted opening blooms and young leaves. This indicates physical interference at a very early formative stage. The description in the question sounds very like the damage resulting from attack by the capsid bug, a small winged insect that sucks the sap, generally from just below the buds. The puncture wound causes the supporting stem to weaken so that the bud flops over with a weak neck. Even if it doesn't collapse completely, the sap flow slows, then stops, and the deprived bud wilts and rots. This explains the internal distortion of the growing bud which is the characteristic that indicates capsid rather than nutrient imbalance.

The insects are very seldom seen – they have a remarkable early warning system and fly off when they see you coming in the distance. You have two basic ways of combating the pest, first, by spraying on a systemic insecticide made up to the strength and instructions on the particular make that you buy. Start in early May before the insects are about so that the sap is already toxic when the first one shows up. This method has to allow the bug to bite, and it is not unlikely, therefore, that you will still lose some buds.

The second method is to cover the buds and stems with a layer of contact killer in such a way that the bug is knocked over before – hopefully – it has time to bite. Again, there are two ways to go about this. The first is dusting, by means of a puffer, a dust based on carboryl or trichlorophon. This is quick-acting but, as you can imagine, it is something of a job to make sure that you get 100 per cent effective coating with dust over such awkward places as underneath all the buds, which is where the bug invariably makes its attack. Even when you get the buds all looking like clowns, a layer of dust is not very durable and can soon be knocked, blown or washed off.

Gamma benzene-hexachloride spray — BHC for short – will dry and leave a toxic layer which the alighting insect picks up on its legs, body and sucking tube as it pierces the plant tissue. It is not so quick acting, and you may not stop the blighters making the fatal pierce with just one coating. You have to build up a thick layer, therefore, by making repeated sprayings, waiting for each to dry before applying the next in order to build up a thick deposit. The buds and their stems are growing fast, so a mist spray each day on them is by no means too much.

There you have the nature of the problem and the disadvantages with each remedial method. Whichever you choose, persistence is the order of the day.

## 54 Egg-spangled rose

*I am intrigued by several bands of insect eggs that I have found round the shoot tips of many of my roses. There is no reference to anything like this in my books. Can you tell me what they are and whether they are dangerous?*

This sounds as though you have found the bracelet bands of the eggs of the Vapourer moth. These are usually laid during late summer and early autumn, but when the weather is right, you may find them somewhat earlier. If they live through the cold of winter and are not removed by pruning, the eggs will hatch in spring into pretty hairy caterpillars with tufts of yellow hairs along the back of a body that is green, red and grey.

However, these pretty little beasts demand a hefty price for their board and lodging, because as soon as they emerge, the caterpillars will feed voraciously on the shoots and foliage of roses, fruit trees, shrubs or other host plants. Roses that are pruned in spring seldom suffer because the eggs are removed with the pruned-off material, but now that you know the moth has been about, you should not take any chances. Any shrub types, climbers and ramblers that are not due to be pruned should be given a precautionary wash when growth is quite dormant and before any new green growth begins to appear. Ovamort or Thiol will clean up any Vapourer eggs and, no doubt, a few other pests waiting for spring before they hatch out and admire your roses.

## 55 Scented roses for the blind and partially sighted

*My father, who is coming to live with us, is almost blind and cannot appreciate colours. I want to plant some roses for him that are really strongly scented. Can you please suggest something suitable?*

If you are to be as helpful as you possibly could be, there is rather more to it than just planting roses for their scent. I realized this many years ago when constructing a sportsground where I put in a garden with sunken paths which were actually to serve as storm catchment ditches to arrest flooding surface water flowing down a vulnerable valley on to tennis courts and a bowling green. I planted sweet smelling and aromatic plants – artemisia, lavender, the old-fashioned clove-scented pinks like Mrs Sinkins, and others – along the tops of the 3ft (1m) high walls either side of the paths, and realized that there was another dimension to what I had planted when I saw blind folk wandering through and running their hands over and through the different textures of the foliage.

There is also the practical problem of a blind person knowing where a rose bush is planted, and just where to bend down to smell the blooms. Standards are better in this respect, or a pergola over which scented varieties of climbers and ramblers can be trained. If you try this latter course, do bear in mind that you will have to make very sure that errant shoots and stems do not protrude to where a blind person can blunder into them, especially at face height.

Think about it and see if you can go a little further than merely planting rose bushes – raised beds, perhaps, and pillars as well as standards and pergolas offer plenty of scope for ideas. Here are some suitable rose varieties.

**Bush types:** 'Blessings', 'Fragrant Cloud', 'Wendy Cussons', 'Deep Secret', 'Alec's Red', 'Papa Meilland', 'Duke of Windsor', 'Elizabeth of Glamis', 'Scented Air', 'Sweetheart', 'Prima Ballerina', 'Paul Shirville', 'Rosemary Harkness'.

**Climbers and Ramblers:** 'Compassion', 'Elizabeth H. Grierson', 'Madame Alfred Carrière', 'Zéphirine Drouhin' (thornless – page 134), 'Albertine', 'Wedding Day' (page 142), and, of course, there are many shrub types that are worth exploring in a good catalogue, and the rose species that have fragrant foliage like *Rosa primula* and *R. rubiginosa* (see Chapter 2).

## 56 Mixing roses

*My rose book – by a well-known author – and a programme I have just watched on TV both say 'never mix varieties'. I can see the reasons advanced, but is it not a counsel of perfection for those with unlimited space? In my small garden, how can I grow different varieties and kinds unless they are mixed?*

I couldn't agree more. Far too much so-called advice is a counsel of perfection by folks who do not put themselves sufficiently into the position of those at whom their advice is directed. Mixing varieties is a case in point. Spoiling mass colour effect is one thing, but space is the controlling factor for the vast majority of gardeners, especially in these modern times of urban development and ever more building plots to the acre. The only way to grow a fair number of varieties is to mix them, and then it becomes a matter of purely personal preference and choice. Do you prefer groups of reds, pinks, yellows and whites, or a mixed-up carnival? It is up to you, and quite presumptuous for anyone to tell you that your preferences, and even your possibilities, are wrong. You do what pleases you with the space at your disposal, and if that means mixing, go ahead and mix.

## 57 Going too far with technical standards

*I have seen a reference in a catalogue to roses that comply with 'BSS specifications' and also to colours relating to numbers on a colour chart. What does this mean? Is it an indication of good varieties?*

Many products stand in need of what is called 'consumer protection', and for codes and standards to be set and maintained in respect of quality of materials, workmanship, service, colour etc. Various EEC regulation marks, British Standard Specifications (BSS) and 'kite marks' are familiar examples.

Setting standards of this kind is by no means new in horticulture and agriculture. Perhaps one of the very first of all standards to be set in this way occurred in the early years of this century when fruit growers in Kent, in a bid to protect and regularize their industry, set up the East Malling Research Station near Maidstone, the forerunner of many such centres of farming research. The first job it had to tackle was the out-of-control mess in the rootstocks upon which apple varieties were being grafted.

Roses are a similar case. The narrative chapters in this book give a fair indication of the extent to which the search for some new colour or hue has gone and, although most gardeners are perfectly well satisfied with 'deep pink', 'rose pink', 'pale pink' and so on in describing bloom colour, growers and breeders have to be much more exact in matching colour to a colour code, something like a very sophisticated paint colour chart, in order to be quite certain that what they may describe as a new colour really is new and not the same as or too close to what somebody else has already bred. Some growers may refer to such a colour code in their catalogues, but without a correct reference chart, which is not at all easy to print and very expensive to reproduce, such information is really academic and rather pointless. Don't worry about it.

I have thought for a long time that there is room for some kind of standardization in having rootstocks cleaned up and certified, like the Malling apple stocks, so that we can have reliance in the uniformity of the subsequent growth of the varieties budded on to them. This work is beginning, but is not yet universal practice. At least the use of colour code details in catalogue descriptions, while it may fly over the heads of most people who read it, nevertheless shows that the grower is aware of such matters, and is paying attention to trying to keep his products up to modern standards.

## 58 The astonishing story of the Banksian rose

*Some time ago we had a most interesting talk at our garden club about the origins of roses, during which the speaker gave what I thought was an enthralling account of the Banksian rose. I have now acquired a* Rosa banksiae *'Lutea' to grow into a tree in my new garden, but I cannot find out much about its history. Books in the local library have given me a little, but nothing like that speaker. I'd love to regale my friends – can you help please? [See page 141]*

It *is* a fascinating story, and you will be something of a raconteur if you can tell your friends all that follows. Many of the plants that adorn our gardens originated far away, and how they got here sometimes makes for a mind-bending tale. The Banksian rose is one such. The rose genus has one of the widest size ranges of all plants. We are quite used to the familiar bush in the garden, and know that they also climb walls and fences, but some of the miniature kinds are scarcely 4–5 inches (10–13cm) tall, whereas 30ft (9m) clambering up into a supporting tree is not at all uncommon with several monsters.

To the Banksian arguably goes the little-known fact and honour of being, or having been, the largest rose ever. Thirty years ago, in Tombstone, Arizona, there was reported to be a double white form, scented, grown and supported to form a large canopy that exceeded 4,600 square feet (427 square metres), with a regular annual bloom count of several hundred thousand! Although many species are native to Europe and Britain in particular, vast numbers come from other climes, and that exuberance of performance is not achieved here, or anything like it, which is perhaps just as well. The Banksian is a remarkable rose, and its story is equally so.

Its natural place of origin is the remote mountainous regions, at an altitude of some 5,000ft (1500m) above sea level, of the Hubei, Yunnan, and Shanxi provinces of central and western China. The story of how it came to Europe is a little tentative but generally accepted. The first introduction to Britain had apparently been unrecognized for a hundred years, while other forms were turning up and making their mark in Europe. In 1909, a celebrated gardener at that time, E. H. Woodall, first observed, no doubt with intense delight, flowers on a completely unknown rose in his garden. The plant had been grown from a cutting taken from an old plant growing at Megginch Castle, Strathspey, Scotland, to where it had been brought with other plants in 1796 by a Robert Drummond, who was the brother of a Royal Navy Admiral, and with whom he had cruised in Far Eastern waters. The rose had apparently been growing at Megginch all that time without blooming because, being a little tender, it had been cut down every year by the severe winter weather in that region.

The flowers observed by Woodall were white, quite small, single, and with a very strong fragrance. Quite likely, this would have been the very first time that this particular form had flowered in Europe. A hundred years earlier, in 1803, William Kerr had been sent to China on a plant-hunting expedition by the Royal Society, and among a lot of 'finds' was a strongly scented double white rose found not growing in the wild, but cultivated in a garden in Canton. This arrived in Britain in 1807, first flowered at Isleworth in what is now west London, and was named in honour of Lady Banks, the wife of the then Director of Kew Gardens. The botanical name now is *Rosa banksiae banksiae*, the second 'banksiae' being added to denote that it is regarded as the type species, and a little incongruous in view of the Megginch specimen. However, another name you will often see listed for the double form is *R. alba plena*.

Some little time later, a yellow form was reported to be growing in a garden in the botanic gardens in Calcutta, India, and J. D. Parks was sent to Asia by the Royal Horticultural Society to obtain specimens. He was successful, and it flowered here in 1824, and is now called *R. banksiae* 'Lutea'. It has a delicate scent, but not so strong as the white forms. In 1870, a single yellow form, *R. banksiae lutescens*, arrived in England from Menton in southern France where it had been growing for some years, and this yellow had as strongly sweet a fragrance as the whites.

It appears that these nineteenth-century introductions were coming from gardens in China's coastal cities. At that time European plant hunters were not penetrating very far into the innermost and wilder country, so the identification in 1909 of a hundred-years-old single white at Megginch was all the more astonishing.

In cultivation, *R. banksiae* has few thorns, and is often quoted as an example of a thornless rose, but this is not entirely true. The best and most prolific bloom is borne on wood that is two, three or even more years old, which imposes a 'no pruning' rule until wood is at least six or seven years old. By this time it can easily be 30ft (9m) or more up into a supporting tree or, as it is most often seen, entirely clothing the walls of a house or for immense distances along a wall. However, by far the best display in our climes is to see it suspending long graceful stems from aloft in a tall tree. I knew a fantastic example running through an ash tree in a sadly neglected wood near Southampton; the sight of sunlight shafting onto tresses of hanging rose blooms is something you never forget. The neglect for several years was just what it had needed to reach a majestic size and flowering, and that illustrates both the need for little pruning and, perhaps most importantly of all given the diminishing size of English gardens, the space it needs. The Banksian roses are far too big for all but those of us fortunate enough to have very large gardens, trees and house walls. Although originating from high up in Chinese mountains, they do not like severe winters and only flower freely where they get protection from cold winds and frosts.

## *59 Dangers of mixing fertilizer chemicals*

*I have several bags of old fertilizers of which I have lost or forgotten the identity. Not wanting to waste any, I wonder if it would be a good idea to mix them altogether so that the result would have a bit of everything like a general fertilizer, and if I could then put it on my roses?*

Mixing fertilizers like this is most unwise – you must know exactly what you are doing, not only because of the chemical intereactions that may take place, but also because the resulting NPK proportions are bound to be quite unbalanced. Read Chapter 7 on feeding, and you will see that, if anything, roses need a bias towards potash. A mixed-up fertilizer of uncertain origin, quite apart from being possibly very dangerous, is likely to do more harm than good to your roses, or to anything else in your garden. Forget the idea, and dispose of those old fertilizers at once.

## 60 Recipe for a safe rose hip syrup

*My three children have always had to have rose hip syrup for the special vitamins it contains. This is rather expensive and we have tried making it ourselves. It seems to be satisfactory when fresh, but it will not keep, even though we have tried various recipes. I wondered if you have ever come across this problem in your gardening dealings and know the answer. Do shop-bought syrups contain some kind of preservative to stop them going off?*

Yes – I can help you. Although I derive enormous satisfaction in growing beautiful flowers, especially roses, there is an extra dimension to growing food, be it vegetables or fruit, and I can never understand those gardeners who say that they like to grow vegetables and fruit but don't have the slightest interest in cooking and preparing them. Taste is vitally important, and so is appearance. I have never met anyone with the same ability as my wife has for cooking greens and keeping the fresh bright natural colour. What a difference that makes on the plate!

With jams, jellies, sauces and syrups the problem often is one of getting them to 'keep'. I'm not sure what you mean by 'going off' but probably you mean a thin film of fungus growth at the surface of the syrup like that which often occurs on home-produced jams and jellies. You are dealing with an organic material that is subject to the natural processes of degeneration and breakdown and, armed only with the utensils of the normal kitchen, you have to extract unharmed the vitamins and constituent parts you need by a method that sterilizes them and prevents breakdown by external influences like bacteria and fungus. For immediate or short term use, the job is not too difficult, but for storage over any useful period it is not easy, rather involved and time consuming.

For the full development of the vitamins that you need, the hips have to be fully ripe and highly coloured, full and plump not dry or shrivelled, and without damage or blemish that may harbour trouble.

Wash them by shaking two or three times in tepid water and grate or finely chop 2 lbs (900g) into 3 pints (1.7 litres) of already boiling water. Bring back to the boil for 20–30 seconds only, no more or you will destroy the vitamin content, and take off the heat. Allow to stand for 15 minutes with the lid on, and strain through a jelly bag or muslin into a scalded clean container that is not metal, and keep it covered.

Tip the pulp back into the saucepan, add half the original quantity of boiling water – 1½ pints (0.85 litres) – bring to the boil again, remove the heat, allow to stand, strain, and add the second straining to the first. Bring to a very slow boil, and adjust the heat to a mere simmer, gradually reducing the liquid quantity to 1½ pints (0.85 litres). This will take some time, and is also a prolonged sterilizing. Slowly mix in 1½ lbs (680g) of preserving sugar, a little at a time, stirring and dissolving it and trying to maintain the simmer as far as possible. When fully dissolved, bring just to the point of boil for 5 minutes, then remove from heat. Keep the lid on as the contents cool, and as soon as cool enough to handle, bottle off into thoroughly clean and ready warmed small capacity bottles. Corks or screw caps must be thoroughly sterilized by boiling. Fill to within 1 inch (2.5cm) of the top and cork or screw cap, loosely for the moment, and stand the bottles in a deep saucepan fitted with a tray or false bottom to prevent burning, immersed in warm water that reaches to just above the level of the syrup. You will need a jam-making thermometer at this point because you now have to heat the water to 170–175°F (77–79°C), and maintain that temperature steadily for 20 minutes. Take off the heat and as soon as cool enough to handle (or wear gloves) seal the cap or cork tight, and move to store in a cool place, but not a freezer or fridge, completely removed from all light.

This may seem a lot of trouble to go to, but within the limitations of the normal kitchen and without artifical preservatives you will have to take all these precautions to avoid a repetition of your previous problems. I would not know how long syrup prepared in this way will last when put to the test, but I have had several correspondents report that it works well from one crop until the next – a whole year!

### 61 Modern varieties do not live so long?

*I was planning to plant a collection of new modern varieties, but an old retired head gardener in the village tells me that the more vivid the colour of modern varieties, the shorter lived the plants will be. Is there anything in this, or is it simply an old wives' tale?*

This is not so much an old wives' tale as the contention held by many gardeners of the 'old school' who have used their eyes and formed their opinions on the basis of their observation. Even allowing for the pressures of competition and the conviction among most growers that several new introductions have to be made each year for them to be regarded as being in the forefront of the job, with the consequent removal from their lists of a similar number of roses at the bottom of the sales tables, it is also a fact that a great many introductions (modern varieties) that make their bows with acclaim and eulogistic promise of flamboyance and scent to match fall at the first hurdles of vigour and resistance to pest, disease and weather. They just don't keep up with the field in a hard tough race, and in a few years they are gone and forgotten. In this respect, the descriptions of 10 or 15 years ago make interesting and amusing reading today. So many false hopes never lived up to what was expected of them. It is no wonder that the old gardeners should hold the opinion that the modern flash Harrys are short-lived, whether that means their life expectancy, their availability in the lists, or both. They will point to several old varieties that have consistently held their place for 30, 40, or even more years, and claim that 'you cannot beat a good old 'un'. Well, that is not true either, because a lot of good old 'uns have been, and continue to be, bettered. However, the fact that some are still around shows that they must have the stamina of reliability and good all-round performance to stay in the race.

Only time will tell with the latest introductions, however well they are written up. It always does, and you would be wise to bear this in mind before launching off on a probably expensive modern collection.

## 62 Roses in a waterlogged situation

*Our garden edges down to the canal and, because the water level is constant, water is always near the soil surface. We cannot get rid of it by draining. Is there anything we can do that would help us to grow roses?*

Modern gardeners in the heavily populated south and east do not have to put up with the climatic conditions and heavy rainfall of those who cultivate the soil in the north-west. In Ireland and the north-west of

Scotland, on soils and in conditions that tend now to be dismissed as incapable of economic cultivation, far bigger populations than those who live there now were once fed and sustained. Not so many generations ago, before the great exodus and the clearances, these people tilled land that was often marshy and boggy with a high annual rainfall. How did they do it?

The obvious first step is to ditch and drain the water from the surface reaches, but that cannot work in a bog or your garden because it has nowhere to go, the water table is too high. So, if you cannot get rid of the water that way, you have to get away from the water by climbing out of it, by raising up areas and patches of land above the water level. A method of cultivation known in Scotland and Ireland as the 'lazy bed system' consists of digging out wide trenches when conditions permit, throwing the spoil up into raised beds and growing on top of these. Very few garden plants will grow with their roots immersed in water, and certainly not roses. If your garden really is as bad as you describe, your only hope is to build up out of it.

I had a customer, a doctor, whose garden backed on to the River Wey near Weybridge in Surrey and had just this problem. He grew roses very well indeed on raised beds, but he objected to them being called 'lazy' – they took him a long time and a lot of hard graft, so they were anything but lazy! In the sunken lower parts from where he had dug out, he had an extensive bog garden with the most wonderful bog primulas I've ever seen, masses and masses of pinks, reds, yellows, orange and blues. It was like the effect of bluebells in a wood, but so much more colourful – and in a bog! The soil that had come out had a very high organic content and high degree of fertility that the roses up nearer to the house revelled in. It took him a long time in between the demands of his job, but where there's a will, there's a way. Out of a waterlogged garden he made something quite enchanting.

### 63 Coping with a rose 'that round the thatch eaves runs'

*We have a rose 25ft (7.5m) up under the eaves of the house. It is years since it was pruned, and as it is old, needs thinning out and some of the roof tiles are being dislodged, I just have to tackle the job and cannot put it off any longer. My pole pruners are neither long enough nor strong enough – any comments on the best way to tackle the job would be appreciated.*

This question is much more important than it appears on the surface, because it has the hallmark of *danger!* With a strong climber high up on a house, even with the 'no pruning' types like the Banksian rose, there comes a time when old gnarled wood becomes too senile and unable to sprout vigorous bloom bearing wood from low down, and the growth bearing the bloom becomes progressively further and further away from the roots. So, judiciously, without creating wholesale slaughter, courage has to be taken in the hands, the older stuff has to come down, and this is where the trouble starts.

It is going to be a long and tedious job, and because it is an irksome job to keep going up and down a ladder and moving it, the temptation is to reach, to overreach – and to overbalance. Long pole pruners are useful tools, *but never ever use them other than with both feet firmly on the ground*. Beyond their reach and ability to cut, there is no other way than going up a ladder.

Precautions with ladders are obvious but necessary, and some mistakes are made so frequently that it is well worth pointing them out. In addition to the normal precautions about soft earth, and never going up without somebody to steady the thing and tick you off when you try to reach out too far, never climb up with tools that are in any way cumbersome, awkward, or too long to handle comfortably with one hand. Always keep one hand on the ladder to steady yourself, and the other for the tool. Try to remove unwanted wood in small pieces – this takes time, but it is safer. Remember, large pieces of rose with thorns can seriously hurt anyone below. When you drop or let it fall, it must always be under control and well clear. Branches that are too big for you to know exactly where they are going as they break away are extremely dangerous to those on the ground, and the ladder. They can run but you cannot, you are up the ladder and at risk.

If you need to change tools, secateurs perhaps, keep them in a deep pocket from which they cannot work their way out and fall. Personally, I even dislike tools in pockets because it is so easy to impale yourself if you stumble and fall, but perhaps I am over-cautious. Two hands need to be free before picking up a saw, for instance – which incidentally should be suspended handily nearby on a strong loop and not rested or wedged into branches, from where it can be dislodged. Falling tools are dangerous.

Don't try to use a carpenter's saw. The teeth cannot clear green sappy sawdust and it will jam. Always use a pruning saw, which has teeth designed for the job, and even before you think of using it make quite sure it is sharp and that the teeth are set properly to keep the cut clear. A blunt or incorrectly set saw is dangerous enough on the ground when the blade jams in the cut, but for this to happen with you up a ladder is to ask for trouble. Any jamming, struggling, or wrestling with tools that won't work as they should means that you exert more force and pressure to try to make the damned thing go, and you are then more liable to slip. Don't lift a leg out to balance while you reach out a bit further – that is going halfway to the cemetery. If you cannot reach comfortably with two feet on the rung, shift the ladder. Finally, don't dismiss this advice and think it cannot happen to you – complacency means carelessness, and that is dangerous.

## 64 Soap in the rose garden?

*We have heard more than one reference to soap spraying to combat greenfly. We don't like dangerous poisonous chemicals in our garden and would like to know more about soap.*

Before all the sophisticated chemical poisons that we have today came into general use, the various substances applied to plants to keep pests at bay were often mixed with soap solution. This helped the solution to 'run' and wet the leaves thoroughly and was in itself something that would leave a nasty-tasting stomach-upsetting coating as it dried for the creatures that ingested it, especially when bitter-tasting stuff like quassia chips has been soaked into it. Many gardeners omitted the insecticidal ingredient of the day and sprayed with only the soap on beans and roses, and swore it was just as effective against soft-bodied creatures like greenfly, blackfly and frog-hoppers.

The soap could be virtually anything from soft soap, sometimes sold in cartons and tins, or loose. Many is the time I've seen it dug out from a barrel, like grease, and weighed and sold by the pound. Crude carbolic washing soap was also much favoured, perhaps because of the disinfectant smell, and also finely shredded and soaked toilet soap. Pieces that had become too small to use normally were avidly saved for this purpose – there were some odd smells in gardens in those days!

There is no reason whatever why you shouldn't be equally thrifty and use the soap ends to make spray solution. Dissolve enough in warm water to make the liquid feel slimy. You may have to open up the spray nozzle just a little, and the spray will be somewhat more coarse than a mist. On roses, this will be first-rate, but if you use it on food, do remember that you will need to wash thoroughly. Soap residue can hang about for a long time – which is why it was used so much.

## 65 What is whalehide?

*We have looked for roses in whalehide pots but our garden centre only uses plastic bags. What is the difference so far as planting is concerned, and what is whalehide, anyway?*

Whalehide pots are really a kind of bitumenized paper or thin cardboard, and were popular before the advent of plastics as a cheaper alternative to the old clay pots. Today, in the interests of economy, plants for sale are mostly grown in plastic bags. Not that there is anything basically wrong in that, except that plastic does not decompose like whalehide does in the soil, and arguably could hinder root development by confining it. The primary purpose of plastic or whalehide pots is to hold soil in a ball and so avoid root disturbance. This may be because the plant does not like its roots disturbed at any time, even when it is dormant, or because the plant is already growing away, even in bloom, and to disturb the roots at this time would mean almost certain flagging and death. Of course, this means that the selling season is greatly extended, and you can buy roses long after they would have been planted had you bought them bare root (the best way to buy them), but occasions do arise when it is a boon to be able to replace a loss with a plant already growing.

However, having said that, the object of the exercise is to plant the subject into the soil, and if it is in a plastic bag, that has to come off. A whalehide pot, being bio-degradable, can be planted as well and will soon rot away. The plant then suffers no root disturbance, whereas stripping off a plastic bag, no matter how carefully it is done, inevitably disturbs and destroys the very fine hair roots that form at the root ends where they come into contact with the plastic.

Even worse can happen. Removing the thin bag sometimes results in the soil ball crumbling and falling apart – so much for no root disturbance. It is then that you find that you have been 'conned', and that the supposed container-grown plant is not container-grown at all: it was potted up recently, and the roots have not had enough time to grow and permeate the soil to hold it together. The container-grown exercise was not done to facilitate planting, but to attract the attention of somebody who wouldn't understand the difference. Be on your guard against this all-too-frequent malpractice.

## 66 Is a thornless rose a chimera?

*My clever daughter tells me that a thornless blackberry is a chimera. I dare not let on that I don't know what a chimera is. Can you explain please, and whether a thornless rose is the same kind of freak? She says it is.*

A chimera (pronounced as in sky, Vera) is sometimes called a graft hybrid and it can occur with plants other than blackberries – the pink or purple flowering laburnum is a familiar example. A graft scion is put onto a rootstock, and in the normal course of events the top scion grows, entirely preserving its own identity in the flower colour, leaf shape and habit, and you see this quite clearly with roses. Many choice varieties are nice enough on their own roots, as you can see when you strike a cutting and get it to grow on its own root system, for example, but are better when grafted or budded onto the stronger-growing stock, which is why we go to all that trouble.

Sometimes, however, things go a little awry, and the stock tissues grow out into the graft, but clothed within a layer or sheath of the scion tissue, rather like a glove. The result then, for example, is a blackberry but with the skin of a thornless type, or the more spectacular laburnum inside the skin of the pink-flowering Cytisus broom grafted on to it. Quite often, the outer skin can become stretched and a hole develop through damage, perhaps, or bad pruning, and the underlying tissue gets a chance to break out and do its own thing. You then get the beginning of a reversion to type, with both thorned and thornless stems and yellow and pink flowers on the same plant, which is not dissimilar to what happens when a stock or briar as it is called in the case of the rose, is allowed to grow and develop. As soon as reversion is detected, it has to be cut out, cleanly and most often relentlessly, because once a breach occurs in the sheathing tissue and the stock tastes freedom, it is quite likely to make another break for it. If you are not vigilant and ruthless in this, you are most likely to have a period when the two forms are borne on the same plant, both thorned and thornless stems, pink flowers alongside yellow, but with the stock form quickly gaining the ascendancy until the chimera recedes and is lost.

Another point to bear in mind is that a chimera 'skin' only exists on the above-ground tissue of the plant, not the roots. It ceases at the point, called the hypocotyl, where the stem structure changes to root structure, and this we have to observe by taking a cross section through and looking at it under a microscope. This explains why a leaf or stem cutting invariably grows with the chimera intact, but a root cutting or sucker never does.

Albeit brief, that is the botanical explanation of a chimera. The question is, do roses have chimeras and is the rose referred to in the question a chimera? I have only ever heard of it referred to as a freak. I remember my university professor saying that she had heard of it, but never seen one, so they must be pretty rare, although neither she nor I would be growing roses in sufficient numbers for the odd chance in a million to happen and for us to see.

In nature, several 'wild' types have very few thorns, just as others have so many that they are almost like hair or fur. Even within these thorn-shy species, considerable variation can occur, and two identical plants can vary noticeably. Some, like 'Zéphirine Drouhin' (see page 134), are called thornless, but I've had heaps of letters asking why a thorn or thorns have appeared, and samples to prove it! While the usual explanation is to say that something from the plant's distant and murky past ancestry makes its presence felt, the true fact of the matter is that genetics is not an exact science and despite our knowledge of chromosome chains and dominant and recessive genes, and our manipulation of them to produce new plants, the unexpected can and does occur. Sometimes this is for the better, and the variation is better able to withstand the competition of natural selection to become a new species. At other times, it is not so good, and the variation dies out as quickly as it appears. That, after all, is the basis of evolution.

Whether your rose is a true chimera could only be proved by taking an extremely thin slice across a stem and examining the cell structure under a microscope to see if the glove effect is present.

## 67 Can rose colour be changed by colourants?

*I use a blue colourant to turn my hydrangeas blue, but it doesn't work on my roses. Why not?*

Plants vary considerably in their toleration of and reaction to degrees of soil acidity and alkalinity, as well as to other conditions and influences. Some, the hydrangea is the familiar example, react almost like litmus, phenolphthalein, and other colour indicators that you may remember from school. The point to remember about the hydrangea is that the colour reaction to acidity is the opposite to the familiar litmus paper: the blue colour so desired in the plant is encouraged by soil acidity and the pink or red colouring by limy alkaline soils. The colourant normally sold for hydrangeas is aluminium sulphate, which, apart from any effect the aluminium may have, is strongly acid, and should be used only with extreme care and concern for the consequences, not where it will run off into a fish pond, for example. This was the chemical which, in 1988, was dumped in the wrong waste tank, found its way into the domestic water supply of a large part of Cornwall, and caused all kinds of distress.

Undoubtedly, rose colours react to soil conditions, but to nothing like the extent that the hydrangea does. Inadequacy of potash is more likely to lead to pale colouring than any effect due to acidity, especially that resulting from artificial colourants. One thing is certain — if you are hoping for a blue rose, you won't get it this way.

## 68 A blue rose?

*All the so-called blue roses I have seen are not blue at all, more a dirty mauve, and I have heard it said that there can never be a true blue rose for botanical reasons. It was also said that there would never be a red delphinium, but now there is one. So what about a really true blue rose?*

There are a number of coloured blooms that don't exist, but which everyone therefore wants, and the quest for them has become something of a legend. So far, no one has produced a really true blue rose, but that doesn't mean that there won't, one day, be such a miracle. New colours do come along from time to time. The red poppy is common enough, the yellow less so, but quite familiar now to most gardeners, and a blue poppy was a dream, until it was found growing wild in Tibet. The red delphinium was another dream, and now we have it. That leaves perhaps the two most sought-after and elusive desirables of all, the blue dahlia and the blue rose.

The quest for a true blue has gone on for a long time, and will no doubt continue. If and when it is achieved, it is in the trial grounds of the Royal National Rose Society at St Albans that it will be proved and acclaimed. As to whether it is botanically possible, old Father Time will have the last word. After all, the blue poppy and the red delphinium were held to be impossible, so who is to say that, with the modern skills of gene manipulation, it cannot and will not happen? It hasn't happened yet, and there is a line of argument that says that the seeking of the elusive blue is more enthralling than the achievement, but it is a challenge to the ingenuity of man that will stand no brooking. There are a lot of breeders trying.

## 69 How do they get roses in bloom for Chelsea?

*My roses never bloom until mid June at the earliest, and some later than that, and yet there are always masses of roses at Chelsea Flower Show in May. How do they do it? And isn't it misleading and unfair?*

Of course, May is early for roses, and months too early for chrysanthemums, just as it is rather late for many spring-flowering bulbs and shrubs. Therefore, to reap the benefit of the extra publicity and attention of the Chelsea Flower Show, the skills of the growers have to be exercised in pushing forward or holding back as the case may require, and even bringing to bloom completely out of season. Roses have to be advanced by a month or two, and that means growing them under glass in controlled and usually warmer conditions, free of pest and disease.

Some varieties respond better than others, providing masses of bloom to fill the Show vases, and some relatively few, requiring many more plants for a given number of blooms. That is just one of the behind the scenes things that have to be taken into account, but which you, the admiring onlooker and potential customer, are not told about. What makes a good show rose, amenable to being made ready for Chelsea, whether easily or with difficulty, does not necessarily make a good rose able to perform well and reliably in the rough and tumble of the outside world, and in the UK there are over 500 miles (800km) of latitude and different climatic conditions to contend with. That is one reason why so many much-heralded new varieties fail to stay the pace when faced with the harsh realities outside the cosseted conditions that prepared them for their Chelsea debut.

The rose is not the worst offender in this respect, because the chrysanthemum blooms are shown completely out of their normal season, and if it is unfair, albeit very clever, to be able to show roses a month or two early, how would you describe an exhibit of chrysanthemums? There is a great deal more 'fiddle' involved here. The chrysanthemum is a plant that responds to length of daylight hours and their continuity. The normally autumn-flowering blooms are produced in May by artificial light and light-excluding blinds during the day to fool the plants into thinking it is autumn when it is only April or May. Spring-flowering bulbs always have to be held back for Chelsea, and this frequently results in their flowers blowing and the petals dropping as the retardation controls cease, especially when they are beset with a warm and stuffy marquee.

The expertise then becomes not merely an exercise in holding blooms back, but a logistical problem in organizing a daily supply of fresh blooms for public scrutiny. The Thursday and Friday of Chelsea often tell a sorry tale compared to the prim fashions of Monday.

By wanting to wait until June, your roses are only doing what comes naturally. Let them bloom in their own time – outwitting nature is fraught with risks.

## 70 Scented leaves

*I heard a passing reference on a radio programme to roses with scented leaves. This sounds most interesting. Can you tell me more, please?*

There are a number of roses with scented foliage. Several have some degree of aroma, but the two that are strong enough to permeate the air for some distance around on a calm summer's day, and are therefore grown for this purpose, are *Rosa rubiginosa*, which you may sometimes see listed as *R. eglanteria*, a robust 8ft (2.5m) shrub from northern Europe with numerous but not particularly notable single pink blooms producing bright red oval hips, and *R. primula*, the 'incense rose' from Turkestan, a graceful 6ft (2m) plant with small pale primrose-yellow blooms, numerous enough to smother the almost fern-like foliage that has a strong and pleasant aroma.

Despite the obvious attractions, garden centres do not go in for this sort of thing and you will most likely have to obtain specimens from specialist nurseries as listed on page 264–5.

## 71 Roses in shaded positions

*The garden of our new house never gets full sun, being shaded for most of the day by the house and nearby trees. Are there any varieties of rose that would be better suited than others to these conditions?*

The rose is basically a plant that enjoys full sun, so you cannot expect it to be happy and give of its best where the light intensity is seriously reduced. This applies particularly to H.T.s and Floribunda types, so you would be wise to think the matter over very carefully before planting them. This problem crops up from time to time and some notice has been taken of types that are perhaps just a little more tolerant, but it should not be more than partial shade. However, the types in question are the older shrubs and species kind, and you will need to go through a catalogue carefully to select the colours and sizes of bush you can accommodate. The Alba section is generally regarded as being the most amenable, followed by the French or Gallica roses, Centifolias and Damasks. The close effect of tree roots will also have bearing and as these type roses can be more expensive than H.T.s and the like, you should consider well before incurring too much expenditure.

There is another point that, as a new resident, you will not have had time yet to experience, and it is quite important. House, trees and shade add up to obstruction of air flow, and in summer that could lead to mildew and other fungus problems that are encouraged by still and stagnant air. Take particular care to leave plenty of air space between eventual full grown sizes when you are planning and planting. Similarly, obstructed air movement could mean that this garden is a frost pocket in winter, and you would be wise, therefore not to prune in late autumn and risk frost split in newly pruned sappy growths, but to wait until spring.

## 72 When they become 'old and past it'

*We have moved to a house that has some very ancient roses in the garden, which raises the question of how long roses live and whether these are worth keeping. What is the best way to treat these plants? They really are old with bark covered bottoms just like tree trunks.*

The very best advice to give anyone who has moved into a new home and is wondering about the plants they have inherited is to be patient, and wait for a whole year to pass so that the bulbs and other plants that may be dormant have a real chance to reveal themselves. There is bound to be plenty of other work around to claim your attention, and a year's grace will give you time to make notes of what, where, when and whether, as in the case of these old veterans, they are capable of performing and earning their keep. Unless they are labelled, you can have no idea of what they are, and there is nothing to be gained, only the possibility of losing a treasure, by impatient removal.

How long can roses live? In addition to native species, many of the plants brought to this country from afar have been well authenticated as over a hundred years old, but any claim to actually being the oldest would be highly contentious and very difficult to prove. Some plants growing in China and Japan are clearly much older than anything in Europe, but exactly how old they are is even more contentious – a couple of hundred years appears to be quite commonplace. There is a renowned case of the Banksian at Megginch in Scotland that didn't flower for over a hundred years – and that monster at Tombstone, Arizona, was no chicken, and yet look at the bloom it produced every year! (See question number 58 on page 214.)

What a normal life expectancy might be is dependent upon so many factors and conditions that it is impossible to say with any accuracy. There are so many variables, and each of your cases has to be treated on its merits. That is why you should give them a year to show what they are made of, whether they can respond to treatment or are already too far gone. If they are bearing any bloom that looks attractive, it may be worth seeing if they can be rejuvenated, but if the bloom has nothing to recommend it, don't waste your time. If they are to have a chance, and at this age and condition it will be a slim one, you will have to be drastic but prudent.

New growth has to be prompted from the base, which means prompting into action any latent growth eyes that will have been dormant for a long time and are becoming progressively buried in a mass of old gnarled overlaying tissue. The odds against a break-out are enormous, but you don't know until you try. The first procedure is to put the pressure on – pressure, not slaughter. Take the very oldest barky woody stem, consider which is the lowest point and the best direction and way to saw through it, and do it. Take it out with a pruning saw, the same with each plant, and then trace the stem up through the top growth, taking it out bit by bit in easy stages, and put it straight on to the fire.

That should concentrate the mind, as they say. It may prompt growth, or it may not. If the rose is a type that is growing on its own roots, such as a shrub or a species – even old antiquated ramblers and climbers can be shaken out of their dotage – you stand a better chance than if it is one that was originally budded or grafted, because then the risk is that, instead of the old barky tissue above the graft breaking out with a new growth, the pressure caused by the removal of the old established safety valve that was taking all the upthrust will cause the rootstock to blow a gasket and relieve itself by putting up sucker growth of its own. If you are lucky, all well and good — next year take out another old stem, and the third year, judging by the way new growth is being produced, you can decide whether to go faster and take out two or even three.

On the other hand, if no new growth breaks out from the base, it is likely that top growth high up will have a shot in the arm. But this is no good at all up there; the old chap is trying alright, but in the wrong direction. Remove any strong growth high up, increase the pressure still further, and continue for a second year. If that doesn't do the trick, don't waste any more time. Take the plants out and start again with something new, paying very careful attention to preparation in soil that is bound to be impoverished. Read the chapters on preparation and feeding very carefully.

Throughout all this, the point to bear in mind is that old and infirm plants are more prone to disease and pests, which can then spread around to the young and healthy.

## *73 Rose petal pot-pourri*

*We bought a rose petal pomander at a country garden fête – it was very nice and lasted a long time. Since then, we have laid sweet smelling rose blooms in the dressing table drawer and linen cupboards, but they always just fade and rot. Can you please tell me something about pomanders and the best way to make use of our roses for this purpose? Any recipes would be most welcome.*

The scents and aromas given off by blooms and foliage are due mainly to volatile oils, pigments, minute pollen grains and similar substances which, being organic, are subject to the natural processes of decomposition just as much as any other part of the plant. Some plants are better than others at resisting decay, for example, lavender flowers and seed heads dried and laid in a drawer retain their scent for a long time, but dried rose petals lose much of the volatility of the scent, and if laid in a drawer undried will simply decay and make a mess.

Pomanders, wash balls and scent bowls are not made of the petals alone – several other aromatic substances are used, some so powerfully aromatic as to quite overpower the rose ingredient. To understand the make-up of the ingredients we have to consider the purpose of pomanders and like articles. Of course, it is nice for us to smell the pleasant aromas in bedrooms and on textiles, but this pleasant aspect hides a truth that is a good deal less pleasant. In an increasingly civilized society there were two main purposes for the use of all manner of scents, aromas, incense and practices to go with them. At a time when sewage was much more primitive and personal hygiene much less effective, the first purpose was to overpower the pervading smells of concentrated human communities with something rather more acceptable. The second purpose was for the insecticidal power of many of these agents to destroy or at least deter vermin. It is quite common practice even today to use camphor, napthalene and lavender to discourage moths and other creatures from laying their eggs among the fibres of clothing and other textiles.

Highly aromatic and exotic substances such as oils, spices, grains, herbs, even powdered wood and roots were and still are mixed with charcoal, ash, and powdered mosses and lichens which both absorbed the odours while they were strong and released them slowly over a longer period and, of course, added body and bulk to the product being sold. Because they rely on the old predominance of highly aromatic materials, many coming from afar, most of the recipes still in use today have very old origins. But there is not the same need, and the loss of demand has meant that some of the ingredients are no longer easy to obtain. You may have to search around chemists, spice merchants, craft and specialist suppliers in your locality.

It is an interesting hobby, and there is no reason why you should not experiment with your own ingredients and ideas, but make sure that petals and leaves collected from your garden are quite dry. Here is a good and reliable recipe:

Grind to a fine powder and mix thoroughly while still powder-dry the following: two tablespoons each of orris root, calamus root, benzoin, and olibanum. One tablespoon each of lavender flowers, bergamot and mace. Now add to and mix with the crushed and dried rose petals of your choice and quantity, although you will probably not want to exceed the equivalent in bulk of the finely ground materials. Add to the mixture three drops only of oil of bergamot, three drops of oil of rosewood, three drops of oil of geranium or oil of cinnamon, three drops of essence of ambergris, one teaspoonful of oil of sandalwood, and finally two teaspoonfuls of salt. Stir and mix thoroughly into the mixture and fill your sachets, bags and pomander bowls. This will last for a long time and, as you can see, it is very far removed from merely laying a rose flower in a drawer. Is it worth all the trouble? Try it, and you'll be keen to try variations and ideas of your own.

If you get bitten by the bug, there are all manner of different recipes and methods, rather like wine making. Here is another one, much more basic and quite likely to go wrong, but worth a try. On a dry day, after all dew has entirely gone, pick the petals and spread them out on paper or cloths to become almost but not completely crisp dry. You will need a plentiful supply because the method is as follows. In an earthenware jug or jar spread in alternate ¼–½ inch (6–12mm) layers, each rammed hard with a wooden spoon or stick, the dried rose petals and bay salt. Repeat the alternate layers until the jar is full. Seal the jar with Sellotape or plastic film so that it is airtight. Place the jar in a cool, dark, cupboard for the contents to mature – usually in about a month – and become ready for use in open bowls or pomanders. Almost any fragrant leaves and petals can be used in this method, and you may like to experiment with a few drops of the previously mentioned oils.

## *74 Rose petal wine*

*We have made wine from all manner of things, some, like pea shucks and potato peelings, quite strange, but often with surprisingly good results. We want to try rose petals, but wonder if the systemic pest and fungus sprays we have had to use would interfere. Your comments please – and do you know a good recipe?*

The juices and liquors of many fruits, flowers, seeds roots and even the sap and leaves of trees can be fermented to make wine. Indeed, one aspect of the DIY wine-making fraternity's enthusiasm seems to be directed at seeing who can make wine from the most unlikely and outlandish ingredients!

However, far from being outlandish, rose petal wine can be very pleasant. Not surprisingly, its particular attributes are first, its 'nose' or 'bouquet' – nothing so out of place as a scented drink, but a delicate faint aroma – and secondly the colour, the original and authentic meaning of rosé (to describe wines).

This is hardly the place for a full discourse on how to make wine, and I must assume at least that you have some experience. If you like a glass of wine, making it yourself – like cooking – is another branch of the gardening art that is well worth getting to know, and guaranteed to bring you lots of friends! Here is a recipe that I have followed quite a few times and found to be reliable and satisfying in the end product. You will need the normal wine-making equipment, of course, and these are the ingredients:

4 pint measures (2.3 litres) of freshly picked rose petals: keep to whites, pinks and reds, at least to start. I find that yellows tend to impart a less sweet flavour, and this should be a sweet wine.

½ pint (0.3 litre) of a red grape juice concentrate, or you can try, as I have quite successfully, 1–1½ pints (0.6–0.85 litre) of the juice squeezed from fully ripe grapes grown in the garden.

2½ lbs (1.1kg) of ordinary white granulated sugar. Brown and demerara sugar will spoil the essential colour of this wine.

1 sulphite or Campden tablet, to prevent the development of mould.

1 level teaspoonful of tannin powder to give a slight astringent flavour, otherwise it could finish up sickly sweet.

½ ounce (14g) of citric acid.

1 nutrient tablet to feed the yeast that is going to do all the work.

1 sachet of yeast. There are several yeasts available; some prefer a burgundy type yeast, but I think a port type yeast makes the best rose wine.

Enough water to make a total of 1 gallon (4.5 litres).

The method, briefly, as I have to assume that the reader will be familiar with the procedure, is as follows. Measure the petals into a large mixing bowl, and pour on 6 pints (3.4 litres) of boiling water. Pummel and pulverize the petals with a wooden spoon or stick in order to extract as much as possible of the aroma and colour. When nearly cool, add the Campden tablet, the tannin, and the acid. Keep covered, preferably with a lid – all manner of spores are in the air at all times, and you don't want any foreigners getting in and upsetting the works – or tip the lot as it cools into a proper fermenting bin that has a close-fitting lid. Allow it to soak for 5 days, giving a good stir twice a day. It is then ready for straining through a fine mesh sieve or clean muslin, pressing or squeezing the pulp to extract every last vestige of colour. Funnel into a demi-john, and add the grape juice, sugar and yeast. Top up with water and set the fermentation lock. Position in a dark place away from bright or artificial light, and very soon it will be popping away merrily.

Rose petal wine should be finished a little sweet, which means a hydrometer reading of 1.010 or a trifle over it. If it reads under this, it will taste dry. Bottle into dark bottles and leave to mature for at least nine months. It is only natural to want a wee taste of what is left over from filling, but don't go too deep into the sediment at the bottom of the jar or it will spoil your anticipation of what is to come.

Take your friends and visitors round the garden to admire the roses, and then treat them to a glass of wine made from last year's blooms, served at room temperature. What could be nicer?

## 75 Is there such a thing as a green rose?

*My wife has become an avid flower arranger since starting evening classes and has already won several small competitions. She complains that there is no such thing as a green rose to add to her displays of green flowers. I wonder if there is a green rose or whether it is just a dream like a blue one. If there is, I should like to get one and surprise her.*

Very many green flowers are not flowers at all, but modified leaves or bracts that become enlarged and enhance, or even take over, the display job of petals. Indeed, in some plants, these modified leaves become highly coloured, are set up in rosettes and bunches, and although they are often called the flowers, in fact hide or make quite insignificant the real flowers. The two most familiar examples of this are the hydrangea – the big white, red, pink, mauve or blue heads that we admire so much are not flowers at all, but modified leaves, the actual flowers being the tiny pips in the middle of each 'flower' – and the poinsettia, with its brilliant scarlet 'flowers' so sought-after at Christmas time. The actual flowers are the tiny yellow pips, and the spectacular red colouring is due entirely to leaves.

However, there are several roses that have a marked tendency to green in the colour of the bloom petals, usually whites and creams where the colour pigmentation is not so strong, and one is so markedly green that its botanical name reflects the fact: *Rosa chinesis* 'Viridiflora'. This small shrub from China has double flowers – the blooms are unmistakably roses – and, despite the increased interest in flower arranging in recent years, it has not enjoyed an increased availability, which is perhaps rather surprising. I doubt that you will find it in a garden centre, and will have to resort to the specialist rose nurseries listed on page 264–5.

## 76 One for the record books

*Can you please settle an argument – what is the biggest growing rose of all?*

It depends on whether you mean the world or just the UK, of all time, or just at present, the tallest, or the area covered. I don't know that such a question has ever been attested and verified to a particular specimen – or ever could be, given all the variables and candidates from far and wide – but I would think that famous Banksian at Tombstone, Arizona (see page 214), would have taken some beating for sheer size, but who knows? There are such incredible plant discoveries from time to time in the hinterlands of China and other parts of the East that one wonders what may be growing there somewhere waiting to be discovered.

As for the UK, there are two or three that may contend for the honour. There is pretty general agreement, I would say, that *Rosa filipes* 'Kiftsgate' is the most vigorous and potentially the biggest, but it only appeared for the first time in 1964, and may not yet have caught up and passed some not quite so rampant but much older plants. The biggest that I have ever actually seen was a double yellow Banksian sprawling all over an ash tree and a few smaller neighbours in a neglected wood near Southampton. Other contenders would be *Rosa gigantea* from northern India, *R. brunonii* from Afghanistan, *R. longicuspis* from western China and the more modern 'Wedding Day' (see page 142) raised here in 1950. All are quite capable of exceeding 30ft (9m) high and as wide, but who can say which, given the best of growing conditions and the time to do it in, would top the lot?

## 77 Smelling of bananas!

*We read your article last week about the many different kinds of roses with great interest because it reminded us of one we saw a few years ago in a large garden not far from Saxmundham that had very large leaves, shoots of a brilliant red, and masses of white flowers that smelled strongly of bananas. We have wondered ever since what it was. Have you any idea?*

The structural description is a little vague. If it is what I think it is, you might have remembered to say that it was a massive great thing climbing all over its neighbours, but the banana scent is fairly conclusive. This must have been *Rosa longicuspis*, a monster from the hinterland of western China and, apart from its unusual scent, all the more remarkable for the extraordinarily large clusters of scarlet orange hips in autumn.

## QUESTIONS AND ANSWERS

### 78 A 'Wedding Day' argument

*One catalogue sent to me says:* R. *'Wedding Day', see* R. *'Kiftsgate', while another lists them separately, and at different prices too, which seems to suggest that they are not the same thing at all. I am confused. Can you tell me which is which? [See page 142]*

The two roses are quite separate. There are similarities, it is true, but I hardly think that that justifies a cursory passing off like this. 'Kiftsgate' is a variety of *Rosa filipes* that was introduced by Murrell in 1964, a climber with grey-green foliage and massive heads of quite small but sweetly scented creamy white flowers in June and July, with well over a hundred to each cluster. Extremely vigorous, it will spread to an enormous size.

*Rosa* 'Wedding Day' first appeared 14 years earlier, introduced by Stern in 1950. It has similar huge flower clusters, but the buds are a definite apricot colour, opening cream with conspicuous golden stamens, and quickly fading to white. It is also fragrant – which doesn't help the confusion – and a vigorous rambler capable of climbing up to 30ft (9m) on a suitable supporting tree (that is similar too), but the bloom comes a month later in July and August. I hope that sorts it out for you.

### 79 Stars and stripes – and blotches

*We have a* Rosa mundi *in our garden, and when visiting a well-known private show garden in the Sussex Weald as part of a garden excursion, we saw what looked very much like a double form of it. Unfortunately, nobody could tell us its name, and we wondered if you could possibly throw any light on it, and if it is possible to get one anywhere.*

There isn't a double form of *Rosa mundi* as such, but there are several varieties with stripes and blotches that could very well be taken for it, and some bi-colours that are equally striking and in which you may be interested. There was an H.T. type available a few years ago called 'Candy Stripe' that would have fitted your description very well, but it has disappeared from the present day lists and you will probably have to resort to the register published by the Rose Growers' Association to see if anybody is still growing it.

Perhaps the most *mundi*-like, and because of its age quite likely the one you saw, was 'Ferdinand Pichard', a Bourbon hybrid raised by

Tanne in 1921. The rounded pale pink blooms are heavily striped with crimson-purple, richly fragrant, and repeat flowering. It is not a large bush, about 4ft (1.2m) high maximum and nearly as wide, so it is not too big for even a smallish garden. It is a spectacular sight in full bloom, and why it is not more popular and widely grown beats me! I doubt very much that you will find it in the ubiquitous garden centre, and you'll have to go to one of the specialists listed on page 264–5. David Austin and John Mattock both have good strains of it. (See page 142.)

Here are some other roses that you will no doubt find interesting and are well worth exploring for.

'Variegata di Bologna', a hybrid raised in Italy in 1909, has fragrant double white flowers flecked with crimson-pink, but in one magnificent flush and then only an occasional repeat bloom. It makes a somewhat larger bush than 'Ferdinand Pichard'.

'Camaieux', a very old Gallica type, dates back to 1830. Its fragrant white flowers are heavily striped and blotched with crimson, which fades with age to rose-pink and later to a blue-grey. It is 3ft (1m) tall and wide.

'Roger Lambelin', a hybrid perpetual, is rather unusual in having the petal edges fringed with white like a picotee carnation. It is unique, but not a 'strong doer', and requires some protection and good conditions to be happy. Similar, but a stronger rose altogether and with even more heavily margined and flamboyant edges, is the modern Floribunda raised by McGredy in 1980 and named after the radio and TV personality 'Sue Lawley' (see page 130).

'Commandant Beaurepaire', a Bourbon, is a dense and larger 5ft (1.5m) shrub that has an abundant flush of large double pink blooms that are flecked and striped with purple and scarlet. An old favourite, over a hundred years old, this is a breathtaking sight in full bloom and another mystery why it is not more widely grown.

'Tricolore de Flandre' is an old Gallica variety that deserves more attention from those gardeners who want a good flowering type – its flowers are white striped with purple – that can also serve as a good hedge. Only 3ft (1m) high, it is impenetrable with masses of thorns.

Finally, one for the lovers of miniature roses, the aptly named 'Stars and Stripes'. I've seen this grown at John Sanday Roses, Bristol, in display patio beds and also pot-grown as individual specimens for the house, and most attractive it is too (see page 143).

As you can see, *R. mundi* is not alone by any means with its stripes and blotches, but it certainly hogs the limelight for this kind of colouring. It is about time some of the others got a look-in; they are just as attractive, if not better in many cases.

## 80 Hanging gardens

*I have taken over as landlord of a public house that has over 60 hanging baskets at the front of the premises. I have to keep them going as it is a main attraction, but it takes a lot of time each day to keep them watered, moving steps about and climbing up and down. One of the customers has suggested small roses which would not need as much watering as geraniums and fuchsias. Do you think that this would work?*

It is not a bad idea, and you wouldn't be the first to try it. I saw an inn alongside the A40 not far from Gloucester festooned with hanging baskets among which were several trailing miniature roses.

However, there will be lots of gardeners other than mine host who will be interested in one or two matters arising from this question. The development in recent years of miniature, patio, and 'ground cover' roses open up possibilities for this kind of use. There are some very good miniature ramblers becoming available now, and which, blooming on the current year's wood, should give a good weeping effect and be ideal for your purpose.

Perhaps the most important point to bear in mind is that a hanging basket is always very susceptible to drying out, exposed as it is on all sides, and the plants within it to the consequent check. Some plants are more tolerant than others of dryness at the roots – geraniums are a case in point, and bloom much better when kept rather dry – but not roses; they won't like it one little bit. They are woody shrubs, their tissues do not move sap about (translocate) as quickly as the 'softer' tissue of geraniums, petunias, verbena and such basket subjects, and take longer to recover if allowed to suffer in this way. Remember also that, once a soil ball becomes dry, especially if it is permeated with roots, water will not readily soak into it when poured on from above, but will run off like the proverbial water off a duck's back.

If this happens, there is only one solution. Each and every dried-out basket will have to come down and be soaked thoroughly by immersion in a tank or bath. Such a task is better avoided altogether, and the precautions begin as you prepare and plant up the baskets.

Line each basket with black plastic, which is not so unsightly as other colours, and will soon be hidden by hanging foliage. This cuts out evaporation through the sides of the basket and is very much better in this respect than moss or peat. Use an organic-rich compost that will soak up and hold moisture, and plant the subjects to grow through a mulch layer not of peat, which will shed water to the sides as soon as it develops a dry crust, but of moss, which does not form a crust, and protects the soil surface from drying just as well. Make a couple of drainage holes by piercing, not at the bottom, but halfway up the side so that a basin of water can collect and be held below the level of the holes and so delay a complete dry out.

Relying on steps and a watering can is dangerous both to yourself in a hurry to get the job done, and to the plants which will not get a long enough drink because you haven't time to do the job properly. There is an old saying in gardening that is very much to the point here: if you find that what you are doing is hard graft and tedious, you are doing it the wrong way. Gardening is meant to be enjoyable at all times, and if you make hard work of it, you don't do it properly. If your back aches, you skimp the job and cut corners. That may ease your back-ache, but it doesn't help the plants. Stop and think how you can make a job easier – you will be better for it, and so will your plants because you are not in such a hurry to leave them.

The ideal tool for the job of watering your hanging baskets is the kind of sprayer that sucks out of a bucket, rather like the old stirrup pump. Fitted with a lance extension or two, and by opening the spray nozzle to very coarse, you'll be able to reach up and direct a stream of water much more easily than climbing steps. If you cannot find this kind of sprayer, an alternative would be one in which you pump air pressure into the liquid container, which then drives the liquid up to the nozzle. Compared with the former type however, the quantity of water you can send up is much less, and you will have to spend longer at the job each time to get the baskets well watered.

Remember too that roses in hanging baskets are just as likely to receive the attentions of aphids as those in the ground, and you will have to spray them with a protective. Systemics will have the advantage over older contact methods, and a spraying once every three weeks should keep them clear, which is where your watering sprayer comes into its own.

## *81 A lemon-scented rose?*

*I heard on a gardening programme a reference to a lemon-scented rose with enormous flowers, but I missed the name. This is a nuisance because I have a passion for lemon-scented plants and would like a rose to add to my large collection. Can you help please?*

The two clues, large flowers and lemon scent, point to the 'Macartney Rose', *Rosa bracteata*, a climbing species from eastern China. The single blooms have large silky white petals, and are fully 4–5 inches (10–13cm) in diameter, with a large group of conspicuous golden stamens at the centre, followed later by orange-red hips. The fully open flowers are preceded by conspicuous leaf-like bracts around each bud, hence the botanical name. It is almost evergreen and, although a climber, is not as tall as many. About 10–12ft (3–4m) will be its maximum height in this country, and it will need the protection of a warm wall or corner about its shoulders to make it happy.

## 82 The rose with only four petals

*I have seen a rose with only four petals! I thought all roses had five or multiples of five, so is this some kind of freak like a four-leaved clover?*

This is an old favourite trick question of gardening quizzes. *Rosa omeliensis pteracantha* is the exception that proves the rule, because it only has four petals – and that is not the only thing unusual about it. If you look at that name carefully (*cantha* means thorns) you may deduce that there is something notable about the thorns. They are crimson red, and virtually transparent like glass! Other than that, it does not have anything to commend it, but is really a botanical curiosity, and more suited to a botanical garden than to a private garden that can have much more beauty to adorn it.

## 83 A real rose hedge

*Almost every rose hedge I've seen is a pathetic disgrace for a hedge and always reminds me of your remarks about using up the left-overs! But now I am in need of a thick barrier alongside my rose garden to keep my new neighbour's animals from coming through. A rose hedge would be very appropriate, but not like the ones I've seen. Is a flowering rose hedge just a dream or can you suggest a genuine repeat-flowering kind that will be certain to keep the dogs out?*

As you say, you cannot grow a good hedge from left-over rubbish any more than you can make a silk purse from a sow's ear. There are several varieties, types and methods that would suit your purpose, both by themselves and in combination with others, but we are dealing with specimen plants and not a cheapened mass production line. If I give you a brief description of a number, you can look them up and research a short list to provide exactly what you want.

'Blanc Double du Coubert' is a *rugosa* type with large semi-double white flowers that begin very early and continue unceasingly throughout summer and autumn. It will get up to 6ft (2m) if left, and you will need to underplant it or bend stems down and interlace them to keep dogs at bay. That will take time, so you have to think of this as a good solid start for interplanting with others.

'Frau Dagmar Hastrup', another *rugosa* type, has pointed buds and flesh-pink blooms. A point of interest could be the hips from the earliest blooms colouring while the later flowers are still appearing. It reaches 5ft (1.5m) and has a similar growth habit to 'Coubert'.

'Roseraie de l'Hay' (see page 134) is yet another *rugosa*, but stronger and more dense than the previous two. The purple buds open to 5-inch (13-cm) flowers with a rich strong perfume. It will make 7ft (2.1m), so has plenty of vigour for lacing and intertwining into an impenetrable thicket.

'Tricolore de Flandre' is a shorter growing, 3-ft (1-m) Gallica with striped blooms. The dense growth with a mass of thorns is ideal for bottoming the taller growing kinds – nothing will get through this.

'Nevada' is a 'modern' shrub type with semi-double creamy-white 4-inch (10-cm) blooms which smother the plant early on and are followed by smaller recurrent flushes. It will make a vigorous 7-ft (2.1-m) plant that will need, and can take, ruthless removal of old wood to promote young bloom-bearing wood from below. Laced into its neighbours, it makes an impassable barrier; the periodic thinning is the only problem (see page 138).

'Constance Spry', perhaps the best known and most popular of David Austin's English roses, has large, clear pink, old-fashioned fully double blooms – more like peonies than roses – and a very strong myrrh fragrance. It is a vigorous shrub that is frequently trained like a climber to pillars and pergolas, and which, interwoven, makes a formidable barrier. It has only one drawback: there is one flush of bloom and no more, but what a bloom to find in a hedge!

'Frühlingsgold' is a modern shrub, and a very tough customer indeed. The large semi-double yellow blooms are strongly fragrant and smother the plant. It is 7ft (2.1m) of flowering barbed wire!

*Rosa paulii*, a hybrid of *R. rugosa* and *R. arvensis*, is a very vigorous 12ft (3.6m) trailing type, tailor-made for low-down interlacing and stopping interlopers. It has 3 inch (7.5cm) pure white clove-scented flowers.

'Zigeuner Knabe', a 5ft (1.5m) modern shrub with dark purple flowers, has dense foliage and masses of strong, wicked, dog-stopping thorns.

Finally, a modern Floribunda, 'Queen Elizabeth', so coarse and rampant that it is too overpowering to be grown in association with other floribundas and H.T.s; it needs growing as a solo specimen or as a hedge. The pink scented H.T.-type flowers are borne singly and in bunches. It is a raucous grower; a hedge is the best place for it.

## 84 Double or fully double – is there any difference?

*Rose catalogues often describe blooms as 'double' and 'fully double'. Is there really any difference or is it merely a figure of speech?*

A lot of licence is taken in the phraseology used to describe rose blooms, which is confusing to anyone wanting to be precise when making comparisons. A lot of opinion – and trying to put the best description on things – comes into it, but a fair description of each type of bloom would be:

Single – the basic type strictly, 5 petals only, but also applied to blooms having 6, 7 and 8 petals, i.e. some malformed and partial petals.

Semi-double – 9 to 15 petals.

Double – 16 to 25 petals.

Full double – 26 to 40 petals.

Very full double – over 40 petals.

It should be borne in mind, however, that petal numbers are seldom if ever precise. Especially with hybrids, it is quite normal to find blooms with different numbers of fully formed and partly formed embryonic petals on the same plant (see also Chapter 2).

## 85 The dutch hoe – a dangerous tool for roses

*I remember you at a lecture saying that a dutch hoe is a dangerous tool which should only be used with great care, and never among roses. I must say that I have never heard anyone else say this. Can you explain, please?*

When I was a youngster and just starting in Dulwich Park, the dutch hoe was used everywhere, and nobody thought or taught that there was anything wrong with it, but when I moved on to work in the propagating nursery at Avery Hill (that place was a university of sheer hard practical experience) I soon learned differently: the dutch hoe can be a menace.

When the soil surface becomes compacted and crusty, it is a simple matter to lose precise control, and to overshoot into small seedlings, as most gardeners will have found to their cost. This is just one reason why hoeing should be frequent and regular, whether there are weeds or not, to keep a loose tilth at all times so that hoe blades move with the minimum of effort.

The trouble with dutch hoeing in roses arises because, when there is a deep mulch (as there should be), and especially if it has been allowed to pack and cake (as it shouldn't be), it is not always so easy to keep the hoe blade in sight, particularly under low foliage, and it is then inevitable that basal stems will be touched, stabbed, cut and snagged. No matter how careful you are, it is inevitable. If the rose is planted correctly, with the bud graft just above the soil level (not below as is persistently and incorrectly advocated), the snag wound must inevitably be in the tissue of the rootstock and, in effect, is a form of pruning. What happens is that callus tissue forms to heal the wound, and this cell formation is the precursor to what is called 'adventitious growth', either root tissue or foliage tissue which forms and breaks out as a sucker. This is why you will often see and hear the advice never to fork deeply near roses in case you snag the roots. It isn't so much the risk in lifting roots to the surface, as the fork tines wounding roots, and starting up the healing tissue and sucker process. If you have to work that deep near a rose, use a spade, then any roots that are encountered will be cut clean through, and you will get a different kind of adventitious growth – fibrous root, which is assimilative, capable of absorbing moisture and nutrient. This in fact is the basis of the practice of root pruning.

The action of a drag hoe, although this can also be dangerous if handled carelessly, is easier to observe and to control around the stems. There are several types; my personal preference is for a swan-necked Stalham, now much treasured and well worn. The bend and crank of the swan neck means that the tool lays perfectly balanced in the hands, with best possible control. Even when soil is caked and crusty, there is no need to use force and 'chop'; that is when the damage occurs. Simply turn the tool through 90° and use the narrow edge of the blade to cut in. It should be a gentle action at all times, with no force, and no cutting damage, and the round swan neck is quite incapable of damaging foliage above.

If you want a good tool that you will come to treasure, find a good tool merchant who stocks Spear & Jackson tools and ask to see their catalogue in which all the many kind of tools are illustrated. Failing that, write to the factory direct, at Handsworth Road, Sheffield S13 9BR.

## 86 Robin's pin-cushion

*I have a very strange thing – I think it must be a growth of some kind because it is firmly attached – growing on some of my roses, some on the leaves and a few on stems. I can only describe them as a small hairy, bristly tufts, and coloured a pinkish red. Can you please tell me what it is, pest or disease, and what I should do about it? Strangely the plants themselves and the growth round about these things don't seem to be affected in any way.*

Many plants are affected by the attentions of insects – wasps and moths for the most part – that inject growth-regulating hormones into the tissue or the sap stream, which then cause abnormal behaviour like leaf curling, or abnormal growths called galls, of which your problem is one. The insect frequently does this as it lays its eggs and the larvae then live in the growth, finding both food and protection. The oak-apple gall to be found among the acorns on an oak tree is a familiar example.

The two main kinds of gall that affect the rose are the crown gall, a brown, corky, wart-like growth usually found on this year's wood that has become half ripened and woody by the time the gall has fully developed, and Robin's pin-cushion, a spongy, red, moss-like patch on leaves and occasionally on the stems. Strange as it may seem, and as serious as they look, these growths do not appear to be measurably harmful to the plants. It has even been suggested that, because of the plants' apparently willing acceptance of these growths, they must derive some mutual benefit from the arrangement – not unlike that which exists between leguminous plants (peas and beans) and the bacteria that invade their roots, causing the nodules that are sometimes mistaken for club root disease, and in which the bacteria perform a useful function for the plants by 'fixing' atmospheric nitrogen in a form that the plants can utilize. Mutual benefit combinations are called symbiosis, and they occur in very many forms of life, animal as well as plant.

You can do two things. Either cut the growths away with a sharp knife and seal the wound with Arbrex protective paint, or leave them as a curiosity.

### 87 Plant Breeders' Rights – what does it mean?

*I have seen references to 'Plant Breeders' Rights' in several catalogues and with many flowers and vegetables, and am not sure what this means. Can you explain, please?*

That grand old showman of the rose, Harry Wheatcroft, figured largely in the proceedings that led to the passing in 1964 of the 'Plant Varieties and Seeds Act'. Since that time, most new varieties of all manner of plants, especially the rose, have been propagated and introduced under the provisions of the Act. This also explains the word, usually in brackets, that appears after a varietal name, and which normally consists of the first letters of the raiser's name, for example Aus for Austin, Har for Harkness, Tan for Tantau, and so on, plus other letters that make up the 'word' and so code the variety.

What this means is that, although you may propagate a coded variety for your own pleasure and satisfaction, you must not propagate and offer it for sale without the express authority of the breeder. In the same way that the law of copyright prevents people copying and profiting from the writings of others, the rights of the plant breeder are protected against any and every other grower being able to propagate and 'cash in' as soon as a new introduction becomes available on the market. This, as used to happen, not only destroyed the scarcity value while the plant was still new and enjoyed a premium price that gave the raiser a fair chance to recoup his investment of money, time and skill, but also led to a mad scramble for the material that could be used for propagation of anything that looked likely to bring a fast profit. The exceptionally fine rose 'Super Star' suffered badly in this respect: so mad was the scramble by unscrupulous growers to get hold of it while the demand was high, that a lot of soft unripe eyes were being budded, with the result that the vigour of many of the bushes that were sold to an unsuspecting public was very poor, blooms fell over on weak necks, and the variety, through no real fault of its own, got the nickname 'Super Flop'. 'Plant Breeders' Rights' can be said to be doing a good job in protecting the plants just as much as they protect the raisers.

## 88 Mineral deficiencies – the tell-tale signs

*I am not at all happy with the general health and condition of my roses, and I have over 100 bushes. They have been fed regularly with a well-advertised rose fertilizer, but for the last three or four years there has been a general decline. I think there may well be a mineral deficiency of some kind that is getting worse. Many of the leaves have dark and withered edges, but I have always assumed that this is due to dryness as our soil is sandy and tends to drain very quickly. Whether these leaf markings are an indication of a shortage I would not know. Do you think it could be? Could you also explain the various deficiency signs to look out for, and what they mean?*

The first point to appreciate is that, on a rapidly draining soil, quickly dissolving artificial chemicals simply wash out before the plants have a chance to absorb much of them. Secondly, unless you make strenuous efforts to get as much organic bulk into that soil as you can – and the artificial chemical fertilizer you are using does absolutely nothing – your soil structure must decline.

You must understand that prevention is better than cure. It is very good to recognize signs, and interpret correctly what they mean, but you really shouldn't see them in any case! Read the chapters in this book dealing with feeding and soil structure, and get hold of Humber 1-1-1 Garden Compound manure before your roses decline any further.

Although I will describe the more important signs of mineral deficiency, I must impress most strongly, and ask you to appreciate, that it is not a question of recognizing one of these descriptions and thinking that all you have to do is to slap down some of the missing chemical – that is to miss the point completely. Plants need balanced feeding according to the laws of nature, not chemicals. If a well-fed athlete takes a stimulant, you can expect a better performance because he has the resources to support the extra effort. But if he is not fed properly with sufficient resources, stimulants simply burn him out.

We will discuss potash (K) deficiency first, because it is the shortage indicated by your symptoms and the soil condition described. Leaves remain green, but with darkened and withering patches at the edges as the cell structure does not develop properly and collapses. Plants decline in vigour and become less able to resist pest and disease attack – mildew can become very prevalent on red-flowering roses. This is a common problem on quick-draining soils, with grossly insufficient organic content, and it is essential to apply and maintain heavy mulching and feed with an NPK-balanced manure.

With nitrogen (N) deficiency the leaves are small, and unable to develop and grow properly. They are a pale colour as the green chlorophyll count is reduced. In severe cases, red-brown spots and areas can develop – the leaves are not working properly, and the plant often aborts them with an early leaf fall. With photosynthesis impaired, stems and all growth becomes stunted. NPK-balanced feeding is essential.

In phosphate (P) deficiency the leaves are small and dark green as they work overtime to compensate. The undersides have a purplish tint. There is poor root action, the stems are weak and the leaves fall early. Again NPK-balanced feed is essential.

The symptoms of magnesium deficiency are very pale leaves green at edges with collapsing areas close to the midrib and veins. The plant tries to support new growth, at the expense of older foliage, which becomes worst affected. Worse on sandy soils, this seldom occurs with organic manure feeding.

Manganese deficiency turns the leaves yellow with green zones only along the veins and midrib. It is common on chalk, so avoid lime. Apply manganese sulphate in a weak solution of 1 ounce (28g) to 4 gallons (18 litres).

With iron deficiency the leaves turn almost entirely yellow, remaining green only at the midrib and veins. Young foliage and shoots are the worst affected. It occurs most often on chalky soils, so avoid liming. Very weak solutions of iron sulphate should solve this problem.

In boron deficiency the leaves become unusually dark green and misshapen, the shoots are malformed and there is a tendency for die-back. It is often associated with calcium shortage.

Finally, a condition that is not a mineral deficiency but often mistaken for one, identifiable by the exact reversal of manganese colours (leaves remain green with the midrib and veins turning yellow), is due to poor drainage and waterlogging. If it is not possible to lift and replant the ailing rose with a better preparation beneath, apply 2 ounces (57g) of gypsum per square yard (square metre) every three months.

## 89 The legendary black rose

*Can you please settle an argument? My friend says there used to be a black rose, and I say there cannot have been because black is an impossible colour in plants.*

The answer to this all depends on what you mean by black. Black is a colour in flowers that has excited plant breeders and growers for ages. Fortunes have been spent trying to achieve it; even the fortunes of nations and dynasties have wobbled. Dumas' *The Black Tulip* is not only a classic work of literature; the story most realistically portrays the intrigue that surrounded the search for the elusive colour at a time when the cult of the tulip not only dominated Dutch domestic politics but virtually ruined the economy. The story of the quest is made all the more intriguing by the widespread belief, even today, that the black tulip was evolved – and lost again in all the tumult of civil strife.

However that may be, such is the demand for a black flower, that all manner of plants have had black and other colours ascribed to them that are wishful thinking at best, and misleading frauds at worst. Nowadays, growers have to be very careful indeed about the colours they claim, but for a long time names were freely used to imply colours or qualities that simply didn't exist.

From about 1850, when the popularity of the Moss rose was at its height, a variety called 'Nuits de Young' became known as The Black Rose. As time went on, and probably because other contenders were appearing, it became 'Old Black Rose', by which name it is still known and grown. It is the darkest rose in cultivation, but in fact is not black at all, rather a very dark maroon purple.

Although capable of making 5ft (1.5m) tall in favourable protected positions, it has sparse foliage, is slender and has all the appearance of being a weak grower – a poor doer. In this characteristic it is not unlike what is widely regarded as being the nearest to all black achieved in a Hybrid Tea, 'Charles Mallerin', which had sooty black velvet suffused into its deep crimson petals. Although it took the highest International honours open to new roses in the early 1950s, it was another poor doer and I very much doubt if it is still grown.

But what is black? Where does scientific analysis have to be reconciled with 'to all intents and purposes'? Some will argue that black is scientifically impossible, others will be equally vehement that such a view is too pedantic, and that the eye is the judge that matters. At any rate, like the black tulip, the black rose hasn't been grown yet, and it will be interesting, as all the skills of genetic manipulation are played about with, to see which colour is achieved first, black or blue.

### 90 Miniature, patio, ground cover: what's the difference?

*I am confused by the abundance of low-growing varieties being offered in all the catalogues. Miniature roses, patio roses and ground cover roses – they all seem to be short growing, and are listed separately with not much explanation of what the differences are.*

It really is remarkable how fashions change, and it happens in gardening just as much as with anything else. I remember how, long before they were fashionable, a well-known grower used to put up a display of tiny little roses at all the big shows. He should have had a gold medal award for sheer dogged persistence because, year after year, the crowds would push and shove to get a good look at the latest wonders in H.T.s, and later the Floribundas, and virtually ignored the stand with the tiny tots!

They were dismissed by most rose-lovers as toys, apologies, not really serious roses – but, as the saying goes, everything goes in circles. Tides, like worms, turn, and now the wee ones are on the crest of a wave. How long the wave will continue to roll in is difficult to judge, and we shall see in a year or two whether it is just a fad, or whether the new trends hang on and become established as regular parts of the rose scene by becoming officially recognized as separate classifications, and then we shall have some form of definition to clarify what is what. Until then, there is a general merging of one into the other.

It adds to the confusion that, at the same time as interest in miniatures grows, there should appear both 'patio' and 'ground cover' types. The names are indicative of the intended purpose, but not very clear on the distinctions, so let's begin with the miniatures. To all intents and purposes, these are scaled-down versions of H.T. and Floribunda bushes with typically shaped buds and blooms. Variable in ultimate size, some can reach 12–15 inches (30–38cm) in height, whereas others have a job to get above 6–8 inches (15–20cm). Care has to be exercised in selecting just the right size for the job in hand. It would be no good, for instance, expecting to be able to restrain a 15 inch (38cm) plant to 8 inches (20cm) by keeping it cut back. Since they are so small there is all the more reason for getting the right size before you buy and plant. They have always been used on rockeries and in window boxes, but now we find them being suggested as ideal for edging beds, balconies, roof gardens, tubs and troughs. A big influence in their popularity has been the supermarket impulse buy; a pretty little rose, small enough to take home with the shopping; which goes into a decorative pot holder and is enjoyed while it remains in bloom and can stand the central heating, and then thrown away for something else.

This does them an injustice, because for the most part they are hardy little things, and deserve to find a more permanent and promising existence in ultra-small bedding in today's ever-diminishing urban gardens. Quite recently, we have seen the development of miniature standards and standard weepers, so there is no sign yet of their star being on the wane.

Patio roses are betwixt and between, not so twee as the miniatures and smaller than the conventional H.T. type bush. The word 'patio' is a little more suggestive of the use than the older name 'dwarf', and with the emphasis on neat and tidy growth habit they are eminently suitable for planting as 'dot' plants in paving, or solo specimens in tubs, and similar uses on patios and in today's smaller gardens. With not such a vast difference in size, this type of rose is more acceptable and popular for the modern smaller areas where the traditional concept, the H.T., has become a little out of proportion. It may seem strange to those with plenty of garden space to think of a rose bush becoming obtrusively big, but that is the way many urban gardeners are having to think. If they want a good collection of roses, there is only one way to get the same numbers in today's smaller gardens, and that is to plant a smaller, more compact version. Many of the bloom colours and types being introduced show just how much attention to this new need is being paid by the growers. In almost every catalogue, the odd one or two in a curiosity corner have now developed into pages and pages of varieties.

Ground cover roses are a different thing altogether. They are not necessarily or particularly low-growing, and with a completely different growth habit. Ostensibly, ground cover plants are intended to be labour-saving by virtue of a dense foliage and spreading habit smothering and suppressing other vegetation with something that is pleasant to look at, floral preferably, and requiring little or no attention. Roses to do this job have developed from basically rambler types, with plenty of side-shooting and a lot of foliage to mask out everything else that tries to compete.

Two main types are evolving, and again, considerable care is needed when choosing from catalogues to know exactly what you are ordering. The differences derive by and large from growth habit and vigour. One type is prostrate and ground-hugging, with a spreading habit and blooms generally held just above the foliage. Differences between the varieties are not in height, but in the area covered by each plant. The other type has a quite different habit, reaching as much as 3ft (1m) in height before arching over to form a spreading, smothering canopy. Some varieties of the latter kind are remarkable for the profusion of bloom and, because of their dimensions and suitability for covering difficult terrain like embankments, slopes and uneven ground, are also sometimes called 'landscape roses'.

By the very nature of what they are expected to do, ground cover roses have to be tough and resistant to pest and disease. It is not going to be easy to go wading into a tangled thicket in order to spray against greenfly, mildew or any of the other troubles that beset the rose, and that is a problem that several gardeners have written to me about, saying that they are sure that their ground cover is a haven for overwintering nasties that then come out and attack the front line beauties. Well, that is gardening I'm afraid: as you close one door, another opens, and there is no form of labour-saving that will permit you to put your feet up and do nothing!

### *91 Bi-colour and multi-colour*

*In the schedule for our local show are classes for 'Bi-colour, not multicolour' and 'Multicolour, not bi-colour'. These seem a bit strict to me, and as I wouldn't want to be disqualified on a technical point which I am not clear about, can you please give me some guidance?*

Despite seeking to be precise, regulations like this one are not as explicit as they might be. You do well to question the meaning of these descriptions in order the avoid the thumbs down on the show bench. However, although I can give you a widely acceptable interpretation, I would strongly advise you to check that this coincides with the requirements of the show committee – they set the rules, not me!

Bi-colour blooms have different colours on the outer and inner facing surfaces of the petals. These may be contrasting, like red and yellow, or similar and blending like red and pink. Multicolour, on the other hand, is something quite different and means blooms of more than one colour, deriving not from differences between obverse and reverse sides of petals, but from chemical changes affecting the pigmentation within the petal tissue and due invariably to the age of the individual flower. This means that you may have blooms of different colours on the same plant, and blooms of different colours within the same flower truss.

Perhaps the most familiar example is 'Masquerade', which has been available for many years, is still quite popular, and is likely to be available for some years yet. The buds and freshly opened blooms are a creamy yellow, which gradually changes through orange to red shades as the pigmentation breaks down and the red-coloured anthocyanins form. As blooms form and develop at different times, we then have blooms of different colours in the same plant, and as with the Floribunda types, within the same truss blooms. Another good multicolour is 'Joseph's Coat'.

## 92 Will the thorns ever be bred out?

*Watching programmes like* Tomorrow's World *and seeing the astonishing things being done with genes and chromosomes to alter plants and animals makes me wonder why thorns haven't yet been eliminated from roses. Will this ever happen?*

Forty odd years ago, when I was a student, a great deal of experimentation was being done with substances that control or influence all kinds of growth and behaviour in plants and animals and which, because they are man-made and do not occur in nature, are called artificial or synthetic hormones. The familiar selective weedkillers used on lawns are just one example. Many such materials, used within certain prescribed limits of intensity, strength and quantity, can have effects that are economically or aesthetically useful. But step outside those limits, and you enter a different world with long-term, hidden and unsuspected side effects.

I have seen a tulip with hundreds of flowers trying to form on one stalk, and a tomato with so many flowers (set to produce fruit, incidentally, by yet another synthetic hormone that is readily available for you to buy) that the artificially fertilized fruit truss had to be supported in a hammock until the plants collapsed under the unnatural strain. Plants were altered beyond recognition by the most minute trace of some man-made chemical. I would like to think that nothing as unpleasant as this will ever be allowed to happen to the rose which, thorns and all gives us a wealth of beauty, colour, form and perfume. If one of the prices we have to pay is the occasional pricked finger, we should pay it gladly, for the rose is one of the most, if not the most, beloved of all plants. It may well be possible that some day, such is the restless ingenuity of man, someone will be able to pinpoint the gene that gives roses their thorns, knock it off and see what happens, but I hope that good sense will prevail and the rose thorns will be left alone.

## 93 Why not put rose leaves on the compost heap?

*You always advocate mulching roses and urge gardeners to make as much compost as possible, and yet you say that rose leaves and prunings must be cleared up and put on the fire. It seems a bit inconsistent to me. It is all organic and will rot down.*

As every rose-grower knows very well, our favourite flower is well liked also by other life forms. They bite it, suck it, eat it, invade it, parasitize and destroy it, and do their damnedest to compete with us for the pleasure. Many of the life cycles of our foes are complicated and bizarre, but they are very successful, not only in maintaining their existence in the dog-eat-dog conditions of the natural world, but also in resisting everything you throw at them. They multiply in extraordinary profusion so that some are bound to avoid slaughter and carry on the fight. You know how clever they are at hiding and protecting themselves to prevent your toxic sprays reaching them. In winter they can even change their life form into something entirely different, that is almost impossible to detect and difficult to destroy. Minute eggs of pests and spores of fungi get into the cracks and crevices of living bark and dead tissue like twigs, fallen leaves, debris and rubbish, waiting only for the signal that a new spring is arriving and it is time to be up and doing again.

Compost is invaluable in the garden, but can you make it properly? Are you able to control the process so that a temperature of 130–160°F (54–71°C) is generated and maintained for several days? This is essential to kill the eggs and spores of pest and disease. The vast majority of garden compost heaps haven't a hope of doing this and therefore cannot self-sterilize. Rose debris is highly likely to be infected in one way or another, and to put it on just such a rubbish tip is simply to provide an over-wintering haven for pest and disease, and to spread that as mulch is to spread trouble. The risk is not worth it; the fire is the only safe place for rose debris, as it is for any plant material that contains thorns. Being hard and woody, these take longer to decompose, and handling compost containing thorns is to ask for a dirty splinter in your hands.

## 94 The strange markings of the rose leaf miner

*Several of the leaves of my roses have strange markings on them. They start as cream-coloured curly lines that day by day get longer and longer until the whole of the leaf is covered with the squiggles. I cannot find any sign of pest or disease. Can you tell me what it is, and what to do about it, as it does not look very nice?*

Several plants have this problem, most noticeable in the leaves of chrysanthemum and holly. The markings are caused by a tiny grub that emerges from an egg laid deep into the leaf tissue while it is still young and soft, and then proceeds to chew its way into the meaty tissue between the upper and lower skins of the leaf, where it is safely out of harm's way from predators, rain, wind and any contact poison that you may spray on the outside surface. Munching its way happily into the filling in the sandwich, it wanders aimlessly about, leaving a tunnel behind it. The skin tissue layers being largely colourless, what you see as 'squiggly marks' are in fact the tunnel where the creature has already been at work. Of course, the leaf soon becomes incapable of performing its function of contributing its share to the photosynthesis total. It may fall or not as the case may be, but the grub remains safely holed up in a perfect hideaway.

There are two basic ways of dealing with leaf miners. Either use systemic insecticides which poison the leaf tissue that the grub is eating (routine precautionary spraying with systemics against aphids would have stopped this from the start), or simply pick off all affected leaves and burn them. No matter how bad and prevalent the attack, the photosynthesis loss to the plant by their removal has to be accepted, and in any case, the leaf efficiency is already seriously depleted. Give the plant a little extra feed and make sure that there is plenty of soil moisture so that it is encouraged to make new growth and get over the leaf loss quickly.

## 95 Chopped straw mulch – a load of trouble

*A few years ago, during a hot dry summer, I saw what appeared to be a good and inexpensive idea in a newspaper article: straw bales chopped up into chaff to make a moisture-saving mulch cover for roses, shrubs and border plants. I had never tried this before, and now I cannot help thinking that this must have been the start of my present trouble: couch grass! I never had it before those straw bales, and now I am having a terrible fight with the stuff. Do you think there is any connection, and do you have any ideas how I can clear the rose beds of it?*

This is another of those ideas which are very good in theory, but which practical experience shows to be anything but. Unless you know a field very well, can be quite sure that it is scrupulously clean of weed, and that any straw bales will consist preferably only of barley or, more risky, of wheat, there is always the risk of introducing something unpleasant like this. Oat straw is even worse, and if you simply buy a bale 'on spec' with the field origin unknown, it is most unwise to chop it and use it as 'dry mulch'.

Even in a clean field, whether it has been 'combined' or baled later as a separate operation, it is almost inevitable that some viable grain will find its way through the baler with the stalks. As these germinate in your rose beds, the seedlings are not difficult to hoe out – but they are not the problem. When the crop is not clean, what you have experienced is quite on the cards because, although the crop may have been sprayed with selective weedkillers to kill out weeds like poppy and fat hen, they do not necessarily do much to clear out rogue and weed grasses.

Couch grass is a very vigorous subject that is able to reproduce and spread in three different ways. That is bad enough in itself for the gardener, but in addition, each of the three ways can also stand a fair degree of adverse conditions, and that makes couch even more difficult to eradicate.

A dirty field at harvest time can mean that the straw bales will contain couch seed or flower heads that ripen seed in the bale. Furthermore, as you will know, couch also spreads by means of tough wiry stems that drive for considerable distances just below the soil surface. In fact, in field conditions these stems can also run in the surface debris, where they are virtually on the surface and are easily picked up by the fingers of the reaping machine. These stems are called rhizomes, and are in fact modified food storage stems with tufts of roots every few inches (centimetres). Every root tuft is also the site of a growth bud that is capable of sending up leaves and thus becoming a fresh individual plant. Even the shortest length of rhizome stem is likely to have a growth bud, which, with the food storage nature of the rhizome tissue, explains why, when digging out couch to eradicate it, every smallest piece has to be removed.

Similarly, the above-ground growth is not unlike the underground stems in that adventitious roots can form from the base of each leaf, arising from a swollen food storage node on a wiry stem. The above-ground stem is called a stolon. It doesn't get up very tall but is inclined to flop around so that it easily becomes covered with other vegetation and leaf fall, whereupon the adventitious roots soon take advantage to strike down and become established.

In Britain, we are quite familiar with the practice of growing grasses by sowing seed, and our climate is so suitable for this method that any other is vitually unheard of and certainly not practised. There are parts of the world, however, where the climate is not so favourable to seed, and a common method then is to harvest grass by reaping, dragging out rhizome stems with a rake from the dusty soil, putting the lot through a chopper and sowing not seed, but the chaff! This contains enough nodes and below-ground tufts to 'germinate', each plantlet having more resources in the dry soil and climate to sustain it than that contained within a seed. Kentucky Blue grass is frequently grown in just this way in the USA.

Now you can see that this is just what you have done in putting down freshly chopped chaff from a dirty bale. The moral is twofold. Firstly, always compost straw and, even if you cannot compost properly enough for it to heat up and kill out living plant matter, at least an inefficient heap does give living stems and roots time to reveal themselves and be dealt with before they can get among your roses. The second moral is not to believe all the good ideas you read in newspapers!

However, you have it now, so what to do about it? You dare not try to dig it out; the roses will not appreciate that amount of root disturbance. Read question number 42 (page 195) concerning another persistent weed, Mares tail, and use the same method – not with selective weedkiller (which will not kill grass) but with the total killer paraquat, or the couch killer Dalapon. It is no good being tough and brutal with couch, because it will beat you every time. This is a case where the soft glove treatment is more effective than brute force. Just one word of warning – keep children and animals out of the way while paraquat is still wet, and keep the bottle locked away safely.

A bale of hay is certain to be much worse than straw for mulching. If it has been made properly, to be nutritious as animal feed, it will contain plants other than grasses, and a lot of it will be at the seeding stage or very nearly so. Putting down a hay mulch is the surest way to turn your rose bed into a hayfield.

## 96 Grey lichen-like tents of the lackey moth

*In this part of Purley every property has to maintain an extensive planting of roses – which gives the road its name – and, as you may imagine there are a vast number of roses involved. Pests and diseases can quickly reach epidemic proportions if we are not very careful. This year a curious problem has affected several of us: leaf stems that are joined to the main stems by masses of grey white fluffy matter, something like the lichen that occurs on many conifers. Nearby leaves have been badly bitten by something, but there is no sign of caterpillars or beetles. Do you think there is any connection, and what should we do about it?*

These patches of 'lichen' are the protective 'tents' in which the grubs of the lackey moth hide themselves between forays to take lumps out of the leaves. If you tear them apart you will very likely find a culprit or two tucked up inside. It is not regarded as a very serious or a frequent pest of the rose, but when it does occur it seems most often to be as a localized outbreak, and of course with the numbers of roses concentrated into Rose Walk, which is not far from where I used to live and therefore know quite well, you are very prone to outbreaks running like wildfire and reaching epidemic proportions.

The individual plants affected are actually at some risk. The whitish grey and orange caterpillars are rather conspicuous, so their hideaway 'tents' are a virtual necessity. When they are out, they chew leaves at a fast rate and quite large bushes can be completely stripped of foliage very quickly. Clearly, they have to be dealt with. Remove the hideaway tents either physically by picking them off or prodding and brushing, and destroy the grubs by a contact killer spray like Derris or with systemics. It is clear that you have not been using systemic insecticides for routine spraying, because then this problem could not have arisen.

## 97 Do coins in the vase water do any good?

*Visiting a very keen rose grower, I was surprised to see coins in the bottom of a vase containing rose blooms. She said they help to keep the water clean. Is there any truth in this?*

There was possibly an atom of truth in this at one time, but it was a bad truth. The old copper coins of the £.s.d. system contained more of that metal than does the bronze of the present coinage, and the theory was that the combined chemical effects of hand perspiration, oxidation in air, and coming into contact with other metals like iron, resulted in the dirt and grime that adhered to the coins containing enough water-soluble copper salts to have a slight anti-algae effect. At any rate that was the theory, and you know what happens to a lot of theories: people believe in them implicity whether they are feasible or balderdash.

The bad truth arises from the assumption that, because coins have been put in the vase water, it will stay clear and need not be renewed so often. Roses are not so bad at fouling their water as are more soft-tissue cut flowers like annuals and herbaceous subjects, but the need is still to replace the water daily, and also take an inch (2.5cm) or so off the ends of the stems. This chore, which the coins are supposed to make unnecessary, is a small price to pay for bringing the beauty of flowers into the house.

## 98 Magnolia – not a good climbing frame

*I thought the idea of setting a climbing rose to grow up into trees a good one, so I planted a 'Danse du Feu' to grow into a* Magnolia soulangiana *to provide bloom and colour after the tree's spring burst of bloom. It hasn't worked: the long rose stems were led up into the tree to give it a start, but the subsequent growth has been very poor with very few flowers. [See page 144]*

Roses are plants for full sun, and those that like to ramble and climb up into trees are happiest in trees that do not have a heavy dense foliage or are not a closely branching form that creates a canopy and seriously obstructs light. As the springtime bloom is finishing, *M. soulangiana* is beginning to clothe itself with leaves that become large, leathery and pale green at first, but gradually turning darker and so reducing the light intensity within the innermost parts and along the branches where the rose stems will want to clamber and compete for the light.

Under the tree, it becomes darker still, and that means that until the rose stems grow enough to get right up and through the magnolia foliage it will not stand much chance, and will always be at a disadvantage. Beautiful as it is, this magnolia is not a suitable support for a rose.

## 99 Clematis not happy on a rose pergola

*I've read about roses growing into trees, but I just cannot get a clematis to climb up on to my rose pergola. I have tried and tried, but they all wither and die. Is it that they dislike each other, or what? I even tried one where a rose died and there was a gap, and that went the same way!*

When climbing and rambling over a pergola, roses are in their element both in being able to expose their leaves to sunlight and in the access of air and sunlight – ventilation – around their bases and the soil they are growing in. This is somewhat different to the natural habitat of the clematis. Although it likes to have its foliage and flowers out in the sunlight and air, it must have its roots deep in cool soil, under a thick shading canopy of other plants. You find the wild clematis at its happiest and most rampant with its roots deep and cool in a hedgerow thicket.

You may be able to help matters by planting a thick shading canopy of ground cover plants and letting the clematis climb from under that. Another point concerns soil drainage. Roses prefer a heavy soil, not waterlogged or badly drained, but certainly dense and inclining towards clay rather than towards a light, fiercely draining, sandy soil. This is another matter over which the rose and the clematis fall out. Clematis likes a cool moist soil, but absolutely abhors waterlogging and poor drainage. If and when you try again, take out a hole at least two full spits deep, half fill it with old plaster rubble, and plant into the replaced top spit above that.

In gardening it is as well to always bear in mind the old saying about 'horses for courses'. Your case shows that horses from different courses do not always make good bedfellows.

## 100 Moles in the rose beds: how to send them packing

*Although there have always been moles in the meadow at the end of our garden, all the years we have been here we have never been troubled by them until this year. Now they are sending up molehills all over the rose beds and half burying some of the plants. I took your advice about three years ago and have kept the soil covered with mulch, but a friend says that this is what is attracting the moles. Could he be right?*

Only indirectly. The moles didn't show interest in you before because your soil must have had very few of its staple food, earthworms. In other words, a low worm count being one of the symptoms, your soil was in poor condition and low in fertility. Mulching is an effective way to get organic matter into the soil, and this has meant a proliferation of the workforce that mines the soil and carried the goodness down. More worms have attracted the attention of one of the worst pests, and one that we can do without – the moles.

Each day the mole has to consume its own weight of worms and other creatures that live in the soil. It will take things like chafer grubs and wireworm, and thus far do some good, but this is far outweighed by the harm it does by taking our best friend, the earthworm, by burying smaller plants, seedlings and even roses under its hills, and by disturbing the roots of sensitive plants like roses. The tunnels it makes are not means of escape but traps for its food: any worm or other soil creature that breaks through into the tunnel has an almighty job in boring its way back into the soil, and is ready to be picked up as the barbarian shuffles through on its routine patrol. Eyesight is not of much use to them in their life style, and has deteriorated to not far short of blindness, but their sense of smell and ability to detect the movement of creatures entering their traps at remarkable distances have developed to an incredible degree. We can use that acute sense of smell to drive them away. I don't like moles, they cause damage and they eat my friends, but I would rather drive them away than kill them with traps and poison.

All you need to do is to put into the tunnel what is to the mole such a powerful stink that he can't smell anything else. It drives him to distraction, and away. An old method was to drop camphor moth balls into the runs, but even more certain is to drop in a few crystals of paradichlorbenzene, which you can buy quite easily at the chemists as a moth repellent.

### 101 The biggest pest of all – deer!

*We live in a lovely house and garden in the countryside, but are plagued with deer that leap with disdain over a 5-ft (1.5-m) high fence to eat our vegetables and roses. We don't wish to harm them by shooting or anything like that – they are such beautiful creatures – but short of surrounding the property with an immensely high fence, I wondered if you have any suggestions.*

Beautiful they may be, but these little montjack deer are ferocious little brutes, and are becoming a very serious pest in many parts of the country. One of the first foremen I worked for had spent his younger days as an apprentice on an estate near Ashurstwood, which is quite close to Ashdown Forest in Sussex. They were troubled by deer, and I remembered him telling me how they had to go around the kitchen garden and other parts of the grounds splashing creosote every so often to keep the deer away. It seemed to work, although nobody knew why! I've heard several times since that this was a familiar method among gamekeepers and the like, and knowing now what great reliance deer place upon their sense of smell, not only to sense danger but also to recognize each other, it seems to me that there is a strong similarity here with moles with whom I have had many a tussle (see question number 100 on page 261).

I suggest you cut a lot of brushwood and twiggy stuff, dip it in a barrel of creosote, then nail and wire it along the top of your fences so that the deer would have to brush through it as they jump over – and get themselves smeared with the stuff. I tried it once, and it worked like a charm, keeping the deer permanently out of a friend's large country garden, who had previously been plagued by them, just as you are.

It was just a hunch then, putting together a little bit of remembered experience from here, a little bit of observation from there, using a little bit of logic, and suggesting that at least it made common sense to try. That is what gardening is all about: a little bit of knowledge, a little bit of experience, a little bit of observation, putting it all together and using your own common sense!

# Bibliography

*Classic Roses*, Peter Beales (Collins Harvill, London, 1985)
*Climbing Roses, Old and New*, Graham Stuart Thomas (Dent, London, 1983)
*The Commonsense of Gardening*, Bill Swain (Michael Joseph, London, 1976)
*The Dictionary of Roses in Colour*, S. Millar Gault and Patrick M. Synge (Michael Joseph, London, 1971)
*Handbook of Roses*, David Austin. The informative annual catalogue by a leading grower of Old, species and hybrid English roses (available direct from the author's nursery)
*The Heritage of the Rose*, David Austin (Antique Collectors Club, Woodbridge, 1988)
*Old Shrub Roses*, Graham Stuart Thomas (Dent, London, 1979)
*Roses*, Michael Gibson (Cassell/The Royal Horticultural Society, London, 1989)
*Roses*, Jack Harkness (available direct from the author's nursery)
*Roses*, Roger Phillips and Martyn Rix (Macmillan, London, 1988)
*Roses for English Gardens*, Gertrude Jekyll (Antique Collectors Club, Woodbridge, 1902)
*The Rose Gardens of England*, Michael Gibson (Collins, London, 1988)
*Shrub Roses of Today*, Graham Stuart Thomas (Dent, London, 1980)
*Twentieth-Century Roses*, Peter Beales (Collins Harvill, London, 1988)

# Rose Nurseries

*Note:* Most nurseries and garden centres are open seven days a week, but times are variable and visitors are advised to telephone and check, especially when a lengthy journey is involved. Unless otherwise stated, all offer mail order and despatch facilities, or personal collection by arrangement. Unless otherwise stated, most nurseries are obliged to charge for their catalogues; a quick phone call will establish their current price.

## Southern England

Cants of Colchester, Nayland Road, Mile End, Colchester, Essex CO4 5EB.
Tel: 0206 844 008.
Rose catalogue free. Rose fields open June to mid September. Garden Centre.

R. Harkness & Co Ltd, The Rose Gardens, Hitchin, Herts SG4 0JT.
Tel: 0462 34027, 34171.
Rose catalogue free (also includes trees and shrubs). Rose gardens open July to September. Garden centre.

Highfield Nurseries, Whitminster, Glos. GL2 7PL. Tel: 0452 740 266, 741 309.
Catalogue free – includes roses, trees, shrubs, fruit and plants. Plant centre.

Hilliers Nurseries Ltd, Ampfield Road, Ampfield, Romsey, Hants SO51 9PA.
Tel: 0794 68733.
Very comprehensive catalogue including roses, trees, shrubs, fruit and plants. Garden centres at Botley near Southampton, Braishfield near Romsey, Liss, Winchester and Sunningdale.

Mattocks Rose Nurseries, Nuneham Courtenay, Oxford OX9 9PY. Tel: 086 738 265.
Rose catalogue free. Rose gardens and fields open June to September. Large Notcutt garden centre with trees, shrubs, plants, sundries etc.

Notcutt Nurseries Ltd, Woodbridge, Suffolk IP12 4AF. Tel: 039 43 7354.

Very comprehensive catalogue including roses, trees, shrubs, fruit and plants. Ten garden centres at: Woodbridge, Colchester, St Albans, Solihull, Norwich, Peterborough, Bagshot, Maidstone, Nuneham Courtenay and Cranleigh.

John Sanday Roses Ltd, Over Lane, Almondsbury, Bristol, Avon BS12 4DA.
Tel: 0454 612 195.
Rose catalogue free. Display gardens.

## *Midlands*

David Austin Roses Ltd, Bowling Green Lane, Albrighton, Wolverhampton WV7 3HB. Tel: 090 722 3931.
Catalogue (*Handbook of Roses*). Large rose garden and display fields open from June. Plant centre.

Gandy Roses Ltd, North Kilworth, Lutterworth, Leics. LE17 6HZ. Tel: 0858 880 398
Catalogue including roses, trees and shrubs, free. Display fields open July to September.

Wheatcroft Ltd, Edwalton, Nottingham NG12 4DE. Tel: 0602 216 061.
Rose fields open July to September. Mail order catalogue *no longer published*. Large garden centre open all year.

## *The North, Scotland and Northern Ireland*

Bees of Chester, Sealand Nurseries, Sealand, Chester CH1 6BA. Tel: 0244 880 501.
Catalogue includes roses, trees, shrubs and plants. Large plant and garden centre.

James Cocker & Sons, Whitemyres, Lang Stracht, Aberdeen, Scotland AB9 2XH.
Tel: 0224 313 261.
Catalogue free. Display garden July to October. Garden centre.

Dickson Nurseries Ltd, Milecross Road, Newtonards, Co. Down, Northern Ireland BT23 4SS.
Tel: 0247 812 206.
This is a remarkable small family nursery that has a tremendous regard in the profession, concentrating on breeding and growing mostly its own varieties. Consequently, the variety list is smaller than most – and without illustrations. Visitors are welcome Monday to Thursday. Don't ever visit Northern Ireland without paying a visit to this intriguing and friendly nursery.

Fryers Nurseries Ltd, Knutsford, Cheshire WA16 0SX. Tel: 0565 55455.
Catalogue free. Display fields open July to October. Garden centre.

# Useful Addresses

The Royal Horticultural Society, Vincent Square, London SW1P 2PE.

The premier horticultural society in UK, the RHS publishes a monthly journal *The Garden*, for its members and organizes the annual Chelsea Flower Show. The RHS owns the Wisley Garden in Surrey, where field trials and research are conducted and extensive show gardens are open throughout the year.

The Royal National Rose Society, Bone Hill, Chiswell Green Lane, St Albans, Herts AL2 3NR.
The premier specialist rose society, the RNRS publishes a quarterly journal and provides numerous services, including the extensive and world-famous trial grounds at St Albans.

The Herb Society, 34 Boscobel Place, London SW1.
Write for a copy of their useful booklet on the use of the rose in conjunction with herbs and other substances for pomanders and similar purposes.

Rose Growers' Association, 303 Mile End Road, Colchester, Essex CO4 5BA.
A professional body that publishes an annual Directory of rose growers and varieties grown. With many varieties now become rare this is a very desirable publication for the general public.

Henry Doubleday Research Association, Ryton on Dunsmore, Coventry CV8 3LD.
The association carries out most important research and publishes work on organic growing and natural control of pest and disease. A very important organization for all gardeners that deserves much more attention and patronage. Its gardens are open all year except at Christmas.

Broad Leys Publishing Co, Buriton House, Station Road, Newport, Saffron Walden, Essex CB11 3PL.
Publications on all aspects of smallholding and allotment management, animal and poultry husbandry, small farming, gardening and organic growing. Also an immensely valuable bi-monthly self sufficiency and crafts magazine *Home Farm*.

USEFUL ADDRESSES

## *Suppliers of organic fertilizers*

Humber Fertilizers PLC, PO Box 27, Stoneferry, Hull HU8 8DQ. Tel: 0482 20458.

Humber organic-based fertilizers – which are referred to frequently in this book – should now be much easier to obtain. Renamed and restyled 'Good Life', a range of four formulations with NPK ratios varied to suit 'All Purpose', 'Lawns', 'Vegetables', and 'Flowers' are to be marketed in re-usable plastic canisters which will be more acceptable to the retail trade than hitherto; there should be very many more stockists. Basically, the products are exactly the same as the old 'Eclipse' fertilizers that have been available, and will continue to be so – albeit in larger unit quantities – to farmers and agricultural merchants. Only the name and packaging has been revised for retail gardening purposes. Useful advice leaflets are still available, as is good advice by telephone, if you will kindly mention this book.

Maskells Fertilizers, Stephenson Street, Canning Town, London E3.

## *Suppliers of pot-pourri materials*

Culpeper shops, situated at Dorking, Guildford, Bruton Street, London W1, Hampstead, Norwich, Cambridge, Brighton, Bath, Winchester, and Salisbury.

# Index

Numbers in *italic* refer to colour plates.

Alba roses 25, 35, 229
'Albertine' 212
'Alec's Red' 212
ammonia, sulphate of 77
aphids 81, 86
Austin, David 25, 29, 147, 238, 242
axil 58

'Baby Jayne' 176
'Ballerina' *135*
   pruning of 186
Banks, Lady 215
bare root 41
bark, use of 76, 170
Benlate 184
bi-colour 252
black rose 249
black spot 91, 92, 202, 203
blackfly 86
'Blanc Double du Coubert' 242
'Blessings' 212
blood, dried 79
blooms, double/fully double 243
   perpetual flowering 17
   quartered 17
   recurrent 17
   *remontant* 17, 70
   repeat 17
   semi-double 16, 243
   single 16, 243
blowing 117
blue roses 226
bone meal 79, 171
Bordeaux mixture 93
boron deficiency 248
Bourbon roses 24, 26, 35, 64, 158, 237
breed names 25
breed types 22
briar 59
British Standard Specifications 213
Broad Leys Publishing Co. 266
bud 58
   opening of 165

budding 59, 101, 166
'Burnett' roses 30
bush rose 17, 43, 64, 66, 155, 166, 173, 178, 212
buttercups 196

calendar work 118
callus 59
'Camaieux' 238
'Canary Bird' *see Rosa xanthina* 'Canary Bird'
   pruning of 185
'Candy Stripe' 237
canker 94, 204
capsid bug 84, 86, 209
catalogues 36, 40, 42
'Cécille Brunner' 147
   pruning of 187
chafer 87
'Charles Mallerin' 23, 145, 249
Chelsea Flower Show 37, 42, 91, 227
chimera 224
China roses 26, 147, 187
chlorosis 96
chrysanthemums 227, 255
clay soil, improvement of 150
clematis 260
climbers 20, 33, 48, 68, 158, 178, 184, 212
'Climbing Shot Silk' 70
climbing sports types 21, 69
colouring 225
'Commandant Beaurepaire' 238
'Compassion' 212
compost 74, 75
'Comte de Chambord' *134*
'Constance Spry' 242
container grown 41
convenience gardening 34
coral spot fungus 76
couch grass 256
'Grimson Glory' 200
cuttings 99, 153, 191

Damask roses 26, 229
'Danse du Feu' *144*, 178, 259

268

dead-heading 62, 153
'Deep Secret' 212
deer 262
die-back 188
diseases 81
'Double White' 30
'Duke of Windsor' 212
dutch hoeing 244

East Malling Research Station 213
'Elizabeth H. Grierson' 212
'Elizabeth of Glamis' 212
Emanuel *134*
English roses 28
Epsom salts 175
exhibiting 113
   timing for 114
eye 58

feeding 73, 115
Felco 54
'Ferdinand Pichard' *142*, 237
fertilizers, chemical 77, 97, 296
   proprietary 76, 134, 175
Floribunda 22, 23, 24, 33, 34, 35, 58, 68, 99, 113, 117, 182, 183, 228, 243, 250
flowering period 17
foliage, scented 228
'Fragrant Cloud' 131, 212
'Frau Dagmar Hastrup' 242
freezing 147
French roses 26, 229
frog-hopper 81, 84, 86
frost, late spring 95
'Frühlingsgold' 242
fungal diseases 82
fungicides, systemic 93, 184, 204

Gallica roses 26, 35, 99, 229
garden centres 37, 40
Gardeners' Benevolent Fund 39
'Geranium' *see Rosa moyesii* 'Geranium'
grafting 59, 108
'Graham Thomas' *138*
green rose 235
greenfly 81, 83, 84, 86, 123, 222
ground cover 250, 251
Growmore 75, 150, 162, 184, 191
growth form 17

habit types 17
'Hannah Gordon' *131*
Harrogate show 37
hedges 165, 241
Henry Doubleday Research Association 89, 161, 266
'Hermosa' 147
holly 255
hoof and horn 79
hover flies 89
Humber Eclipse Fish manure 75, 127, 150, 162, 177, 184, 191
Humber Fertilizers PLC 267
Humber 1-1-1 Garden Compound Manure 247
Hybrid Musks 27, 186
Hybrid Perpetual 24
Hybrid Tea 11, 17, 22, 24, 30, 33, 34, 35, 58, 67, 69, 99, 113, 117, 148, 180, 182, 183, 202, 228, 237, 243, 250
hybridizing 110

'Iceberg' 68, *130*, 146
Ichneumon fly 89
insects, beneficial 88
internode 61
iron shortage 95, 248
iron sulphate 79

Japanese roses 27
'Joseph's Coat' 253

'Kiftsgate' 236, 237
'Korona Red' 183

'La France' 23

lacewing 89
lackey moth 258
ladybird 88
lateral 59
leader 59
leaf-cutter bee 84
leaf mould 74
leaf-roll sawfly 84, 208
lemon-scented rose 240
life expectancy 230
*Limnanthes douglasii* 161

'Macartney Rose' 241
'Madame Alfred Carrière' 212
*Magnolia soulangiana* 259
magnesium deficiency 175, 248
'Maiden's Blush' *142*
manganese shortage 96, 248
manure 74
   farmyard 80
   horse 168
   organic 79
mare's tail weed 195
'Masquerade' 253
Mattock, John 238
'May Bug' 87
mildew 90, 126, 200
   powdery rose 91
mineral deficiency 247
miniature roses 22, 72, 178, 179
   for hanging baskets 239
'Mme Isaac Pereire' 26, *132*
moles 261
'Monthly Rose' 147
moss 149, 198
Moss roses 28, 249
moths, tortrix 85
moving plants 155, 158, 160, 163
multi-colour 252
muriate of potash 79
mushroom compost 80
Musk roses 27, 64, 99

'Nevada' *138*, 242
New English roses 28
nitrate of potash, saltpetre and bonfire ash 78
nitro-chalk 78
nitrogen 73, 77, 95
   deficiency 248
node 60
Noisette roses 27
Northern Horticultural Society 39
Nottingham marl 151
'Nuits de Young' 249
nurseries, rose 39, 264

'Old Black Rose' 249
'Old Blush China' 147

'Papa Meilland' 212
patio roses 22, 72, 250, 251
'Paul Shirville' *130*, 212
'Peace' 25, 68, 155, 160
peat 74, 75, 170
'Peaudouce' *130*
Pemberton Musks 27
'Penelope' *136*
pergolas 260
'Perle d'Or' 147
Pernetiana roses 24
pests 81
   fungal 90
   insect 83
phosphate 73, 95
   deficiency 248
physiological problems 94
Pillar roses 21, 50, 70
Plant Breeders' Rights 246
Plant Varieties and Seeds Act 246
planting 44, 47
   preparations for 42, 50
Polyantha roses 22, 24
pomanders 231
Portland roses 26
potash 73, 95
potash, deficiency 173, 247
pot-pourri 231, 267
'Prima Ballerina' 212
propagation 98
   asexual 99
   sexual 109
Provence roses 28
pruning 53, 54
   definition of terms 58
   old roses 220
   principles of 61
   saw 55
   species 67
   timing for 65
purple spot 94, 174

'Queen Elizabeth' 25, 68, 147, 180, 243

ramblers 19, 33, 48, 58, 66, 70, 99, 117, 212
Regent's Park 39
rhododendrons 164
Roath Park, Cardiff 39

Robin's pin-cushion 245
'Roger Lambelin' 238
rootstock 59
*Rosa*
　*alba maxima* 25
　*alba plena* 215
　*arvensis* 243
　*banksiae banksiae* 215, 220
　*banksiae* 'Lutea' *141*, 214, 215
　*banksiae lutescens* 215
　*bracteata* 241
　*brunonii* 236
　*canina* 107
　*centifolia* 28, 35, 99, 229
　*chinesis* 235
　*damascena* 26
　*ecae* 29
　*eglanteria* 228
　*filipes* 236, 237
　*gallica* 'Versicolor' *133*
　*gigantea* 236
　*hempisphaerica* 29
　*indica* 26
　*longicuspis* 236
　*moschata* 27
　*moyesii* 30, 109, 162
　　'Geranium' 30, *138, 142*, 162
　*multiflora* 24
　*mundi* 27, 237
　*omeliensis pteracantha* 241
　*paulii* 243
　*pimpinellifolia* 30
　*primula* 30, 212, 228
　*rubiginosa* 30, 193, 212, 228
　*rubrifolia* 30
　*rugosa* 36, 107, 181, 182, 183, 193, 243
　　'Roseraie de l'Hay' *134*, 192, 242
　　'Rubra' *138*
　*spinosissima* 30
　*wichuraiana* 19, 20
　*xanthina* 30, 185
　　'Canary Bird' 30, *139, 140*
rose debris 254
Rose Growers' Association 146, 266
rose hip syrup 217–18
rose leaf miner 255
rose petal wine 233
rose rust 94, 206

rose slugworm 85
'Rosemary Harkness' 212
'Roseraie de l'Hay' *see Rosa rugosa*
Royal Horticultural Society 215, 266
　Gardens, Wisley 39
Royal National Rose Society Gardens,
　St Albans 39, 266

Sanday, John 238
Saughton Park, Edinburgh 39
sawfly 81
'Scented Air' 212
scented roses 211
scion 59
seaweed, use of 169
secateurs 54
seed propagation 193
serphid flies 89
shady positions 228
'Shot Silk' 70
show schedule 115
Shrewsbury show 37
shrub roses 21, 43, 48, 64, 66, 72, 191, 242
side-shoot 59
slag, basic 78
snag 59
soap spraying 222
soda, nitrate of 78
soil, composition of 44
　conditions 175
　sickness 149
　waterlogged 219
species names 25
　roses 29, 72
spittle-bug *see* frog-hopper
spur 59
staking 47
standard roses 18, 19, 49, 51, 64, 108, 163, 173, 186
　half 18
　weeping 19, 20, 50, 66, 108
'Stars and Stripes' *143*, 238
stock 59
straw mulch 256
sucker 59, 165, 183
'Sue Lawley' *130*, 238
'Super Star' 23, 126, *129*
superphosphate 79

'sweet briar' 192
'Sweetheart Rose' 147, 187, 212

terms, clarification of 16
thornless roses 158, 212, 225
thrips 88
thumbing 116
'Tricolore de Flandre' 238, 242
tubs, roses for 176

underplanting 35, 160

Vapourer moth 211
'Variegata di Bologna' 238
'Viridiflora' 235

watering 177
'Wedding Day' *142*, 212, 236, 237
weedkillers for rose beds 197
'Wendy Cussons' 212
whalehide pots 223
Wheatcroft, Harry 91, 246
Wilkinson Sword 55
William Shakespeare *137*
wood, new 58
  old 58

'Zambra' 91, 145
'Zéphirine Drouhin' *134*, 158, 212, 225
'Zigeuner Knabe' 243